Last Man Standing

Communication, Media, and Politics
Series Editor: Robert E. Denton, Jr., Virginia Tech

This series features a range of work dealing with the role and function of communication in the realm of politics, broadly defined, including general academic books and texts for use in graduate and advanced undergraduate courses, the series encompasses humanistic, critical, historical, and empirical studies in political communication in the United States. Primary subject areas include campaigns and elections, media, and political institutions. Communication, Media, and Politics books will be of interest to students, teachers, and scholars of political communication from the disciplines of communication, rhetorical studies, political science, journalism, and political sociology.

Titles in the Series

Last Man Standing

Media, Framing, and the 2012 Republican Primaries

Danielle Sarver Coombs

ROWMAN & LITTLEFIELD
Lanham • Boulder • New York • Toronto • Plymouth, UK

Published by Rowman & Littlefield
4501 Forbes Boulevard, Suite 200, Lanham, Maryland 20706
www.rowman.com

10 Thornbury Road, Plymouth PL6 7PP, United Kingdom

British Library Cataloguing in Publication Information Available

Library of Congress Cataloging-in-Publication Data

Coombs, Danielle Sarver.
Last man standing : media, framing, and the 2012 Republican primaries / Danielle Sarver Coombs.
pages cm. -- (Communication, media, and politics)
Includes bibliographical references and index.
ISBN 978-1-4422-2035-5 (cloth : alk. paper) -- ISBN 978-1-4422-2036-2 (electronic)
1. Presidents--United States--Election--2012. 2. Primaries--United States--History--21st century. 3. Presidents--United States--Nomination--History--21st century. 4. Press and politics--United States. 5. Mass media--Political aspects--United States. 6. Republican Party (U.S. : 1854-)--History--21st century. I. Title.
E910.C66 2013
324.973932--dc23
2013026986

To my parents, William and Patricia Sarver,
for their limitless support.

And dedicated to the memory of my godfather,
David Troutman,
who loved politics and loved life.
We still miss you, Uncle Dave.

Contents

Acknowledgments

There are too many people to thank and acknowledge to possibly fit in this section, but I would be remiss without specifically thanking those without whom I never could have written this book. Special thanks go to series editor Dr. Robert E. Denton, an intellectual inspiration and scholarly champion. Bob, thanks for seeing the potential in this work and your encouragement along the way! Thanks also go to David Trebing for organizing the National Communication Association 2011 convention panel where Bob was first introduced to my work and to Paul Haridakis for recommending me to David. At Rowman & Littlefield, big thanks to Marissa Parks for her original support of this project and to Charles Harmon for patience and grace while seeing it home. Finally, thank you to my bosses, Dean Stanley Wearden and Director Thor Wasbotten, for their support and encouragement during this process.

Managing data on a project of this scope and scale is a daunting and almost Herculean task. I could not have done this without the help of a fantastic and generous research team. Special thanks go to the excellent graduate students who worked on this project: Randy Brown, Caitrin Cardosi, Kathryn Coduto, and Connie Collins. Norma Jones, the world's greatest research assistant and all-around fantastic human being, was invaluable during all phases of this process. Norma, you are a star. Your tireless effort, ready availability, boundless energy, and constant positivity were appreciated more than you could ever know.

When push came to shove, two evergreens volunteered their unwavering support. To my Beautiful Research Assistants, Christine Alexander and Patricia A. Sarver, I cannot thank you enough. You made sure this got done, and your persistence and faith were invaluable. During the writing process, I had the great good fortune to have a first-read critic at my disposal. William

Sarver, your insights and thoughtful commentary made this a richer, more edifying product. This book is much stronger thanks to your intellect and rigor. Thank you.

I also need to give a solid shout-out to those who suffered along with me during the final push to get this written, including the students enrolled in my Spring 2012 classes, Audience Analysis and Research, Global Advertising and Public Relations, and Qualitative Research Methods: Data Collection. Your patience and kindness did not go unnoticed. To my colleagues and friends who endured analytical test-runs, you guys are the best. Thank you. And thanks to those who love to talk politics with me, including Mary Josephine Alexander and Lisa Brabach Skruck

Finally, to my husband, Lindsey, and daughters, Alexandra and Genevieve: Thank you for your love, your hugs, your patience, and your reminders that there is so much good around me. I'm the luckiest person in the world to be able to do a job I love and then come home to my three favorite people. Thank you for being my everything.

Chapter One

Setting the Stage

As polls began to close on Tuesday, November 6, pundits warned that viewers should buckle in for a long, bumpy night. They speculated that the election would be too close to call for hours, with some going so far as to openly question whether Americans would wake up Wednesday morning without knowing who their president would be. After all, this was in the wake of the "most polarized and bitterly contested presidential election of modern times"[1] and Obama "was a very vulnerable incumbent. His party was trounced in the 2010 congressional elections and his healthcare reform, rammed through without a single Republican vote, was highly controversial."[2] Republican candidate Mitt Romney went into the night feeling confident about his chances to come out on top; in fact, he had only prepared a victory speech.[3] Despite these lofty expectations, the night ended fairly early. By 11:15 PM on the Eastern Seaboard, the race was effectively over: "A young man cupped his hands to his mouth—half in prayer and half in shock. Fox News had just called Ohio for President Obama, bringing a deafening silence to the ballroom at Mitt Romney's election night party at the Boston Convention Center."[4] President Barack Obama would remain in the White House. Romney had lost.

In a far cry from predictions of a closely split electorate and an election that would be decided by the smallest of margins, Obama's margin of victory was considerable across all metrics. He won 332 Electoral College votes, 126 more than Romney. His popular vote—62,611,250 to Romney's 59,134,475—was equally impressive. Perhaps more tellingly in an electoral context that had been characterized as conflicted and split, Obama won all but one of the anticipated swing states. Rather than a late-night nail-biter, this was a good old-fashioned rout. Despite presiding over a sluggish economic recovery and lacking widespread approval in the months leading up to the election, Obama managed to persuade voters that he was, in fact, the best choice to lead the country—or at least a better choice than Romney.

As Republicans and conservative pundits scrambled to explain the disaster that had befallen them on election night, fingers almost immediately pointed at their presidential nominee. According to some, Romney had moved so far to the right on key social issues during the primary he could not manage to move back to the center convincingly during the general election campaign. His positions on illegal immigration were considered particularly problematic: "For Mitt Romney to have used the immigration debate as a way of feeding red meat to the party faithful, and to have alienated so many Latinos as a result, could have been a costlier decision in swing states than suggesting Detroit should go bankrupt."[5] Others disagreed, arguing instead that he was too moderate and that the Republicans would have won if an authentic conservative had won the nomination. Another related perspective argued that Romney had no "core values," that he was not a "true conservative"—instead, they speculated that he had adopted conservative values during the primary to win the nomination but never really had the necessary conviction to embody the Tea Party brand of conservatism.

Even Romney's strongest argument to validate his conservative bona fides was questioned in the wake of his loss. While Romney had pointed to his business experience as evidence of his ability to fix the American economy, he never explained how that expertise would translate to the Oval Office. Instead of offering credibility, references to his tenure at Bain Capital often were linked to his extraordinary wealth, at times implying that these financial gains were at the expense of everyday Americans who had been downsized out of jobs as their companies either shut down or moved overseas. As the embodiment of the "one-percent" of the wealthiest Americans vilified by the Occupy movement, Romney was characterized as an out-of-touch millionaire who was incapable of reaching or inspiring the middle class.

Not all rationalizations were focused on Romney's character. His loss also was explained through structural deficiencies and limitations. An extended primary was thought to have depleted his resources at a pivotal time, meaning he had to go fundraise instead of reaching out directly to voters during the lull between being named the presumptive nominee and the party convention. He also was criticized for his "embarrassingly ineffective"[6] get-out-the-vote operation on Election Day and having a strained relationship with the media. Romney and the rest of the Republican elite were thought to have underestimated Obama, unable (or refusing) to see his appeal. Finally, some felt that "Romney's problem—in terms of how he's perceived—is that what he most values is empirical data, which he thinks complement his natural management skill."[7] As Andrew O'Hehir wrote on *Salon.com*, "We just spent an entire year and $2 billion to end up with the same president, the same House, and the same Senate. That sounds a lot like everybody losing, but at least Mitt Romney and those who financed him and pumped him full of hot air lost most of all."[8]

While nerves were raw, the negativity surrounding the Romney candidacy was palpable. If Romney truly embodied even some of these negative characterizations, we have to ask: How did he become the nominee? What happened during the primary contests that led to the nomination of a candidate who could be—and was—critiqued on so many fronts? More importantly, what does this tell us about the influence and impact of the Tea Party, a passionately conservative group that was fighting to redefine the Republican Party? By exploring and understanding these questions we can better understand the state of the Republican Party and, more broadly, electoral politics in the United States.

UNDERSTANDING THE CONTEXT

The 2012 Republican presidential nomination process provides a unique opportunity to witness what in many ways was a battle for the soul of the party. In the wake of President Barack Obama's 2008 election,[9] a new power base emerged in conservative America: the Tea Party. Growing exponentially during the Obama administration, Tea Partiers enjoyed a fair amount of success in 2010 midterm elections, bringing new blood—and a specific philosophy—to Congress. Three key frames defined the movement: advocating for limited government, promoting an "us versus them" dynamic toward "liberal" political media elites, and actively highlighting the concept of those who are "deserving versus undeserving."[10]

Tea Party activists wrapped themselves in the Constitution, with some going so far as to don clothing reminiscent of the Revolutionary War era to reinforce the perception that they represented the fundamental American values of our Founding Fathers. This association with war and revolution was no coincidence; as Edward Ashbee wrote, "The clashes between the movement and the Republican 'establishment' around some of the institutional arrangements that govern the party and structure electoral processes have added to the anger and rage that the movement feels towards the Obama administration."[11] While the Tea Party had aligned with the Republican Party, it was by no means an easy and effortless merger. For Tea Partiers, the 2012 candidate needed to represent their interests, and potential Republican nominees actively courted their support.

Media Framing

While there are varying approaches to understanding what happened during the GOP's 2012 nominating contest, one approach is to examine news coverage. As posited by Plato's Allegory of the Cave, media create "shadows on the cave" that shape and create our understanding of the world outside. Most of us will never see presidential candidates in person, let alone have any sort of meaningful engagement with them. Because we are not able to draw our own conclusions or make our electoral decisions based on firsthand experience, we rely on the mainstream media to help us learn about and get to know our potential leaders.

Although we depend on the media to show us the world outside our everyday lives, even the most casual of media observers would note that those shadows often differ. The media do not reflect one consistent, objective version of the world; instead, they frame news to help us make sense of what we are seeing.[12] Grounded in Goffman's seminal 1974 book *Frame Analysis*, framing "refers to the way events and issues are organized and made sense of, especially by media, media professionals, and their audiences."[13] At its core, framing is "the process of culling a few elements of perceived reality and assembling a narrative that highlights connections among them to promote a particular interpretation"[14] and "is based on the assumption that how an issue is characterized in news reports can have an influence on how it is understood by audiences."[15] When frames are "at their most powerful, [they] invite people to think about an issue in particular ways."[16]

While the study of framing is too complex to cover in detail here, one particular model within this "fractured paradigm"[17] was particularly helpful in shaping this analysis: cascading network activation. As Entman describes in his cascading network activation model,[18] powerful political elites attempt to create and promote frames that advance their purposes. These frames are then reinforced through other elites, including elected officials, staffers, and experts. The media become the filter for these frames, either opting (whether consciously or unconsciously) to reflect or reject the elite-perpetuated frames. The news frames themselves then emerge: the consistent symbols, words, phrases, and images that constitute a systematic representation of the candidate. Finally, the public accepts or rejects these frames, as evidenced through polls, focus groups, and grassroots activity. The public's response to these frames then filters back up the framing food chain, informing and potentially redefining the frames that are used. While Entman created this model to understand issue-based framing (particularly foreign policy), it provides a useful means of exploring the frames that emerge during electoral campaigns as well.

Primaries

Elections provide ample fodder for political and media scholars. Elaborate rallies, bold claims of questionable veracity, and time-tested horserace coverage give us abundant angles with which to explore media narratives. The vast majority of the time, however, these stories focus on the general election, picking up the story after the candidates have been selected. They often start with the party conventions, constructed spectacles designed to rally the base, "bump" poll numbers, and gain momentum as the candidates move toward the first Tuesday in November. Debates provide additional events to analyze, and then the holy grail—the election itself—and the postmortem examinations of what went right for one candidate, and very, very wrong for the other.

While the motivations for this focus on the general election are clear— after all, the final contest between the Democratic and Republican candidates is one of the greatest spectacles in American politics—it also means we have a limited understanding of what led to that event. As the authors of *The Primary Decision* posited, "it is distinctly possible that the primary race ultimately determined who would be president, by deciding who won the right to face a weak opponent. This would make these primary races, in a very important sense, more important than the general campaign."[19] They also identified several ways primary campaigns differ from the general election, including candidates being members of the same parties (thus negating the impact of party membership on candidate support and introducing the challenge of attacking an opponent within the same party), the abundance of candidates, and the "constant state of flux"[20] as candidates move in and out of the race. The lack of a national primary means the geographical locus of the primary campaign moves throughout the race, and the impact of early voting states and their ensuing media coverage is disproportionate to their actual size and representativeness of the American population.[21]

As scholar and political expert Elaine C. Kamarck explains in her excellent book *Primary Politics*, changes to the nominating process "almost always are made in the context of preceding presidential elections. . . . But while the Democrats have been the most frenetic tinkerers, the Republicans too have fallen prey to the desire to 'fix' the system."[22] Before the 2012 primary contest began, the Republican Party opted to make structural changes to respond to what they saw as flaws in the 2008 process, including trying to start the nominating contests later in the year and spreading out the primaries through spring.[23] They also moved away from a "winner take all" delegate strategy, opting instead to allow states to assign delegates to a range of candidates based on the electoral outcome. These decisions were intended to facilitate greater excitement among voters and generate additional interest in the campaign, as they believed the Democrats had enjoyed in 2008 when Barack Obama surprised the political world by winning the nomination in place of early frontrunner Hillary Rodham Clinton.

For candidates running for the nomination, their path to the general election often is slow, labored, and exhausting. Long before they actually face off on a ballot, candidates engage in an "invisible primary"[24] where they try to raise money, increase name recognition, and bring voters into their camps.

During this period, candidates (both declared and potential) need to attain approval from both voters and the party elite.[25] This latter group's influence cannot—and should not—be discounted. They "participate in an extended conversation to pick a presidential nominee . . . [and] make a collective decision regarding which presidential primary candidate is most likely to preserve party orthodoxy and win in the general election."[26]

The impact of elites on the nominating process has been codified through primary policies, including the Republican National Committee's decision to stack the deck in favor of the establishment by giving the RNC chair "greater discretion"[27] in appointing representatives to the Temporary Delegate Selection Committee, a group that made substantive structural changes in the 2012 process. Historically, the Republican Party had enjoyed fairly straightforward nominating contests, largely avoiding the interparty "squabbling" Democrats seemed to suffer with alarming regularity. The active involvement of party elites could help ensure this would continue.

Because the party primaries often involved candidates with almost no recognition on the national stage, media coverage of this period is of particular import. Electoral contest coverage often is framed as a "horse race," with media emphasizing polls and perceptions of momentum to predict who might win (even if only by a nose). In this model, the emphasis is on victory rather than viability or morality. Because the primary campaigns are almost exclusively event driven, the tendency to focus on the horse race likely is exacerbated. At times during this extended season, there is little to write or talk about other than the latest polls or fundraising figures; thus, winning drives the narrative.

Debates are a tool frequently used to generate attention and increase voter awareness of candidates during primary campaigns. They are an important part of the process, since "political debates offer a framework for examining the arguments and issues within a political campaign that help shape potential voters' perceptions about each candidate's character and fitness for office."[28] For voters, debates can be an essential tool for learning about the candidates. Previous research indicates that debate viewing can be a significant predictor of knowledge about issue positions held by candidates[29] and thus change perceptions of who can or should win the nomination.[30] Furthermore, "primary season debates may provide candidates with the best opportunity to influence viewers' perceptions."[31] Instead of flat, two-dimensional names and faces, debates allow candidates to come alive. They can show their personalities, use humor to engage, offer substantive responses to policy- and issue-based questions, and—perhaps most importantly—jockey for position among their competitors, often attempting to define the parameters around which their opponents will be critiqued and evaluated. This is an opportunity for a candidate to demonstrate both viability and electability; in other words, that he or she is capable of leading the party, and also the country.[32]

Citizens United versus Federal Election Commission

In 2010, the U.S. Supreme Court issued a decision that fundamentally changed campaign finance in American elections. In Citizens United versus the Federal Election Commission, "a bitterly divided Supreme Court . . . ruled that the government may not ban political spending by corporations in candidate elections."[33] While justices who voted in favor of the decision hailed this as a "vindication . . . of the First Amendment's most basic free speech principle—that the government has no business regulating political speech," it has resulted in "a deluge of campaign spending, much of it essentially undisclosed. . . . The era of 'dark money' is upon us."[34]

Although direct contributions to candidates were still limited, wealthy donors and organizations could spend as much as they wanted through so-called super PACs, political action committees that ostensibly were not coordinating with campaigns. The decision was characterized as having "freed corporations and unions to spend unlimited sums on politics,"[35] vastly increasing the money available to sustain candidacies and campaigns during the nominating contest. While the *Citizens United* decision was immediately controversial, it established a new reality for the Republican primaries: Candidates now could, and likely would, have extraordinary sums of money working in their corner. This was a game-changer.

UNDERSTANDING FRAMING IN THE 2012 REPUBLICAN PRIMARIES

This study begins just before the first official event designed to determine the Republican candidate: an early debate in May 2011, almost exactly eighteen months before the election. I continue through a year characterized by numerous debates, seemingly endless scandals of varying degrees of import, and cutthroat campaigning, ending in April 2012 with the emergence of Mitt Romney as the Republican nominee. Specifically, I collect and analyze how the mainstream media—including both major print and broadcast outlets—covered this period, looking at the frames that were used to describe the ten Republican candidates[36] and how they shifted over time.[37] Tens of thousands of pages of articles and transcripts were used in this analysis, distilled into the central frames presented in the ensuing pages. In order to best represent the ebb and flow of candidate frames as their fortunes shifted, the narrative is presented chronologically.

To be clear, this book is about the media, not about Republicans. I neither address nor assess the fairness and/or accuracy of mediated depictions of the

Republican candidates or constituents; to do so is well outside the scope of this book. Instead, I came to this work as an interested observer—a scholar intrigued by how we, the people, learned about our candidates through coverage of events often held too far in advance for anyone but the most dedicated and passionate "true believers" to notice, let alone care. The first Republican debate was held a full eighteen months before the general election, and the ever-changing pool of candidates provided a fascinating glimpse into the struggle for the soul of the Grand Old Party. As a Democrat, I knew I would not play a part in the selection of the candidate. I did not have a horse in this race, so to speak—I could look at this impartially, as a media scholar, rather than as a citizen actively making a decision about who should represent me in the general election.

With that clarification and disclaimer fully in place, let us move to May 2012. The onset of spring brings sunshine, warm weather, and the official kick-off of the Republican presidential race . . .

NOTES

1. *Guardian* (U.K.) Editorial, "Barack Obama's Second Term: Change He Can Believe In," *TheGuardian.com*, November 7, 2012, www.guardian.co.uk/commentisfree/2012/nov/07/obama-second-term-change.

2. Toby Harnden, "Hindsight Will View Romney as a Poor Candidate with No Core Values Who Looked Deeply Uncomfortable," *MailOnline.com*, November 7, 2012, http://www.dailymail.co.uk/news/article-2229083/US-Election-2012-analysis-Hindsight-view-Mitt-Romney-poor-candidate-says-Toby-Harnden.html.

3. "Romney Prepared Victory Speech for Election, but Delivered Concession Speech Instead," *Washington Post*, November 7, 2012, http://articles.washingtonpost.com/2012-11-07/politics/35504045_1_mitt-romney-romney-plane-romney-first.

4. Ashley Parker, "The Scene at Romney Headquarters," *NewYorkTimes.com: Live Coverage of the Election Day*, November 29, 2012, http://elections.nytimes.com/2012/results/live-coverage.

5. *Guardian*, "Barack Obama's Second Term."

6. *The Week Editorial*, "Mitt Romney's Disastrous Ground Game and 7 Other Behind-the-Scenes Revelations," *Yahoo!News.com*, November 9, 2012, news.yahoo.com/mitt-romneys-disastrous-ground-game-7-other-behind-113000893-election.html.

7. Tom Bevan and Carl M. Cannon, "21 Reasons for Obama's Victory and Romney's Defeat," *RealClearPolitics.com*, November 7, 2012, http://www.realclearpolitics.com/articles/2012/11/07/21_reasons_for_obamas_victory_and_romneys_defeat_116090-full.html.

8. Andrew O'Hehir, "Fox News' Dark Night of the Soul," *Salon.com*, November 7, 2012, http://www.salon.com/2012/11/07/fox_news_dark_night_of_the_soul/.

9. David A. Weaver and Joshua M. Scacco, "Revisiting the Protest Paradigm: The Tea Party as Filtered through Prime-Time Cable News," *International Journal of Press/Politics* 18 (2013), doi: 10.1177/1940161212462872.

10. Edward Ashbee, "Bewitched—The Tea Party Movement: Ideas, Interests and Institutions," *Political Quarterly* 82 (2011), doi: 10.1111/j.1467-923X.2011.02175.x.

11. Ibid., 164.

12. For an excellent assessment of framing, I suggest *Framing Public Life* (Routledge, 2010), edited by Stephen D. Reese, Oscar H. Gandy Jr., and August E. Grant.

13. Stephen D. Reese, "Framing Public Life: A Bridging Model for Media Research," in *Framing Public Life: Perspectives on Media and Our Understanding of the Social World*, ed. Stephen D. Reese, Oscar H. Gandy Jr., and August E. Grant (New York: Routledge, 2001).

14. Robert M. Entman, "Framing Bias: Media in the Distribution of Power," *Journal of Communication* 57 (2007): 164, doi: 10.1111/j.1460-2466.2006.00336.x.

15. Dietram A. Scheufele and David Tewksbury, "Framing, Agenda Setting, and Priming: The Evolution of Three Media Effects Models," *Journal of Communication* 57 (2007): 11, doi: 10.1111/j.0021-9916.2007.00326.x.

16. David Tewksbury and Dietram A. Scheufele, "News Framing Theory and Research," in *Media Effects: Advances in Theory and Research*, 3rd ed., ed. Jennings Bryant and Mary Beth Oliver (New York: Routledge, 2009), 19.

17. Robert M. Entman, "Framing: Toward Clarification of a Fractured Paradigm," *Journal of Communication* 43 (1993): 51, doi: 10.1111/j.1460-2466.1993.tb01304.x. Also see D'Angelo and Kuyper's introduction in their wonderful *Doing News Analysis: Empirical and Theoretical Perspectives* for an overview of the disparate strands and uses in framing research and theory.

18. Robert M. Entman, *Projections of Power: Framing News, Public Opinion, and U.S. Foreign Policy* (Chicago: University of Chicago Press, 2004), 4. The cascading activation model is explained beginning on page 4.

19. William L. Benoit, P. M. Pier, LeAnn M. Brazeal, John P. McHale, Andrew Klyukovski and David Airne, *The Primary Decision: A Functional Analysis of Debates in Presidential Primaries* (Westport: Praeger, 2002), 3.

20. Ibid.

21. The Benoit book referenced above is an excellent resource for understanding the issues around and importance of primary debates.

22. Elaine C. Kamarck, *Primary Politics: How Presidential Candidates Have Shaped the Modern Nominating System* (Washington, D.C.: Brookings, 2009), xi.

23. Joshua T. Putnam, "The Impact of Rules Changes on the 2012 Republican Presidential Primary Process," *Society* 49 (2012): 400–4.

24. Jack Citrin and David Karol, "Introduction," in *Nominating the President: Evolution and Revolution in 2008 and Beyond*, ed. Jack Citrin and David Karol (Lanham: Rowman & Littlefield, 2009).

25. Marty Cohen, David Karol, Hans Noel, and John Zaller, *The Party Decides: Presidential Nominations Before and After Reform* (Chicago: University of Chicago Press, 2008).

26. Ibid, 71.

27. Citrin and Karol, "Introduction," 23.

28. Diana P. Carlin, "Presidential Debates as Focal Points for Campaign Arguments," *Political Communication* 9 (1992): 252, doi:10.1080/10584609.1992.9962949.

29. Dan Drew and David Weaver, "Voter Learning in the 1988 Presidential Election: Did the Debates and the Media Matter?" *Journalism & Mass Communication Quarterly* 68 (1991), doi: 10.1177/107769909106800104.

30. Mike Yawn, Kevin Ellsworth, Bob Beatty, and Kim Fridkin Kahn, "How a Presidential Primary Debate Changed Attitudes of Audience Members," *Political Behavior* 20 (1998), doi: 10.1023/A:1024832830083.

31. David J. Lanoue and Peter R. Schrott, "The Effects of Primary Season Debates on Public Opinion," *Political Behavior* 11 (1989): 291, doi: 10.1007/BF00992301.

32. Yawn et al., "How a Presidential Primary Debate," 168.

33. Adam Liptak, "Justices, 5-4, Reject Corporate Spending Limit," *NewYorkTimes.com: Politics*, January 21, 2010, http://www.nytimes.com/2010/01/22/us/politics/22scotus.html?pagewanted=all.

34. Jessica Levinson, "Will the SEC save us from Citizens United?" *SacamentoBee.com: Viewpoints*, March 5, 2013, http://www.sacbee.com/2013/05/04/5394092/will-the-sec-save-us-from-citizens.html.

35. "The Supreme Court's Cowardice," *Bloomberg.com: Opinion*, June 26, 2012, http://www.bloomberg.com/news/2012-06-26/the-supreme-court-s-cowardice.html.

36. Only candidates who took part in a nationally televised debate were included in this analysis.

37. For a more complete explanation of and justification for the methods used in this book, please refer to the Appendix.

Chapter Two

Unsettled Field

May–June 2011

With the onset of spring, the Republican Party was poised to officially launch the search for its presidential candidate. In years past, candidates would traipse through early voting states to give speeches, charm voters, and solicit donors. The denizens of Iowa and New Hampshire, seasoned political veterans of campaigns past, reveled in their first-in-the-nation status. They were accustomed to candidates currying their favor and offering face-to-face attention, often calling candidates by their first names due to the frequency of their interactions. Typically the field would be fairly set by now: who was running, who was competitive, and who was wasting their time. The race looked a bit different in early 2011, however. While the pool of Republican nominees was beginning to emerge, this was an uncertain field. Unlike GOP presidential contests of the recent past, there was no preordained nominee.[1] Widely considered the frontrunner, Romney had not yet managed to convincingly make his case that he was the best choice. Voters and the Republican establishment spent early May expressing concern about the field as it stood, hoping that either a stronger favorite would emerge from the pack or that other, more appealing potential candidates would throw their hats in the ring. This active search for alternative options led to some interesting commentary, including *Saturday Night Live*'s Seth Meyers's joke at the 2011 White House Correspondents' Association dinner: "Just look at the options the Republicans are kicking around, Palin, Huckabee, Gingrich, Trump. That doesn't sound like a field of candidates, that sounds like season 13 of 'Dancing with the Stars.'"[2]

MEET THE CANDIDATES

While some still hoped for additional names in the race, favorites Mike Huckabee, a former Mississippi governor and prominent social conservative, and Mitch Daniels, the Indiana governor respected for his fiscal conservatism and appeal to mainstream Republicans, both declined to join. New Jersey governor Chris Christie, Texas governor Rick Perry, Wisconsin congressman Paul Ryan, and Florida senator Marco Rubio all repeatedly insisted they would not be running in 2012, and even businessman and reality television star Donald Trump eventually made clear he was out. With these possibilities falling by the wayside, a defined pool of candidates was beginning to emerge. At this point, the media consistently framed the candidates as being in three broad groups: top-tier candidates (Jon Huntsman, Tim Pawlenty, and Romney); Tea Party conservatives (Michele Bachmann, Herman Cain, Newt Gingrich, and Rick Santorum); and the libertarian fringe (Gary Johnson and Ron Paul). These depictions represent the ways most Americans were introduced to or reminded of these candidates in the earliest stages of the nominating process and thus help set the baseline for exploring how potential nominees were framed throughout their campaigns.

Top-Tier Candidates

The three media-defined top-tier candidates in early May—Huntsman, Pawlenty, and Romney—were all former governors. Only one, Romney, had wide name recognition at this point, based on his candidacy in the 2008 nominating contest. While the other two benefited from their inclusion in this top tier, they knew they faced an uphill battle in getting their names out and building recognition among voters. Despite this, the media frame was clear: These were the only legitimate choices at this point in the race. A *Washington Post* article quoted Republican consultant Alex Castellanos as saying, "Electability is going to matter. That means, unless the field changes, only one of these three can win the nomination."[3] During a discussion about the Republican candidates' somewhat grumbling reactions to the killing of Osama bin Laden, David Frum echoed this sentiment on CNN, noting that Pawlenty and Romney were "normal American political figures" in contrast to the likes of Cain and Bachmann, "who are in politics for very different kinds of reasons. And there comes a point where you have to stop pretending that they are the same kind of candidate. There are people who are likely to be— who have a chance of being Republican presidential nominees and people who just don't."[4]

Jon Huntsman

Former Utah governor Jon Huntsman stepped off an airplane from Beijing and into his campaign. As the returning U.S. ambassador to China, Huntsman found himself working with political pros who had actively recruited him to run—some without even having met the candidate. Among his team were a number of former McCain staffers, seasoned veterans of the early nominating battles in Iowa and New Hampshire. While they knew Huntsman's campaign would face considerable challenges due to low name recognition and his Obama association, they believed he marked the best chance to nominate a candidate who could appeal to independent voters and win against the incumbent president in a general election. CNN correspondent Jim Acosta referred to the "presidential politics baptism" Huntsman was undergoing in early May, noting that his arrival comes at a time when some Republicans were less than confident about their choices: "and that's why a lot of Washington experts are looking at Jon Huntsman right now as sort of the tantalizing prospect, sort of the flavor of the moment, if you will. That's because not only is Jon Huntsman telegenic, he is also very campaign savvy."[5]

Early coverage of Huntsman typically referred to him as the dreaded M-word: moderate. Despite his branding as such based on a limited number of social issues, Huntsman offered some of the most fiscally conservative positions on social issues among all of the candidates, particularly in terms of foreign policy. When asked about U.S. military involvement in Libya, Huntsman's response clearly indicated his belief that engagement should be based not strictly on national security, but also on the financial realities of military involvement. He was quoted in the *New York Times* as saying, "It's an affordability issue. . . . With all of our deployments and all of our engagements abroad, we need to ask a fundamental question: Can we afford to do this? That should be driven by the second point, which is whether or not it's in our national security interest."[6] Huntsman also quickly developed a riposte to criticisms that he had worked for the Obama administration and thus would not be a credible Republican candidate, reframing the debate as a demonstration of his patriotism: "I'm the kind of person when asked by my president to stand up and serve my country. When asked, I do it."[7]

Some pundits speculated whether being known as a moderate could work to his advantage: "But the Huntsman campaign thinks—excuse me, he's not officially a candidate, but they believe there's space for him in the field for kind of a moderate, fresh face."[8] The frame of bringing something new and different to the table—implying a respite from the same old, same old drudgery represented by other candidates like Romney—permeated early coverage of Huntsman. Notwithstanding a strong history of socially conservative positions on some key issues, including abortion, and an unimpeachable record as a fiscal conservative, support for domestic partnerships for same-sex partners and a history with cap-and-trade environmental regulations coupled with a refusal to offer knee-jerk anti-Obama rhetoric meant he was by default framed as the moderate in the race. According to the *New York Times*'s Jeff Zeleny, Huntsman "presented himself as a sunny alternative to the Republican field. If he decides to run, he will test whether the party has an opening for a candidate who sits in the middle, rather than the right, of the Republican spectrum."[9]

"Moderate" was not the only M-word presenting a challenge for Huntsman's campaign; as a Mormon, Huntsman faced the same difficulties appealing to a conservative Christian base as fellow candidate (and fellow Mormon) Romney. During May, media pundits pondered over what this meant for him in Iowa, speculating that this would lead to increased importance of New Hampshire, a state with a much weaker conservative Christian influence, in his campaign strategy. They also suspected that Huntsman and his campaign team would not be attempting to compete with conservative values candidates, including one of his perceived top-tier competitors, Tim Pawlenty.

One of the most interesting frames to emerge about Huntsman during this time was that he was a different kind of candidate: Rather than pounding his fist and calling for blood, Huntsman's campaign would be "soothing in tone to the American people."[10] He intended to have thoughtful, reasoned debates, focused on moving the country forward instead of battling to a standstill. While this certainly had appeal for some voters (and provided an interesting hook for media looking for a story), this approach reinforced the difficulty Huntsman—a self-described "margin of error"[11] candidate with very low name recognition—would face in breaking through to Republican voters. If Huntsman were not willing to yell, how would he be heard among the cacophony created by other candidates?

Tim Pawlenty

Early May coverage of Tim Pawlenty emphasized that he was a top-tier candidate in large part because he had been working the electoral system the traditional way: paying dues to kingmakers in the early voting states and spending as much time on the ground as possible to garner name recognition and appeal among key constituencies. As *Washington Post*'s Chris Cillizza wrote, "Former Minnesota governor Tim Pawlenty holds the pole position to be the anti-Romney, having benefited over the past few months from hard work and luck."[12] A favorite of both the media and the elite, Pawlenty profited from other politicians opting out of the race; when Huckabee decided not to run, Pawlenty was positioned to absorb those Christian values voters, and when Daniels declined he hoped to pick up the fiscal conservatives from that camp as well. Much like Huntsman, however, Pawlenty's most significant challenge was that he had very little name recognition among voters.

Regardless of his low awareness among voters, Pawlenty commonly was tapped as a real contender in this election. On MSNBC's "The Last Word," host Lawrence O'Donnell and guest Steve Schmidt speculated that Pawlenty would go far in the nominating process. Schmidt's assessment of Pawlenty's speechmaking was generally positive, if not overly enthusiastic: "He's not bad at all. He's pretty good. He can connect with an audience. He has an ability to communicate to the middle of the country."[13] The last part of this message was central to Pawlenty's appeal: As a Minnesotan, pundits believed he could appeal to voters in key Midwestern states, including Ohio and Michigan.

In an effort to differentiate himself from his competition, particularly Romney, Pawlenty attempted to frame himself as a candidate who would be candid instead of political—even when those truths and positions are unpopular. In the speech in which he declared his candidacy, entitled "A Time for Truth," Pawlenty made "repeated references to honesty and truth, a word that he used 16 times during the course of a 20-minute speech."[14] Claiming that the difficult economic conditions faced by Americans in 2011 were created by politicians unwilling to tell hard certainties, he took great strides to be perceived as the opposite. Pawlenty deliberately discussed his support for eliminating ethanol subsidies in Iowa, a state where a substantial corn farming industry greatly profited from this program. He also broached the need to revisit Social Security to voters in Florida, much of whose elderly population relied on the system to survive. While taking these unpopular positions was a conscious decision to reinforce his authenticity as a fiscal conservative as well as the embodiment of the new kind of "truth-telling" politician, these bold statements certainly were risky for a mostly unknown candidate who had not built reserves of goodwill among voters.

While he was consistently referred to as a top-tier candidate during this period, as spring rolled on a frame emerged addressing his inability to excite the Republican base. He continued to put in exhaustive hours to win over voters and kingmakers in Iowa, a state considered essential to establishing the momentum that would catapult him to the top of the pack once voting began. Despite his considerable efforts, Pawlenty was not connecting with Iowans in a way that would help him effectively leapfrog Romney. While he was doing all he was supposed to do, Pawlenty was not quite catching fire. In an article exploring Pawlenty's efforts in Sioux, Iowa, journalist Michael Leahy notes that despite the hard work Pawlenty had put into building a base there, he was not able to completely win over voters: "But all this qualified praise for Pawlenty betrays a muted leeriness: Few in Sioux have been deeply turned on by anyone, including him. Potential backers are 'leaning' his way, or 'getting close.' In a largely empty field, Pawlenty has made an impression, but that's all for now."[15]

Mitt Romney

While Huntsman and Pawlenty had to fight to build name recognition, Willard "Mitt" Romney found himself in a very different position. A familiar face in both Iowa and New Hampshire, Romney's campaign was in many ways a continuation of what he began to build when attempting to gain the Republican nomination in 2008. After spending his last campaign introducing himself to voters in an effort to build name recognition, he had the advantage this go-around of being the perceived frontrunner, albeit considered "the weakest frontrunner in any recent Republican nomination campaign,"[16] and generally was thought to be the establishment choice.

The scion of former Michigan governor George W. Romney, Mitt grew up in an affluent environment. He went to elite schools, including simultaneously earning law (J.D.) and business (M.B.A.) degrees at Harvard University. An experienced governor and campaigner and a successful businessman in his own right, Romney was lauded as a candidate who understood the economy and knew how to create jobs. This expertise led him to develop a campaign message that was "devoted almost exclusively to the economy,"[17] emphasizing his experience with investment firm Bain Capital. Republican strategist Christian Ferry noted that "Romney has been running an incredibly disciplined campaign,"[18] refusing to let other candidates or events distract him from his singular focus. Romney and his advisers were clear: he would "stake his candidacy on the economy. They say that is the key to winning the nomination and the White House, and on that they sound defiant."[19]

Romney's campaign certainly benefited from his 2008 candidacy in terms of structure and name recognition, but his time in the spotlight clearly created problems for the candidate. He still carried baggage from the previous campaign, particularly in the early voting states where memories are long and voters pay close attention. Romney's biography and bank account, while in some ways ideal for a Republican running for office, reinforced perceptions that he was formal and distant, unable to connect with the everyday men and women who would be heading to the polls. More problematically, there was a strong perception that Romney had a sometimes-passing acquaintance with the truth. This fed into and reinforced what was probably the most damaging personal frame he faced: that Romney was a political flip-flopper, willing to change his mind on a whim in order to better appeal to the voters in front of him at that time.

More diplomatically referred to as Romney's authenticity problem, this meant that every political statement and decision made by Romney during the campaign was considered a marketing choice rather than a reflection of his true beliefs. This frame was made clear in a June 2011 *Washington Post* article about climate change, in which Philip Rucker and Peter Wallsten discussed the potential political repercussions of Romney's stated belief that global warming is occurring and is being exacerbated by humans. An anathema to most conservative Republicans, this was a statement guaranteed to raise additional concerns about Romney's bona fides. Rather than framing Romney's decision as being grounded in true convictions and/or science, the reporters write: "The episode suggests that Romney and his team, trying to market the candidate as authentic, see more of a benefit in sticking with his position and taking heat than in shifting to win over a crucial segment of the conservative base."[20] This demonstrates the difficulties faced by a candidate who is suspected of shifting too often on issues: No matter what Romney had said here, the decision would have been framed as a marketing ploy rather than an honest response. During an appearance on Fox News, *New York Daily News* publisher Mort Zuckerman voiced the concern felt by many Republicans: "But I think he's a serious candidate. He's a talented man. He was an effective governor in Massachusetts. But he does have this tendency to go from one state to another and have different views."[21]

While Romney's personal challenges as a candidate were numerous, his feared Achilles heel[22] was found in a piece of legislation passed while governor of Massachusetts. In the build-up to the 2012 elections, Republican candidates repeatedly and regularly derided the Affordable Care Act passed as a signature piece of legislation for the Obama administration in 2010. Republicans were outraged at what they considered the insidious invasion of government in private lives, and they expected their candidates to clearly and unequivocally reject "Obamacare" and its requirements. For Romney, that was "tricky territory," with media noting that "the new national health-care law, enacted last year, is similar in design and ambition to the greatest achievement of his tenure as governor—a landmark 2006 law that established Massachusetts as the first state in the nation to guarantee health insurance coverage for all its residents."[23]

Pundits noted the difficulties Romney would face in parsing his support for the state bill from his rejection of the federal equivalent. His first effort was an early May PowerPoint presentation in Michigan, where Romney pointed to the Tenth Amendment as justification for his position, citing the states' rights position held dear by Tea Partiers and conservatives in an effort to explain away this contradiction. "It was the start of a treacherous balancing act for Mr. Romney, one that forced him to confront not just the complexities and passions surrounding health policy but also questions about his willingness to stick to his principles under political pressure."[24]

The obvious challenges presented by health care legislation coupled with the lingering questions around Romney's character and convictions remaining from his previous races meant some Republicans—even those who had supported him during the 2008 campaign—were hedging their bets. Several stories noted that high-profile endorsers were either holding off or offering their support to others, while other stories cited big donors who were reconsidering their support. The media framed this hesitancy as directly related to concerns about Romney and his potential to win; since donors and high-profile politicians were not convinced that Romney could take the election, they were biding their time to see what else might happen. On Fox News, guest Mara Liasson of National Public Radio got to the heart of the matter when she acknowledged "there is a huge hunger in the party for (an) established alternative to Mitt Romney."[25]

In the face of this, Romney and his team focused in these early days on doing what needed to be done to reinforce and maintain the perception of Romney as the clear frontrunner while keeping a low enough profile to avoid direct attacks from his fellow candidates. Fundraising was a major part of this, including a one-day phone bank event in Las Vegas that raised over $10 million.[26] Grooming potential donors was central to Romney's strategy, and he spent much of his time during this period meeting with potential patrons rather than doing the traditional meet-and-greets on the campaign trail. Media speculated that this was part of Romney's "shock-and-awe"[27] approach to fundraising, intended to "keep his rivals at bay by frightening them with his fund-raising . . . aimed at amassing a money total that dwarfs the competition when the first official tallies are released in early July."[28]

Further efforts to reinforce perceptions that Romney was the inevitable nominee included campaign decisions to skip any events that might indicate otherwise. Romney did not participate in the May 5 debate in South Carolina, and he decided to opt out of Iowa's Ames Straw Poll along with all other straw polls held prior to the nominating kick-off in January. These decisions were made in the wake of spending millions to win the Ames event in 2007 and then coming in second in the actual 2008 caucus, a result that he and his team believe stalled his campaign. This decision also reinforced the recognition that Romney was a hard sell in Iowa. Social conservatives did not trust his commitment to core conservative values, and evangelical Christians did not trust him because he was a devout Mormon.

While media were quick to note the challenges of Romney as a candidate and his coverage often included references to his limitations, one of the most consistent frames throughout this period was that Romney was running a smart, calculated campaign, with every decision carefully considered to maximize his electability. After all, "Romney's goal, according to advisers, is to keep his eyes on the bigger prize and to run his own race. . . . His hope is to convince Republican voters that, whatever flaws they may see in him, he is still the strongest candidate for the general election."[29]

Tea Party Conservatives

Despite the gains made by the Tea Party and its undeniable impact in the 2010 midterm elections, early May media coverage did not seem to take the potential influence of these candidates particularly seriously. While certainly representing the voices of the Tea Party movement, including leaders of various Tea Party organizations and voters aligned with them, the candidates most favored by or trying to appeal to the group—Bachmann, Cain, Santorum, and to a lesser extent Gingrich—were not considered likely candidates in the early days of the race.

Michele Bachmann

First elected to Congress as a representative from Minnesota, native Iowan Michele Bachmann rose to national attention as a firebrand conservative, willing to buck her party's leadership in order to be as true as possible to her conservative values. She was unafraid to be out of step with her Republican colleagues in Congress, and she was known as one of the most passionate—and strident—voices in the House. A regular presence on cable news networks, where she often could be found making what were considered by many to be outrageous claims about Obama, his administration, Democrats in Congress, and White House staffers, Bachmann had developed a reputation that she was more of a provocateur than a legislator. As such, she was framed during this early period as a vanity candidate, running to increase her public profile and negotiating power but with no real chance at winning.

In fact, one of the few in-depth pieces on Bachmann in these early days highlighted her lack of legislative success. In an article published on May 2, 2011, the *Washington Post*'s Philip Rucker and Paul Kane noted that, despite her national popularity, Bachmann had done almost nothing of note in Congress: "Despite her fame and her skill at attracting controversial headlines, Bachmann has yet to leave her mark as a policymaker or legislator. On Capitol Hill, she holds little sway with her colleagues and has guided no substantial legislation into law."[30] The article intimated that Bachmann's prioritizing public appearances and media ranting over governing had soured relations with some of her Republican colleagues: "In March, several freshmen spoke out at a closed-door party meeting. Although none singled out Bachmann by name, the freshmen accused some colleagues of provocative media appearances that distracted from the party's overall goals."[31] They then noted, "Bachmann did not hear the criticism. She had left the meeting early to scurry back to her office. She was scheduled to be the call-in guest on Laura Ingraham's nationally syndicated conservative radio show."[32]

While Bachmann's media presence might be considered somewhat of a distraction for her colleagues, it certainly was a boon as a presidential candidate. As she raised her visibility via cable news and talk radio, Bachmann became known in the media as the de facto face of the Tea Party movement. Almost every article and transcript in these early months referred to her in some context as the Tea Party "darling" or "heroine," citing her absolute positions on issues near and dear to the collective Tea Party heart. She also was framed as a masterful moneymaker, with Fox News calling her a "fund-raising powerhouse."[33]

Bachmann was not considered the only woman representing the Tea Party and its constituents, however. In most of the early Bachmann coverage, references to her candidacy were considered in conjunction with former Alaska governor and 2008 Republican vice presidential nominee Sarah Palin. During this period, Palin was still publicly considering a run. She had organized bus tours in key states, but refused to give clear indication of her plans. With Palin's name still in the mix, media pundits typically speculated about their potential candidacies in relation to each other, often noting that these two women would be positioned to energize what was a somewhat desultory contest at this point. In fact, a May 18, 2011, *Wall Street Journal* article by Jonathan Weisman and Neil King Jr. quoted GOP strategist and former Huckabee campaign manager Ed Rollins as saying, "The girls are the exciting candidates. They're the ones that can create a stir."[34] As evidenced by this quote, much of the Bachmann (and Bachmann and Palin) coverage either implicitly or explicitly focused on appearance and gender. At this point, however, the primary focus was on whether or not Bachmann could appeal outside of the Tea Party.

Questions about Bachmann's legitimacy as a candidate were frequently raised among the media examined, particularly in terms of her ability to understand complex economic issues (despite her background as a tax attorney working for the Internal Revenue Service). She also faced scrutiny due to her historical tendency to overstate or misrepresent "facts" to better suit her argument, including public and notable misstatements on the history of slavery and accusations of "secret funds" in Obama's health care law. Bachmann rarely let these errors put her off stride, however. When asked on Fox News about a speech in which she mistakenly said Lexington and Concord were in New Hampshire instead of Massachusetts, she played it off with a joke: "I made a mistake and promise never again [to] use President Obama's tele-prompter. I intend to keep that promise."[35] While Bachmann seemed ready and willing to laugh off these gaffes, Republican elites and the mainstream media wondered out loud whether or not she would have the discipline to run a national, presidential campaign.

Herman Cain

Businessman Herman Cain first entered the public eye when he told President Bill Clinton that "in the competitive marketplace, it simply doesn't work that way"[36] during the late 1990s health care reform push. Within the context of a nominating contest that focused a tremendous amount of discussion on the repeal of Obama's health care law, Cain's authority on the topic from the business perspective—and his belief in the need for a repeal—was notable. This was part of an overarching frame that focused on Cain's business background, giving him credibility on job creation and the economy, two extremely important issues in the 2012 election.

Unlike his competition for the nomination, Cain had never held an elected office. While some might have considered this a mark against a candidate running for the highest office in the land, Cain wore this "outsider status" as a badge of honor (although he rarely mentioned his loss in the primaries when running for an open U.S. Senate seat in his native Georgia or his time as the head of the Washington, D.C., lobbying group, the National Restaurant Association). His campaign and coverage at this point often emphasized his fiery personality, including how excited crowds would get while hearing him speak. While Cain was light on political experience and substance, he was long on character and intangible appeal. Coverage of Cain at this time often mentioned his Horatio Alger-esque background as the son of a domestic worker and chauffeur who rose to be chief executive at a national restaurant chain.

The only racial minority running for the Republican nomination, Cain was in the unique position to provide a living, breathing refutation to accusations that the Tea Party was anti-Obama not because of his policies, but because of his skin. As a fellow black man, Cain could address race and racial politics in a way his compatriots could not. He also kept winning: the South Carolina debate, a Washington State straw poll, and momentum in a field in desperate need of energy. His traction was a surprise, since "he's a blip on national polls, a newcomer to presidential politics and has never held elected office. He's an African-American in a party that remains overwhelmingly white. He brushes all that aside, describing himself at a recent rally as 'the black guy who keeps winning stuff.'"[37]

Newt Gingrich

As Speaker of the House in the 1990s and the chief architect of the Republican's "Contract with America" during that period, Georgia native Newt Gingrich was the intellectual driver behind the GOP for a number of years. After leaving office under the cloud of heavy Republican losses, a Congressional reprimand for an ethics violation, and personal scandals including multiple ex-wives and an admission of adultery (notably the revelation of a six-year affair with a Congressional staffer, his now-wife Callista), Gingrich had spent the ensuing decades building numerous centers and organizations, including a multimedia production company creating content designed to promote issues and ideas near and dear to his heart. The latest topic of note was American exceptionalism,[38] a concept around which he hoped to build his campaign.

In early May, questions abounded about the sincerity of Gingrich's candidacy. Media pundits and Republican commentators wondered about how seriously he was taking this venture, debating whether Gingrich's true intent was to raise his profile in order to help him sell more books and movies and keep him in the public eye. His insistence that he was absolutely committed to winning and his hiring of experienced political strategists and campaign team members to join his long-term staffers slowly quieted those concerns. Quickly, however, coverage turned to his ability to actually succeed in the day-to-day operations of this venture. His doubters noted that Gingrich had not run a political campaign of any sort for years and that the campaigns he *had* run were not for a national office. Furthermore, it was not enough that Gingrich had good ideas—and no one doubted he had ideas in abundance—but he needed to be able to focus on "ideas that have relevance to the people he needs to energize,"[39] translating "his many ideas into one larger and consistent vision for the country that connects with people."[40] This abundance of ideas but inability to evaluate and edit fit into an overarching frame for Gingrich's campaign: His lack of discipline would make surviving a tough campaign even more difficult. Not only did he have difficulty focusing; he also was known for speaking off the cuff and without thinking through consequences—a common foible for someone considered "one of the smartest people in American politics."[41]

Because of his scandal-ridden past, Gingrich's attempts to appeal to the socially conservative Tea Party voters were not a natural fit. Media frames during this period emphasized this disconnect. While Gingrich converted to Catholicism for his current wife (the aforementioned Congressional staffer, Callista) and was by all accounts fairly devout, his history of peccadillos was considered a hard sell to the morally focused conservative Christian voters who made up much of the Tea Party constituency, particularly in Iowa. As the *New York Times*'s Matt Bai wrote, "Mr. Gingrich, a bit of a rogue in his personal life, has never been a favorite of his party's powerful social conservatives, who tend to think of scandalous affairs as the purview of Democrats, and maybe Rudy Giuliani."[42] Despite this, Gingrich was convinced that his brand of conservatism would appeal to the Tea Party voters as long as he could address the issues head on: "Mr. Gingrich is well aware that social conservatives are skeptical of him because he did not emphasize their issues in Congress, but also because of his two divorces and admissions of infidelity. He has been meeting with religious leaders around the country to address their concerns."[43]

Gingrich's faith in his candidacy was rooted in what he believed was historical precedence and impetus—for him, running for president had a sense of destiny about it. Media coverage of him during this period often referenced his fascination with history, quoting Gingrich drawing parallels between his candidacy and those of Ronald Reagan (the golden god of the Tea Party), Abraham Lincoln, and Thomas Jefferson.[44] Others were not quite as quick to hold Gingrich in as high esteem as the political luminaries he mentioned. Somewhat surprisingly, coverage of Gingrich included considerably more outright jokes about him and his past (including the Giuliani quip above) than other candidates. These sometimes were worked in as quotes from voters; for example, an article about Pawlenty included a section where Iowans debated about the different candidates. The following conversation was chronicled: "'His track record on marriage isn't all that good,' Goemaat said. 'Forgiveness is important, but he carries a lot of baggage.' Lantinga raised his finger and grinned, having just remembered something. 'I heard that [Kentucky Sen.] Rand Paul said that Gingrich has more positions on Libya than wives.' The two men laughed. Gingrich was out for them."[45] Clearly, appealing to the Tea Party and socially conservative voters would be an uphill battle for the former Speaker.

Rick Santorum

During these early months of the campaign, coverage of Rick Santorum presented him almost exclusively as a "culture warrior."[46] While other candidates and prominent Republicans wanted to keep the nominating debates focused on the economy, perceived to be Obama's weakest front, Santorum refused, saying, "Anybody who would suggest we call a truce on moral issues doesn't understand what America's all about."[47] Known as a rigid social conservative due to his staunch Roman Catholic beliefs, Santorum fought during this period to be perceived as a candidate with broader appeal. He talked about his record, pointing out that during his time in the Senate he had one major piece of legislation on social issues but two on foreign policy. Despite these efforts, Santorum's coverage rarely included any consistent or prominent frames other than his strong conservative positions on social issues.

What is somewhat surprising during this period is how little coverage there actually was about Santorum. As a two-term senator from Pennsylvania, a state likely to play an important role during the general election, Santorum should have generated more coverage than the limited amount he did during this period. While various explanations are possible, one likely factor in this dearth of media attention is exactly what drove the coverage he did receive: he was considered *so* conservative—much more so than the average American—that he could not possibly be elected to the presidency during the general election. Past statements about same-sex marriage and abortion and the ensuing coverage defined Santorum as a slightly ridiculous, rabid right-winger, and even though these characterizations were not explicitly discussed in this early coverage, it certainly is likely that they informed perceptions of Santorum and his electability among media and political elites.

The Libertarian Fringe

The remaining two known candidates in early May, Gary Johnson and Ron Paul, were both running for the nomination as libertarians. While this certainly did not preclude them from running, it did limit framing of their viability as candidates. Johnson, in fact, almost disappears from coverage after the first debate in South Carolina, while Paul's continuous candidacy and populist appeal kept him in the mix.

Gary Johnson

Despite being the first Republican to officially declare his candidacy, former New Mexico governor Gary Johnson received surprisingly little coverage, particularly among the newspapers. His media coverage climaxed with the May 5 debate, where he joined fellow libertarian Ron Paul on stage with other GOP candidates. While it is never stated outright, the lack of coverage for Johnson considered in conjunction with Paul's past experience indicates that the media just do not believe a libertarian has a realistic shot at the Republican nomination. Without being considered a viable candidate, Johnson did not offer the other incentives for media coverage: scandal and/or entertainment value. As such, he was almost entirely omitted from both newspaper and cable television during this period.

Ron Paul

While Johnson's experience points to the real challenges faced by non-mainstream Republicans,[48] Paul's repeated efforts to obtain the Republican nomination and his passionate fan base means he was given much more coverage than Johnson in the press. As a "self-described contrarian,"[49] the "irrepressible"[50] Paul repeatedly demonstrated during this period that he was unafraid to speak his mind, regardless of the party position or the popularity of his perspective. Despite the knowledge that most values-based conservative voters would object to drug use, Paul advocated for the legalization of heroin during the South Carolina debate: "'How many people here would use heroin if it was legal?' he asked the audience, which again erupted in applause."[51]

Paul's framing during this period characterized him as a powerful fundraiser with a passionate base. During the May 5 debate, his campaign organized a one-day "money bomb"[52] that raised over $1 million for his campaign. While that pales in comparison to what others raised, it certainly was impressive for a candidate with little realistic shot at the White House. After all, Paul "has none of the typical attributes of a successful presidential candidate, except one: he can raise money."[53]

One particularly interesting aspect of Paul's coverage during this early May period is how little association the media drew between Paul and the Tea Party. Despite being one of the earliest voices calling for fiscal responsibility and limited government, press coverage during this time primarily emphasized Paul's libertarian leanings. This could be due to the increased association with conservative Christian values emphasized by the Tea Party; while Paul advocated for the pure financial elements supported by the Tea Party, his positions on social issues at times put him at odds with the organization.

THE RACE BEGINS

The First Debate: South Carolina

On May 5, 2011, five declared or potential candidates joined in what was the first official debate of the Republican primary season. While for some this marked the contest moving into full swing, the palpable lack of excitement around the candidates meant expectations were lowered: "Normally, the first debate of the presidential primary season serves as a starting gun. The one that will take place Thursday night could sound more like a distress call."[54] As several journalists noted, the debate was more notable for the candidates who were not there than those who were. Headlines for articles about the event demonstrated this phenomenon, including the *Wall Street Journal*'s "First Debate for GOP Has Sharp Exchanges, But Lacks Big Guns,"[55] the *Washington Post*'s "Stage Set for First GOP Debate. So Where Are the Candidates?,"[56] and the *New York Times*'s "5 GOP Hopefuls (Who?) Flock to the First Debate of '12 Race."[57] Even the Republican leadership was not particularly interested in what happened in this debate, with Speaker of the House John Boehner opting to dine out at a steakhouse rather than tune in.[58]

Sponsored by Fox News and the Republican Party of South Carolina, Cain, Johnson, Paul, Pawlenty, and Santorum spent their time focusing on introducing themselves to potential voters and beginning to establish some name recognition; although "candidates in presidential debates often need no introduction, the participants who filed onto the stage at the Peace Center for the Performing Arts offered an exception to that rule."[59] Prior to the debate, not one of the five participants had received more than 10 percent support in any polling,[60] and only Pawlenty was considered at that time to be a top-tier candidate.[61] Despite the low turnout for this event, it still marked an important opportunity for candidates seeking to define themselves, and "they arrived hoping to take advantage of one of the most slow-to-develop Republican primary contests in recent years, an opportunity to reach a nationwide cable television audience."[62]

No official reason was given for why Romney declined to attend, although some speculated that this decision reflected his approach to the campaign at this point: stay under the radar, rather than "becoming a punching bag for Ron Paul or some of the marginal candidates who could be in the debate."[63] By declining to join his competitors onstage, Romney was buying more time to build strength as the perceived frontrunner without attracting the negative attention associated with that position. Even without Romney present as a target, however, his specter loomed large. Romney's name was mentioned repeatedly throughout the debate, particularly in terms of the health care law he signed in Massachusetts. While Romney's weak spot proved irresistible, the debate participants generally focused their attacks on Obama. In fact, when asked to remark upon their absent brethren, they declined, with "all of them (doing) their best to stick to former President Ronald Reagan's rule of not speaking ill of fellow Republicans."[64]

While the debate was expected to focus on the economy and jobs, the killing of Osama bin Laden by Navy SEALs—an act ordered by President Obama—shifted the narrative. This one act changed the dynamic of what was to be discussed in the debate and, more importantly, how candidates needed to draw themselves in comparison to the president. As William McGurn wrote in the *Wall Street Journal*, "In death, the al Qaeda terrorist now presents a new challenge, mostly to Republicans hoping to run in 2012. The message is this: You better have a coherent foreign policy to go along with your fiscal agenda."[65] Rather than facing a Carter-esque incumbent president who could be defined by weakness, bin Laden's death put Obama into a position of strength: "Nevertheless, in going after and getting bin Laden as forcefully as he did, Mr. Obama has just undermined one of the primary narratives against him—that of an indecisive president who worries more about the rights of our enemies than the freedom and safety of our citizens."[66]

Despite the late change in focus, the debate, while certainly a low-key affair, was generally considered a successful kick-off to the GOP race. The candidates' "spirited exchanges"[67] on a wide variety of topics served as a solid testing ground for their still-developing sound bites and position statements. Through questions about social issues, the debate also served to better separate the libertarian candidates—Johnson and Paul—from the Tea Party conservatives and the GOP mainstream.[68] While the candidates drew distinctions among their positions, the debate was characterized by generally friendly tones, with the potential nominees hesitating to be the first to draw blood. For a group of mostly unknown politicians, this first foray into the national spotlight had a more important objective: to begin grabbing the attention of the American public. One candidate in particular, Herman Cain, successfully managed to achieve this. A post-debate focus group conducted by GOP researcher Frank Luntz for Fox News enthusiastically declared Cain the "overwhelming winner,"[69] calling him a "breath of fresh air" and proclaiming, "he won us over. I think he can win America over."[70]

Gingrich Implodes: Parts I and II

As discussed earlier, concerns always surrounded Gingrich's ability to run a disciplined, effective campaign. Only days after officially declaring his candidacy on May 9, 2011, Gingrich set off a major explosion among Republicans when he publicly questioned Paul Ryan's budget plan on *Meet the Press*, including criticisms of his Medicare plan: "I'm against Obamacare, which is imposing radical change, and I would be against a conservative imposing radical change. . . . I don't think right-wing social engineering is any more desirable than left-wing social engineering." Although Gingrich apologized to Ryan within days, his comments fueled the frame questioning whether Gingrich had the discipline to remain on message: "Gingrich has undermined his candidacy not simply because, in the eyes of many Republicans, he attacked [Ryan's] plan to overhaul Medicare. His greater problem is that he reminded people, friend and foe alike, of his inability to keep his rhetoric under control."[71]

Perhaps more importantly, his comments damaged his credibility with the Tea Party audience considered essential for a successful bid. Ryan, a favorite among fiscal and social conservatives, had won rave reviews among Tea Partiers for his budget plan, particularly because he was considered willing to take on what had long been considered sacred cows—including entitlement programs like Medicare. Through his criticisms, Gingrich opened the door for questions about his true conservative values. Furthermore, his comments were perceived to be critical of the new "intellectual leader of the House Republicans, a role that Gingrich once played."[72] This theme subtly reinforced Gingrich's age and time out of office, implicitly questioning whether Republicans would want a return to the old guard. The most painful part of coverage for Gingrich and his campaign, however, likely was how little attention his competition paid to his statement: "Aides and advisors to Mr. Romney and former Minnesota Gov. Tim Pawlenty, another White House hopeful, dismissed the significance of Mr. Gingrich's early stumble, in large part because they said they did not see him as a threat."[73]

The fallout from Gingrich's Medicare comments was just beginning to abate when phase two of his implosion began: the revelation that he and his wife had a $500,000 rolling credit account at Tiffany & Co., a high-end jewelry store that was well out of reach for most Americans. While this was not new news—the information came from a financial disclosure document filed by Mrs. Gingrich while working for the House Agriculture Committee (a position she left in 2007)—it raised further questions about Gingrich's judgment and electability in a time of economic crisis. More problematically, as Democratic strategist Chris Lehane articulated, this was a double-barreled challenge for Gingrich, making it "particularly damaging. . . . It raises questions about his commitment to fiscal restraint . . . and 'plays into a prevailing story line about lack of discipline and being reckless, which has been a consistent part of his political and public life.'"[74]

This invariably led to more jokes, including Comedy Central's Stephen Colbert poking fun on the *Colbert Report*: "'Five hundred thousand at Tiffany's?' the comedian Stephen Colbert asked. 'There's a simple explanation. The guy clearly buys his engagement rings in bulk.'"[75] This simple jest on a cable faux-news show neatly encapsulates the challenges this scandal wrought for Gingrich and his campaign: It highlighted his wealth and history of poor judgment, and provided more opportunities to hearken back to his scandalous past.

The Evangelical Vote

As calendars turned to June, Republican eyes turned from the early voting states to the home base of Washington, D.C. On June 3 and 4, Ralph Reed and his Faith and Freedom Coalition held the Faith and Freedom Conference, a forum for nearly all of the Republican candidates to make their cases to the evangelical Christians in attendance.[76] Reed, the former head of the powerful Christian Coalition—a dominant force in American politics during the 1990s and early 2000s—had come back from disgrace and was rebuilding his career as the go-to guy for getting out the conservative evangelical vote. His early June conference brought the potential Republican nominees in front of a captive audience of Christian conservatives, offering each an opportunity to make his or her case for attendees' votes while simultaneously reminding the candidates of how important this group was to their electoral success. As CNN's Carol Costello put it on June 3, "Republican presidential hopefuls and conservative power brokers have packed a Washington hotel for the first day of the Faith and Freedom Conference. Their goal: to reach out to evangelicals and to score their support in the 2012 race."[77]

While economic issues featured prominently in most of the candidates' speeches, they also brought out their best conservative moralizing for the attendees. After opening and closing his speech with passages from the Bible, Pawlenty informed the audience that his "top four 'common-sense principles' for the nation were to turn toward God, protect the unborn, support traditional marriage, and keep Americans secure."[78] Bachmann went even further, with MSNBC reporting that she was putting on her best Palin impression "insofar as she is spouting half-truths and wildly incorrect data. Today [at the conference] she was saying that Planned Parenthood is engaging in trafficking of underage girls and women. She is saying things that conservatives want to hear, and in that way I think has learned some great lessons from Sarah Palin."[79]

This event underscored the importance of the conservative Christian vote for the Republican candidates. On CNN, Cheri Jacobus noted, "They've always been an important block, but Republicans still have to fight for that vote. More and more, the evangelicals in this country [focus on] fiscal issues as [well as] moral and family issues. So, I think it fits well with the Republican agenda and Tea Party agenda."[80]

Gingrich Implodes—Again

What many considered the third strike for Gingrich came on the heels of the Tiffany's scandal. On June 9, his campaign was thrown into upheaval when almost his entire team quit: "Newt Gingrich's campaign manager and top aides resigned en masse Thursday, a remarkable setback that could prove fatal to a presidential run that has stumbled from the outset."[81] This was not just a falling out between a mercenary strategist and a candidate; in one fell swoop, Gingrich lost his entire Iowa team along with staffers in New Hampshire and South Carolina. Top aides, including his campaign manager, made the decision to resign when aggravations with Gingrich's willingness to be the candidate they needed him to be became unbearable.

Gingrich's decision to take a two-week cruise to the Greek islands with his wife instead of spending time glad-handing and networking in early voting states was the tipping point for already-frustrated staffers. One long-time aide, Rick Tyler, told the *Wall Street Journal*'s Neil King, "'The problem is that Newt just couldn't transition into the role of a candidate. He remained what he has been for years, basically an educator and analyst.'"[82] This included the prominent role his wife took in his campaign, including running his schedule and deeply influencing Gingrich's decisions. This sentiment was reinforced for his departing team with the realization that Gingrich took their call from New Hampshire, where he was promoting one of their movies instead of campaigning.

The Second Debate: New Hampshire

Expectations ran high for the second debate. With more candidates planning to take part, including frontrunner Romney, observers speculated that this might finally be the point where candidates started to go on the attack. Pundits particularly were interested to watch Pawlenty's performance, since he "won praise on the political right last week for an economic plan focused on tax cuts intended to produce economic growth. His campaign is finding its first dollop of momentum amid improving poll numbers."[83] The night before the debate, Pawlenty coined the portmanteau "Obamneycare" on the *Chris Wallace Show*, sparking speculation that he would go on the offensive during the debate and putting Romney's feet to the fire on what was considered his greatest vulnerability. For Romney, this was the first real test of his campaign. Until now, his competitors had avoided pressing him on his potential trouble spots, but that grace period was likely to end. Media observers wondered: Could Romney maintain his frontrunner status once he was under attack?

Despite anticipation of fireworks, the debate itself did not offer much in the way of drama. Romney did exactly what he needed to do to maintain his frontrunner status, helped along by his opponents' avoidance of direct attacks even when given an opportunity by moderator John King from CNN. Pawlenty refused to directly address Romney's health care problem, avoiding any barbed commentary when King asked him about Obamneycare. Likewise, despite King opening the door, Santorum did not go after Romney on his changed positions on abortions. During CNN's immediate post-debate deconstruction, senior political analyst David Gergen commented on how this translated into a positive result for Romney: "And overall I think it wound up to be a very good night for Mitt Romney. Nobody laid a glove on him really, and he had a very consistent message about what he argued was the failure of President Obama."[84] In general, the debate offered few surprises. Said one undecided voter interviewed on CNN, "They all seem to be speaking the Republican playbook, and I'm looking—as an undecided voter, I'm looking for a candidate who has a real plan of attack and not just blaming President Obama. And I'm not sure I saw that last night."[85]

In the days following the debate, Pawlenty's stock dropped even further. He was perceived to have passed up the opportunity to say to Romney's face what he had said behind his back, making him look weak. He had "hoped to use the debate to establish himself as the clear alternative to Romney. He may yet become that candidate. But he left New Hampshire with fresh doubts about his campaign. His decision to set up a confrontation with Romney over health care Sunday and then duck it in the debate left other Republicans more than puzzled."[86] Pawlenty attempted to negotiate the fallout by admitting he made a mistake, appearing on Hannity's Fox News show to clarify: "I don't think that we can have a nominee that was involved in the development and construction of Obamacare and then continues to defend it. And that was the question. I should have answered it directly."[87]

Larry Sabato, director for the Center for Politics at the University of Virginia, offered his take to Fox News's Bill Hemmer: "He admitted that goof, and he made a major, major mistake in the Monday night debate. And woulda, coulda, shoulda, it's not the same as saying it on cable TV when your opponent isn't there. He had Romney in position to take a strong hit on the issue that could sink Romney potentially. But look, Pawlenty blinked.

There's no question about it."[88] Others were harsher in their evaluations of his damage control efforts. According to GOP strategist Ed Rogers, the back-tracking only served to remind audiences that "when he had the chance to be forthright and mano-a-mano with Romney, he took a pass, and when he's behind his back he swung at him."[89] Rogers continued: "The worst thing you do in politics is play to your negative stereotype. He has a negative stereotype that suggests he is a somewhat bland, mechanical politician and that he's not great on his feet and he's not unrehearsed. This reminded everybody of that."[90]

Bachmann's Buzz

If Pawlenty's candidacy was damaged during the debate, Bachmann emerged as a force to be reckoned with. She came across as a true conservative, boasting a real ability to connect with voters and establishing herself as a contender. Former Bush chief of staff Andrew Card lauded her performance on CNN, commenting, "she really did a very credible job. She was a cheerleader, but she was also quite substantive. And she seemed calm, cool, and deliberate."[91] These last three characteristics were particularly important for Bachmann as she attempted to supplant the perception that she was little more than a firebrand and ideologue. "By turning in a confident and savvy performance, the Minnesotan at least temporarily carved a spot as a serious candidate—one whose presence will almost certainly affect the race no matter how far she goes."[92] Bachmann's success had real implications for the other candidates fighting for the same voters, both declared (Pawlenty, Cain, Gingrich, and Santorum) and still considering options (Palin). After all, if she could energize Tea Party voters and keep them in her camp, her opponents would have difficulty finding the support needed to continue their campaigns. More broadly, her success could mean Bachmann's rigid, uncompromising brand of conservatism would drive other candidates further to the right in order to win in early states, particularly Iowa.

Bachmann's momentum carried her into late June, and she was credited with injecting energy into a contest that sorely needed it. While questions lingered about her overall electability, there was no doubt that Bachmann could get a conservative crowd excited. "To liberals, Michele Bachmann is a ring wing extremist who plays loose with the facts. To Tea Party activists, she is a hero willing to stand up not just to the Obama agenda, but to her own party's leadership. Like her or not, there is no disputing this. At the moment, she is the candidate making the greatest impact on the race for the Republican nomination."[93] Polling showed her in a statistical tie with Romney in Iowa, and she was given plaudits for "moderating her tone without moderating her views,"[94] recognizing the importance of broadening her appeal.

With success comes media scrutiny, however. For a politician closely associated with the Tea Party and its financial conservatism, a story in the *Los Angeles Times* reporting that "Bachmann and her family have benefited personally from government aid even as the congresswoman campaigns against federal spending"[95] tolled warning bells; the story was picked up by a number of other media. Undaunted, Bachmann formally declared her candidacy in her birthplace of Waterloo, Iowa, on June 25. While she managed to avoid making any major faux pas, she mischaracterized Waterloo as the home of actor John Wayne when it was actually the home of serial killer John Wayne Gacy. Albeit a somewhat minor mistake, it did reinforce the narrative that Bachmann was careless with facts: "She has a long list of falsehoods she's made and she—this matters."[96]

Campaigns in Trouble

As the close of June approached, several campaigns found themselves facing difficulties. Two more of Gingrich's aides quit, leaving him even more understaffed. Huntsman admitted that he was tired during a campaign event, then canceled his scheduled appearance at the Republican Leadership Conference due to illness. Johnson was no longer on the media's radar at all, with his name not included in the list of candidates contained in a brief article about Huntsman's official declaration of candidacy.[97]

Despite starting off as a top-tier candidate, late June found Pawlenty scrambling to resuscitate what was starting to look like a terminally ill campaign. Word got out that his top aides were working for little or no pay, raising questions about the long-term viability of his campaign. The bad news continued for Pawlenty with the release of the *Des Moines Register* poll on June 25, where he only received six percent: "For Pawlenty, who has invested more time and money in Iowa this month than perhaps any other candidate, the poll was a sobering sign of the difficulties he appears to be having raising money nationally and breaking out in the early voting states."[98] He attempted to turn this around with a fiery foreign relations speech in which he attacked Romney and Huntsman, which was framed as an effort to reinvigorate his campaign and separate himself from his rivals.

Rick Perry: A New Alternative to Romney?

Late June coverage crystallized the post-debate sentiment that other candidates were competing to be the alternative to Romney. His superior fundraising and organization meant he had staying power and was unlikely to falter in the earliest races; thus, other candidates needed to shake each other off in order to develop a large enough base to compete. Despite Romney's strength, there was still widespread recognition that he was not the candidate of Republican—and especially Tea Party—dreams. This resistance to Romney, coupled with a dearth of candidates widely considered to be electable in both a socially conservative-driven primary campaign and a general election, meant some Republicans closed June with the same mission with which they opened May: to find another candidate who could credibly compete against Romney. An envoy of Iowa businessmen flew to New Jersey in an effort to sweet-talk Governor Chris Christie into running, but he refused.

One glimmer of hope was on the horizon, however. Just when it seemed the field was settled, for better or for worse, Rick Perry uttered a two-sentence phrase that threw the contest wide open—a "game changer,"[99] according to CNN. In late May, when asked if he was planning to run—as he had been asked so many times before—Perry changed his response: "Mr. Perry, a staunch conservative and a Tea Party favorite, said without a hint of irony: 'Yes, sir. I'm going to think about it.' Then a couple of beats later, he smiled and added, 'But I think about a lot of things.'"[100]

By the end of June, the drumbeats encouraging Perry to run were almost deafening. He had spent the month testing the waters, bringing advisers who had left to work with Gingrich back into the fold. Perry gave a series of "rowdy"[101] speeches around the country designed to generate excitement for his campaign while painting himself as the true conservative in the field. In mid-June he appeared at the Republican Leadership Conference where he "wowed" the crowd: "Delivering a barn burner of a campaign-style speech he exited the stage to chant[s] of 'Run, Rick, run.'"[102] His words during that speech certainly sounded like a campaign was afoot: "Doesn't matter what your zip code is or where you're from. We're all facing the same challenges in America. I stand before you today a disciplined conservative Texan, a committed Republican and a proud American, united with you in the desire to restore our nation and revive the American dream."[103]

As the longest-serving governor in Texas history, Perry boasted a tremendous appeal to evangelical voters. His potential candidacy was considered a threat to almost all of the current crop of candidates, particularly Romney and Bachmann, since he could appeal to Republicans of all stripes: "He's good-looking and telegenic, great at working a crowd, both at the handshake level and at the microphone. He actually enjoys campaign hokum. He has become a good public speaker. . . . He's good with the fiscal conservatives, the social conservatives, the Tea Partiers and the Christians, and he subdued the establishment Republicans in Texas."[104] Powerful conservative voices like Rush Limbaugh encouraged him to jump in the field, citing his electability and conservative appeal as factors that would lead to his victory. According to Limbaugh, Perry and his conservative colleagues were the White House's greatest fear: "They think they can beat a moderate Republican. They know they can beat a liberal Republican. They know they can beat a

Republican who is afraid to be a Republican. But they are mostly afraid of a genuine, full-throated, passionate, articulate conservative."[105]

NOTES

1. Karen Tumulty, "Stage Set for First GOP Debate. So Where Are the Candidates?" *Washington Post*, May 5, 2011, A-Section, Factiva.

2. Don Lemon, "Interview with Donald Trump; Politics, Race & Trump; Washington One-Liners: Highlights of White House Correspondents' Dinner," *CNN: CNN Newsroom*, May 1, 2011, LexisNexis Academic.

3. Chris Cillizza, "On This Day Off, the Real Work Starts for GOP Contenders," *Washington Post*, May 30, 2011, A-Section, Factiva.

4. Wolf Blitzer, Nic Robertson, Jeanne Meserve, Dan Lothian, Barbara Starr, Mary Snow, Ed Lavandera, Lisa Sylvester, David Frum, Paul Begala, and Fan Townsen, "Al Qaeda: Bin Laden Won't Die in Vain; Videotapes Seized from bin Laden's Compound; President Says No Gloating; Raid Exposes Secret Forces & Weapons; A Non-Covert Covert Operation; Jobs and Unemployment Both Up; Afghanistan War Dead Remembered; 'Strategy Session'; Hunting Osama bin Laden's Heir Apparent," *CNN: The Situation Room*, May 6, 2011, LexisNexis Academic.

5. Richard Roth, Dan Simon, T. J. Holmes, Susan Candiotti, Jim Acosta, Thelma Gutierrez, Alison Kosik, Chad Myers, Wolf Blitzer, and Joe Johns, "Unabomber Involved in Tylenol Scare?; Former IMF Chief Indicted But Gets Bail; Schwarzenegger's Mistress, Love Child; LinkedIn Stock Soars; Three to Six Major Hurricanes Predicted; Secret Service Twitter Oops," *CNN: CNN Newsroom*, May 19, 2011, LexisNexis Academic.

6. Jeff Zeleny, "Huntsman Takes his Potential Campaign for Test Drive in New Hampshire," *New York Times*, May 21, 2011, National Desk, Factiva.

7. Bret Baier, Mike Emanuel, James Rosen, and Karl Cameron, "Political Headlines," *Fox News Network: Fox Special Report with Bret Baier*, May 20, 2011, LexisNexis Academic.

8. T. J. Holmes, Reynolds Wolf, Alexandra Steele, Brian Todd, Peter Hamby, and Ray D'Alessio, "CIA Did Surveillance on Bin Laden Compound For Months Before Raid; Two Islamic Clerics Not Allowed on American Flight By Pilot; Storms and Tornadoes Devastate Southern States; Analysts Debate Political Significance of Bin Laden Killing; New Candidate Enters Republican Field of Presidential Hopefuls; Female Jockey to be Riding In Kentucky Derby," *CNN: CNN Newsroom*, May 7, 2011, LexisNexis Academic.

9. Zeleny, "Huntsman Takes his Potential."

10. Lawrence O'Donnell and Eugene Robinson, "The Last Word for May 9, 2011," *MSNBC: The Last Word with Lawrence O 'Donnell*, May 9, 2011, LexisNexis Academic.

11. Nia-Malika Henderson, "Huntsman Joins the Presidential Race," *Washington Post*, June 22, 2011, A-Section, Factiva.

12. Cillizza, "On This Day Off."

13. O'Donnell and Robinson, "The Last Word."

14. Jeff Zeleny, "Pawlenty Declares Candidacy and Takes on Politically Popular Programs," *New York Times*, May 24, 2011, National Desk, Factiva.

15. Michael Leahy, "In Iowa's Largely Empty Field, Pawlenty First to Make Inroads," *Washington Post*, May 1, 2011, A-Section, Factiva.

16. Dan Balz, "Romney's Focusing His Bid on One Thing: The Economy," *Washington Post*, May 29, 2011, A-Section, Factiva.

17. Ibid.

18. Cillizza, "On This Day Off."

19. Balz, "Romney's Focusing His Bid on One Thing."

20. Philip Rucker and Peter Wallsten, "Romney in Hot Seat on Warming," *Washington Post*, June 9, 2011, A-Section, Factiva.

21. Chris Wallace, Brit Hume, Nina Easton, Kimberly Strassel, and Mort Zuckerman, "Fox News Sunday Panel," *Fox News Network: Fox News Sunday*, May 15, 2011, LexisNexis Academic.

22. Suzanne Malveaux, Barbara Starr, Carol Costello, Holly Firfer, Rob Marciano, Alison Kosik, Ed Lavandera, Reynolds Wolf, Sara Sidner, T. J. Holmes, and Paul Steinhauser, "Osama bin Laden's Handwritten Diary; Losing Homes in Flood; Government Flood Insurance Broke; Bringing Baseball to Inner City Youth; Residents Brace for Troubled Waters in Louisiana; Rebels Claim Misrata," *CNN: CNN Newsroom*, May 12, 2011, LexisNexis Academic.

23. Karen Tumulty, "Romney to Outline Plan for Health Care," *Washington Post*, May 11, 2011, A-Section, Factiva.

24. Jim Rutenberg, "Romney Defends Massachusetts Health Plan, but Concedes Flaws," *New York Times*, May 13, 2011, National Desk, Factiva.

25. Bret Baier, Charles Krauthammer, Mara Liasson, and Charles Lane, "Fox News All-Stars," *Fox News Network: Fox Special Report with Bret Baier*, May 16, 2011, LexisNexis Academic.

26. Eliot Spitzer, Richard Roth, Deborah Feyerick, E. D. Hill, Fareed Zakaria, and John King, "IMF Chief Held without Bail; Trump Will Not Run for President," *CNN: In the Arena*, May 16, 2011, LexisNexis Academic.

27. Cillizza, "On This Day Off."

28. Jonathan Weisman and Neil King Jr., "U.S. News: As Field Thins, Search Goes On—Romney is Putative Frontrunner as Huckabee, Trump Exit; GOP Leaders Push Others to Enter Race," *Wall Street Journal*, May 18, 2011, A4, Factiva.

29. Balz, "Romney's Focusing His Bid on One Thing."

30. Philip Rucker and Paul Kane, "Long on Ambition but Short on Record," *Washington Post*, May 2, 2011, A-Section, Factiva.

31. Ibid.

32. Ibid.

33. Chris Wallace, Carl Cameron, Jennifer Griffin, Catherine Herridge, Mike Emanuel, Shannon Bream, and James Rosen, "Political Headlines," *Fox News Network: Fox Special Report with Bret Baier*, May 18, 2011, LexisNexis Academic.

34. Weisman and King, "U.S. News: As Field Thins."

35. Wallace et al., "Political Headlines.

36. Eric Lichtblau, "Former Restaurant Executive Enters 2012 Republican Race," *New York Times*, May 22, 2011, National Desk, Factiva.

37. Neil King Jr., "U.S. News—Election 2012: GOP Debate Fuels a Long Shot," *Wall Street Journal*, May 9, 2011, A4, Factiva.

38. In this context, American exceptionalism relates to the idea that the United States is by definition exceptional and that it stands above the rest of the world. A common accusation against Obama at this time was that he did not support this concept and thus was not representing America's exceptionalism to the world.

39. Brooke Baldwin, Patrick Oppmann, Casey Wian, Deborah Feyerick, Mark Preston, and Sara Sidner, "Where Is Moammar Gadhafi?; Bin Laden's Sons Speak Out," *CNN: CNN Newsroom*, May 11, 2011, LexisNexis Academic.

40. Dan Balz, "A Student of History, Gingrich Has His Own to Overcome," *Washington Post*, May 12, 2011, A-Section, Factiva.

41. Wolf Blitzer, Mark Preston, Barbara Starr, Ivan Watson, Hala Gorani, Jack Cafferty, Don Lothian, Deborah Feyerick, Brian Todd, Max Foster, Jill Dougherty, and Rafael Romo, "Mass Exodus From Gingrich Campaign; U.S. Airstrikes Against Al Qaeda in Yemen; Hundreds of Syrians Flee to Turkey; President Obama's Biggest Challenges; Your Personal Information at Risk; Royal Family Hacked?; Leon Panetta Under Fire Over Afghanistan; Massive Blow to Gingrich Campaign," *CNN: The Situation Room*, June 9, 2011, LexisNexis Academic.

42. Matt Bai, "Gingrich's Run Reflects His Sense of History," *New York Times*, May 11, 2011, National Desk: Political Memo, Factiva.

43. Sheryl Gay Stolberg and Barclay Walsh, "Gingrich Set to Run, with Wife in Central Role," *New York Times*, May 10, 2011, National Desk, Factiva.

44. Neil King, Jr. and Patrick O'Connor, "Gingrich's Secret Weapon: Newt Inc.," *Wall Street Journal*, May 9, 2011, A1, Factiva.

45. Leahy, "In Iowa's Largely Empty Field."

46. Katharine Q. Seelye, "'Culture Warrior' Looks to Broaden the Battle," *Washington Post*, June 6, 2011, National Desk, Factiva.

47. Karen Tumulty and Nia-Malika Henderson, "GOP Debaters Hail Bin Laden Death," *Washington Post*, May 6, 2011, A-Section, Factiva.

48. Based on the importance and success of the Tea Party in the 2010 midterm elections, I am including them as mainstream Republicans in this statement.

49. Michael D. Shear, "A 'Money Bomb' Delivers for Ron Paul's Campaign," *New York Times*, May 7, 2011, National Desk, Factiva.

50. William McGurn, "Main Street: Bin Laden's Last Challenge—to Republicans," *Wall Street Journal*, May 3, 2011, A15, Factiva.

51. Jeff Zeleny, "5 GOP Hopefuls (Who?) Flock to First Debate of '12 Race," *New York Times*, May 6, 2011, National Desk, Factiva.

52. Shear, "Money Bomb."

53. Ibid.

54. Tumulty, "Stage Set."

55. Neil King Jr., "U.S. News—Election 2012: First Debate for GOP has Sharp Exchanges, but Lacks Big Guns," *Wall Street Journal,* May 6, 2011, A4, Factiva.

56. Tumulty, "Stage Set."

57. Zeleny, "5 GOP Hopefuls."

58. Ibid.

59. Ibid.

60. King, "First Debate for GOP has Sharp Exchanges."

61. Tumulty and Henderson, "GOP Debaters Hail Bin Laden Death."

62. Zeleny, "5 GOP Hopefuls."

63. Dan Balz, "Romney, the Invisible Frontrunner," *Washington Post*, May 1, 2011, A-Section, Factiva.

64. Tumulty and Henderson, "GOP Debaters Hail Bin Laden Death."

65. McGurn, "Main Street: Bin Laden's Last Challenge."

66. Ibid.

67. King, "First Debate for GOP has Sharp Exchanges."

68. Ibid.

69. King, "GOP Debate Fuels a Long Shot."

70. Sean Hannity, "Analysis of the GOP Debate," *Fox News Network: Fox Hannity*, May 5, 2011, LexisNexis.

71. Dan Balz, "Newt Gingrich's Apology Tour," *Washington Post*, May 19, 2011, A-Section, Factiva.

72. Ibid.

73. Weisman and King, "U.S. News: As Field Thins."

74. Sheryl Gay Stolberg, "All That Glitters May Redefine Run by Gingrich," *New York Times*, May 25, 2011, National Desk, Political Memo, Factiva.

75. Ibid.

76. The only declared candidate not in attendance was Gary Johnson, reflecting the media perception that he was not a legitimate candidate for the Republican nomination.

77. Carol Costello, Jeffrey Toobin, Dan Gilgoff, Max Foster, Steve Perry, Ed Henry, Poppy Harlow, Chris Lawrence, Jeff Fischel, Jeanne Moos, Joe Johns, Max Foster, and Paul Steinhauser, "Moody's May Review U.S. Rating; Yemeni PM, Officials Wounded; Seven Republicans to Join Debate; Edwards Indictment Expected Today; 2012 GOP Contenders Talk Faith; 'Education Makeover' Helps 9th Grader; Mavs Come Back to Beat Heat; NHL Player Picks up Hitchhiking Bono," *CNN: CNN Newsroom*, June 3, 2011, LexisNexis Academic.

78. Associated Press, "Conference Offers Tryout for Hopefuls," *New York Times*, June 5, 2011, National Desk, Factiva.

79. Chris Matthews, Ed Rendell, Michael Steele, Karen Finney, Pete Williams, Brian Sullivan, David Corn, and Alex Wagner, "Obama's 2012 Opponent; John Edwards Indicted on Six

Counts; Faith and Freedom Conference; Weiner's Week in Review," *MSNBC: Hardball*, June 3, 2011, LexisNexis Academic.

80. Carol Costello, Ed Henry, Joe Johns, Mohammed Jamjoom, Jeffrey Toobin, Poppy Harlow, Gloria Borger, and Suzanne Malveaux, "Jack Kevorkian Dead at 83; Obama Visits Ohio, Talks Chrysler; 2012 GOP Contenders Talk Faith; Charges Likely Today Against Edwards; Job Growth Slows; Weiner Picture Scandal Goes Global; John Edwards Indicted; Yemen's Presidential Compound Shelled," *CNN: CNN Newsroom*, June 3, 2011, LexisNexis Academic.

81. Neil King Jr., "U.S. News—Election 2012: Gingrich Campaign Aides Abandon Ship—Staffers Questioned GOP Candidate's Commitment to Rigors of Presidential Run; Greek Cruise Drew Chorus of Complaints," *Wall Street Journal*, June 10, 2011, A4, Factiva.

82. Ibid.

83. Neil King Jr., "U.S. News: Aiming to Connect at the GOP Debate," *Wall Street Journal*, June 13, 2011, A4, Factiva.

84. Wolf Blitzer, Cornell Belcher, John King, Gloria Borger, David Gergen, and Anderson Cooper, "Analysis of GOP Presidential Debate," *CNN: Anderson Cooper, 360 Degrees*, June 13, 2011, LexisNexis Academic.

85. Ali Velshi, Christine Romans, Kiran Chetry, Jessica Yellin, Mark Preston, Rob Marciano, Martin Savidge, and John King, "GOP Debate: Blasting Obama, Jobs, Health Care; Winners and Losers in GOP Debate; Did the GOP Candidates Connect?; Yemen: Transfer Of Power; Interview with Michele Bachmann; Obama Weighs in on Rep. Anthony Weiner," *CNN: American Morning*, June 14, 2011, LexisNexis Academic.

86. Dan Balz, "Romney, Bachmann Scramble the GOP Race," *Washington Post*, June 15, 2011, A-Section, Factiva.

87. Bret Baier, William La Jeunesse, Carl Cameron, Jim Angle, Peter Barnes, Jennifer Griffin, Reena Ninan, Mike Emanuel, Rick Leventhal, and Catherine Herridge, "Political Headlines," *Fox News Network: Fox Special Report with Bret Baier*, June 17, 2011, LexisNexis Academic.

88. Bill Hemmer, "Interview with Larry Sabato," *Fox News Network: Live Event*, June 17, 2011, LexisNexis Academic.

89. Amy Gardner and Philip Rucker, "Questions Emerge over Pawlenty's boldness," *Washington Post*, June 18, 2011, A-Section, Factiva.

90. Ibid.

91. Cooper et al., "Analysis of GOP Presidential Debate."

92. Amy Gardner and Sandhya Somashekhar, "Basking in New Momentum, Bachmann Plots Path Ahead," *Washington Post*, June 15, 2011, A-Section, Factiva.

93. John King, Jessica Yellin, Ben Wedeman, Jim Clancy, Nic Robertson, Arwa Damon, and Hala Gorani, "Exclusive Reports from Syria, Yemen; President Takes Personal Role in Debt Ceiling Negotiation; Rep. Bachmann Enters Presidential Race," *CNN: John King*, June 27, 2011, LexisNexis Academic.

94. Sandhya Somashekhar, "In Iowa, Bachmann Makes it Official," *Washington Post*, June 28, 2011, A-Section, Factiva.

95. Chris Wallace, "Interview with Michele Bachmann," *Fox News Network: Fox News Sunday*, June 26, 2011, LexisNexis.

96. King et al., "Exclusive Reports from Syria, Yemen."

97. Chris Cillizza and Aaron Blake, "Huntsman to Join 2012 GOP Race," *Washington Post*, June 15, 2011, A-Section, Factiva.

98. Philip Rucker, "For Bachmann, Fresh Scrutiny Accompanies New Popularity," *Washington Post*, June 27, 2011, A-Section, Factiva.

99. King et al., "Exclusive Reports from Syria, Yemen."

100. James C. McKinley Jr., "Texas Governor Hints at GOP Run for White House," *New York Times*, May 28, 2011, National Desk, Factiva.

101. Cenk Uygur, "MSNBC Live with Cenk Uygur for June 15, 2011," *MSNBC: MSNBC Live with Cenk Uyger*, June 15, 2011, LexisNexis Academic.

102. Martha MacCallum, "Interview with Larry Sabato," *Fox News Network: Live Event*, June 21, 2011, LexisNexis Academic.

103. Ibid.

104. Ross Ramsey, "Saying He's Not Running Puts Perry in a Good Spot." *New York Times*, May 20, 2011, National Desk, Factiva.

105. Martha MacCallum and Sarah Palin, "Hard Feelings Over Rapper's White House Appearance," *Fox News Network: Fox on the Record with Greta Van Susteren*, May 11, 2011, LexisNexis.

Chapter Three

The Race Intensifies

July–August 2011

The lethargy that often comes with summer heat waves also characterized the state of the race in the beginning of July, described by the *Washington Post*'s Dan Balz as "a sleepy, shapeless and uninspired affair punctuated by comedic interludes."[1] While candidates had been campaigning for months (and for some, years), the competition still felt like it was in first gear. To fill column inches and on-air minutes, journalists and pundits found themselves looking for and analyzing any pieces of information that could help make sense of the race; poll results and fundraising totals were pored over and endlessly debated in an effort to suss out the relative strength of each candidate. A weak jobs report issued at the beginning of the month offered fodder for Republican attacks on President Obama and increased perceptions among the media, political insiders, and potential primary voters that a GOP candidate could, in fact, take back the White House—if only the right candidate could be found.

The difficulty of finding that candidate became even clearer during the heart of summer. As the race wore on and contenders' fortunes rose and fell, recognition grew that the eventual nominee ideally needed to "even more than normal . . . check two contradictory boxes: He or she has to appeal to the GOP's energized Tea-Party and social-conservative wings, while also assuring the party's elites of the ability to reach out to more moderate swing voters who usually decide general elections."[2] Despite the ever-increasing likelihood that Perry intended to officially throw his hat in the ring, a lack of consensus around or confidence in the current crop of candidates fed speculation that there might still be a winner waiting in the wings. Republican National Committee member and former Nevada governor Bob List articulated concerns with the current field: "We're looking for a convincing, compelling, dynamic, intelligent person that we feel can win. . . . That person might or might not be in the race."[3] Thus far, "the race has been marked by two realities—a lack of enthusiasm for Romney as the potential GOP standard bearer and an inability of any other candidate to take advantage of that perceived weakness."[4]

During this period, a disproportionate amount of attention was paid to Iowa—considerably more than other early voting states, including New Hampshire and South Carolina. This likely was at least in part because Ames, Iowa, was host to two high-profile events during August: the third candidate debate and the Ames Straw Poll. Perhaps more importantly, the state represented a key battleground for those candidates who built their campaign strategies around winning the "values voters": the conservative evangelical Christians who made up much of the Iowa GOP electorate. According to the media, two candidates in particular—the Minnesota contingent of Bachmann and Pawlenty—needed to appeal to and attract these voters to sustain their campaigns. When asked by a CNN reporter in early July why candidates spent so much time and money on winning over Iowa voters, Bachmann acknowledged the impact of the August straw poll and the January caucuses. She commented, "Well, because Iowa is first in the nation. It's very important to be here and have a presence here, because the values and opinions that people have in Iowa count. They count for the nation."[5]

One of the first and most important indicators of campaign health during this period was insight into how much money candidates had raised and had on hand to spend on the primary battle. The Federal Election Commission required candidates to release their totals by July 15, so much of the early part of the month was spent anticipating what would be revealed and what it would mean. As Wolf Blitzer noted on CNN, "In politics, like so much else, money talks."[6]

When the numbers began trickling in, no one was surprised to learn that Romney had far exceeded his competition, raising more than $18 million. While this number was impressive within the context of the Republican primary campaigns, it fell short of his announced goal and was less than what he had raised in 2008. Paul came in a distant second, raising over $4.5 million. The two other candidates who had been considered "top tier" just a couple of months earlier did not fare well in these reports. Concern was raised about the viability of Pawlenty's campaign, particularly since his release did not make clear what of his $4.3 million would be available for the primaries versus earmarked for a general campaign. Huntsman had raised $4.1 million, but $2 million of that was from his own personal funds. Pundits noted that this was "a bit of a contradiction," noting he "told reporters in early May that he would not put in his own money."[7] This did not bode well for his campaign.

A number of explanations were given for these fairly disappointing numbers, including a still-sluggish economy and the speculation that large donors were giving to super PACs instead of directly to candidates. For some, however, this was a clear indicator that the party had not yet found the right person for the job: "But many GOP advisers also acknowledge that the numbers show a remarkable lack of excitement for the current Republican field, which includes two candidates—Romney and former Minnesota governor Tim Pawlenty—who have effectively been running for president since Obama was elected."[8] The bad economy and super PAC explanations were undermined when Obama released his own fundraising numbers, singlehandedly raising more than all of his potential Republican competitors combined. As *Washington Post* reporters Dan Eggen and Perry Bacon rhetorically asked in an article headlined "GOP Candidates' War Chests Mostly Empty," "Are Republicans suffering from an enthusiasm gap?"[9] According to media frames at this point, the answer seemed to be a resounding (albeit somewhat disinterested) "yes."

THE RISE OF MICHELE BACHMANN

While national polls did not seem to indicate any one candidate had wholly captured the public's imagination, the bright spot in early July was Congresswoman Michele Bachmann. During this period, Bachmann was "[drawing] some of the biggest and most enthusiastic crowds of the season"[10] at her campaign events. By July 12, Bachmann surged ahead of Romney in Iowa polls, landing "on top of the pack of those running for the GOP presidential nomination"[11] and dominating cable news coverage. While national polls still showed Romney in the lead, Bachmann's insurgent campaign clearly enjoyed considerable momentum, providing a shot in the arm to what was otherwise a fairly dry race so far. Donna Brazile, a CNN political contributor who had served as campaign manager for Democratic candidate Vice President Al Gore in 2000, offered this assessment of Bachmann's rise to the top tier: "She's leading the polls in Iowa. She has a terrific organization. She's a hometown girl. I know she was born there, in Waterloo. But you know what? She is really rallying the faithful."[12]

With fellow competitors being framed as unassuming and boring (Pawlenty) or overly political and inauthentic (Romney), Bachmann benefited from the perception that she was exactly what she said she was—even if you did not like her, you could not question her absolute commitment to her own moral code and sense of righteousness. While her incendiary rhetoric and factual inaccuracies had led to earlier perceptions that Bachmann was unelectable, these same characteristics fed the fire and fanned the flames among Republicans frustrated with what they felt was inefficiency, ineptitude, and a rejection of fundamental American values in Washington. Bachmann was willing to speak the truth, even if those truths were in opposition to her party's leaders, because she was perceived to prioritize conservative values over popular appeal; for her audience, there was no question that at her core she meant every word she said. During an interview with Wolf Blitzer, former president Bill Clinton noted, "I'm not surprised that Congresswoman Bachmann is off to a good start, because I think she's a compelling public figure. I don't agree with her on a lot of things, but I think she comes across as real."[13]

Bachmann's success in polls and on the campaign trail meant the media had to move away from the "unelectable" frame that had been commonly used in coverage before her success in the mid-June New Hampshire debate catapulted her into the top tier. In July and August, the question became can she maintain this position? There was little doubt that Bachmann would do well in Iowa; not only was she a native daughter, but their socially conservative voters and Tea Partiers fit right into her sweet spot. New Hampshire, however, was considered tougher terrain. Republican strategist Alex Castellanos characterized the race as such: "There's the conservative Tea Party contest. Michele Bachmann is winning that. If she wins Iowa, then the party is going to go to New Hampshire . . . and they're going to look for the anti-Bachmann."[14]

While the media often reflected the voter's perception (and Bachmann's self-portrayal) of the candidate as being absolutely, authentically conservative, a subtler frame permeated coverage of Bachmann. Stories about Bachmann often were quietly critical, continuing to develop the frame that she made for great television and entertaining campaign stops, but she just did not have the experience or ability to truly lead. This was reinforced by frequent jabs from Pawlenty, whose none-too-subtle attacks included a new campaign slogan that alluded to Bachmann offering rhetoric, not results. Questions were raised about her lack of executive experience and how little she had accomplished as a sitting representative. An anonymous former staffer revealed that Bachmann suffered from chronic, debilitating migraines, and these headaches became a top news story as debates raged about Bachmann's physical ability to do the job. Eventually, the House of Representatives' doctor issued a letter clarifying Bachmann's condition to put concerns to rest.

Some of these stories were the result of increased scrutiny in the wake of Bachmann's quick ascension into the top tier of candidates. While Bachmann had been a regular on cable news networks for quite some time and thus had a national presence, she had never run a campaign of this scope or scale. As her electoral fortunes improved and she began to be perceived as a legitimate candidate, her background, family, and finances became fair game for media examination. Speculation abounded when it was discovered that Bachmann and her husband officially had left their conservative Lutheran Minnesota congregation after not attending services for two years. The investigation into the 2008 financing of their mortgage indicated that the Bachmanns had benefited from federal subsidies, despite her publicly railing against the Fannie Mae and Freddie Mac programs—including calling for their dismantling—during a House Financial Services Committee hearing just weeks before.[15] Her professional experience was questioned, with the *Wall Street Journal* noting that while she claimed to have been a "federal tax litigation attorney . . . others might call it a tax collector."[16]

Bachmann's husband, Marcus, was a flashpoint for much of the critical coverage. His counseling center in Minnesota was "caught in a swirl of media attention over whether the clinic practices 'reparative therapy' or so-called gay-to-straight counseling."[17] This put a spotlight on Bachmann's longstanding and vociferous opposition to gay marriage, which she had referred to as "'an immediate loss of civil liberties for five million Minnesotans. . . . In our public schools, whether they want to or not, they'll be forced to start teaching that same-sex marriage is equal, that it is normal and that children should try it.'"[18] In July, the candidate signed a pledge that "compared same-sex couples to polygamists. That's a comparison Bachmann made as a state lawmaker in 2004, when she called for an amendment to block gay marriages in other states from being recognized in Minnesota."[19]

Perhaps most damaging to Bachmann at this point were concerns that she did not understand the real implications of her rhetoric, at least in part because she had so little legislative experience. Pawlenty criticized her on *Meet the Press*, saying, "I like Congresswoman Bachmann. I've campaigned for her, I respect her. But her record for accomplishment in Congress is nonexistent. It's nonexistent."[20] Her competitors were quick to jump on moments that demonstrated these foibles, including her claim that as president she would bring gasoline prices back down under $2 per gallon. Huntsman "scoffed" at this claim, saying, "'I just don't know what world that comment would come from. . . . That is completely unrealistic. And, again, it's talking about things that, you know, may pander to a particular group or sound good at the time, but it just simply is not founded in reality.'"[21] She also refused to vote to increase the debt ceiling in early July, a position that was derided as showing a complete lack of understanding about how the economy actually worked. For some Republicans, these types of ideological dogmatic positions hindered Bachmann's political fortunes. On Fox News, Margaret Hoover offered this analysis of the difficulties Bachmann's positions would hold for attracting young voters and independents: "And that's one of the things about this generation. Their politics is pragmatic not ideological. And so when they see exactly as you say, Michele Bachmann and these new freshman who are buckling down and they're harboring purism over any sort of pragmatism—that turns them off."[22]

While Bachmann undoubtedly held strong appeal for the audiences clamoring to see her live and in person on the campaign trail, she continued to make misstatements that were at times more charitably interpreted as gaffes. During an interview in early July, Bachmann claimed that the Founding Fathers had actively opposed slavery, declaring: "And I think it is high time we recognize the contribution of our forebears who worked tirelessly, men like John Quincy Adams, who would not rest until slavery was extinguished in the country."[23] When it was pointed out to her that Washington and Jefferson among others owned slaves and that John Quincy Adams was not a Founding Father (and was, in fact, only eight years old when the Declaration of Independence was signed), Bachmann justified her statement by noting that he was from the Revolutionary War era. Media coverage of these gaffes, particularly on the cable news networks, often included discussion on whether her gender and appearance played into the critiques of her misstatements and hyperbole. Rarely, however, were these incidents considered in context with her pre-campaign appearances, where a history of over-the-top claims shaped a career "where nobody batted an eye when she proposed amending the United States Constitution to stop our country from adopting the yen as our currency instead of the dollar because she thought that was a threat" and she "[warned] about secret concentration camps being set up by the government."[24]

Despite these negative elements in her coverage, Bachmann was credited with bringing energy and enthusiasm to an otherwise uninspiring race. Her campaign stops featured large crowds cheering at her stump speeches, inspired by her passionate conservative rhetoric. Bachmann's ability to invigorate her audience often led to favorable comparisons to her Minnesota counterpart, Tim Pawlenty. As she cemented her position in the top tier, the media often framed her success against Pawlenty's decline.

PAWLENTY'S "FAILURE TO LAUNCH"

By now, Pawlenty was framed as having a "failure to launch,"[25] despite doing everything according to the Republican campaign playbook. His lack of success was considered "one of the big mysteries of the early 2012 campaign,"[26] particularly since expectations had been so high. While Pawlenty had been considered a top-tier candidate only a month ago, his campaign was perceived to have stalled almost entirely by mid-summer. Often credited to his poor performance during the June debate, Pawlenty "suffered from being pegged as mild-mannered or unwilling to go on the attack."[27] Media pundits and partisan analysts speculated that the voters wanted a bulldog that would never compromise or back down, and Pawlenty was the antithesis. At this point, Pawlenty was characterized as failing on all fronts: "He had a lackluster performance in the first major presidential debate last month in New Hampshire, has been unimpressive with fundraising and thus far has barely made a dent in the polls."[28] Eventually, the explanatory frame crystallized: "His decline in Iowa has less to do with any policy stance than merely a hardening perception among detractors—and a worry among supporters— that he is not as charismatic or rhetorically tough as some of his rivals, particularly Bachmann."[29]

In an effort to improve his standing and simultaneously fight against the Bachmann tsunami, Pawlenty increasingly focused his attention on her during the summer months, even if not always calling her out by name. He was quoted in the *New York Times* as saying, "Any bobblehead can stand up here and give you the words of the Republican checklist. That doesn't take any particular talent. . . . The question is, have you actually done it?"[30] While Pawlenty was careful not to identify Bachmann specifically (and thus likely reinforcing the narrative that he did not have the guts to engage in actual combat), there was no mistaking to whom he was referring. The two candidates began to feud, with both "staying to type. . . . He offers a cautious slap . . . and she smacks back with dramatic comparisons between him and President Obama."[31] This reinforced frame echoed throughout coverage: she was perceived by voters to be an authentic, passionate conservative, but he was not. Instead, he was perceived to be wishy-washy and weak, paling in comparison to her "titanium spine."[32]

In many ways, their presidential campaign dynamics mirrored their Minnesota experiences: Pawlenty paid his dues and took his time, while Bachmann stole his thunder through incendiary speechmaking and savvy positioning. Pawlenty worked within the system, following procedures both written and implicit. Bachmann went outside of it through her own brand of populism. His stoic and methodical approach to campaigning and governing translated into a perception that voters were not going to get too excited about his "everyman image—some call it blandness."[33] Rather than being used positively, Pawlenty's oft-used "Minnesota nice" label was a code for lacking the charisma and passion required for the 2012 GOP candidate. According to Republican strategist John Feehery, Pawlenty "suffers from two problems. He's got a charisma gap. He has no charisma, and Michele Bachmann is killing him on charisma. And he's got a money gap. He's not raised any money. . . . Tim Pawlenty is not famous. And without money, it's awfully hard to get famous."[34]

HUNTSMAN'S "DIFFICULTY GAINING TRACTION"

Unlike Pawlenty, Huntsman's personal and family fortunes meant he could feasibly fund his own campaign long enough to build awareness and momentum among voters in key states, even though he had initially stated that he was not in favor of this strategy. Unfortunately, the two candidates shared the frame that they had not quite been able to live up to their springtime hype. Both had "difficulty gaining traction in national polls,"[35] and Huntsman's campaign showed signs of internal struggle when his campaign manager, Susie Wiles, quit on July 22. Wiles had been criticized for her handling of Huntsman's campaign launch "which was riddled with errors, from a mis-spelling of the candidate's name to an announcement speech that was staged poorly for television."[36] He was criticized for not having a strong message, and media frames began to emerge questioning whether or not Huntsman really had what it took to earn the nomination.

Soon after Wiles's departure, Huntsman aides announced he was "over-hauling his struggling presidential campaign . . . with plans to strike a more aggressive tone against his GOP rivals and President Obama, step up appear-ances in key states and emphasize his conservatism."[37] This was a notable departure from Huntsman's strategy in spring and early summer, which had "presented [him] as a candidate eager to follow a more civil style of cam-paigning and appeal to voters in both parties."[38] By late July, Huntsman was directly attacking Romney as well as other candidates in an effort to boost his own campaign while attempting to increase their negatives as well. CNN Deputy Political Director Paul Steinhauser commented that Huntsman "looks like he's getting a little tough and maybe shutting that Mr. Nice Guy im-age."[39] With Huntsman clearly dropped from the top tier of candidates, this shift was framed as essential if he had any hope for success.

Part of his newly aggressive approach to the nominating contest was adopting the mantle of truth-teller. In the wake of candidate statements on gasoline prices and global warming that he found problematic, Huntsman "warned against the Republican Party becoming what he called 'the anti-science' party."[40] As he continued to lose ground against his rivals and became more firmly blocked out of the top tier by values candidates, Hunts-man continued to develop "a broader strategy to stake out a part of the Republican primary field that is not so crowded: the moderate part,"[41] in-cluding standing alone as the sole Republican candidate to publicly support the controversial and hard-fought debt deal reached between President Oba-ma and Congressional leaders in late July.

ROMNEY'S FOCUSED CAMPAIGN

While other candidates lobbed accusations and hurled thinly veiled (or not veiled at all, in some cases) insults at each other, Romney continued to try to remain above the fray. He acted as if his nomination was a done deal, even though the nominating contest was just starting to heat up. While Bachmann's rise in Iowa (and some national polls) might have concerned Romney's camp, the candidate did not let it—or her—become a distraction from his campaign strategy. It continued to operate with deliberate, focused precision: "'He's not shooting a machine gun at an artillery,' said Tim Albrecht, a veteran of Romney's 2008 campaign who now works for Iowa Gov. Terry Branstad (R). 'He's going out to the shooting range and taking precision shots.'"[42]

Romney's presidential persona was convincing enough that the media began to realistically assess and anticipate the challenges he would face as the nominee. While being interviewed on CNN, Michigan governor and Democrat Jennifer Granholm was asked who would win Michigan if Romney won the nomination. She immediately brought up Romney's now-infamous *New York Times* op-ed piece, headlined "Let Detroit Go Bankrupt." She then commented, "The president saved the auto industry. And Mitt Romney has got a problem." While (not surprisingly) a Democratic governor predicted the difficulties the Republican would face running against Obama in Michigan, this exchange highlights one of the most important Romney frames during this unsettled period in the race: Even if he did not yet have the nomination locked up (and, in fact, voting was still months away), his nomination was considered likely enough that media pundits and other politicians were treating his match-up against President Obama as a legitimate scenario.

In an effort to "polish up his foreign policy credentials"[43] and burnish his credibility as a statesman, in early July Romney undertook a "romp across the pond"[44] to the United Kingdom. While this is common practice for presidential candidates, Romney's trip primarily was characterized as a fundraising tour, with Fox News's chief political correspondent Carl Cameron commenting, "Comfortably ahead in the polls and fundraising, Republican presidential candidate Mitt Romney has left the United States to raise money overseas. A $2,500 a head dinner in London could rake in $1 million from U.S. citizens living abroad. He'll also meet some British officials."[45] These British officials—unnamed in this report and in most others—included former and current prime ministers Tony Blair and David Cameron. Rather than this trip reinforcing Romney's abilities as a diplomat and statesman, however, the emphasis was on how much money he would make from wealthy expats.

Despite Romney's best efforts to embody the future Republican presidential candidate, he continued to have difficulty inspiring excitement or a unifying energy among GOP voters. Media noted his lack of charisma, often in a negative comparison to other, more engaging candidates like Bachmann. Referring to the 2008 nominating contest, the *Washington Post*'s Chris Cillizza noted, "But Romney struggled then—as he still does—to connect with voters. He seemed to vacillate between overly stiff and overly solicitous, never finding a balance that seemed genuine."[46] A later *Post* article by Philip

Rucker included a conversation the reporter had with Iowa voters Chris and Brenda Malcolm. After Brenda commented, "Everybody's on a first-name basis with Mitt," Rucker followed up with a question: "Does she trust him?" The answer: "No. . . . We're looking for something different, something real."[47]

This perception of Romney as someone with no true north was symbiotic with the contention that he did not hold strong positions on key issues; according to media frames, Romney had very little in the way of either charisma or conviction. The media continued to frame him as a flip-flopper, at times explicitly, as guest host Chuck Todd did on MSNBC's *Hardball*: "All right, up next: Is Mitt Romney flip-flopping again? Talking about President Obama's handling of the economy, he now says he never said that things were worse. Trouble is, he did, and he did it a couple of times."[48] Prominent Democrats picked up and reinforced the perception that Romney was chronically inconsistent on issues, including when "at a breakfast with reporters Wednesday, David Plouffe, Obama's top political adviser, described Romney as 'a world-class political contortionist.'"[49]

During this period, one particular frame began to gain prominence within the Romney coverage: the out-of-touch millionaire. At an August campaign rally, he generated controversy when he responded to hecklers by stating, "Corporations are people, my friend. . . . Everything corporations earn ultimately goes to people."[50] For voters still reeling from a severe economic crisis, this comment was quite jarring. Soon after, his personal fortune was reported to be in the range of $90–$250 million; this was quickly followed by a "renovation plan that is going to do little to change some people's perceptions that he's—he lives in a rarefied environment. [Romney] is reportedly planning to demolish his $12 million, 3,000 square foot ocean front home in California and replace it with a property that's nearly four times larger."[51] The quick onslaught of information about Romney's vast wealth was characterized by MSNBC's Rachel Maddow as a deliberate strategy to go "for the full Thurston," referring to the incredibly wealthy character on *Gilligan's Island*, by no longer trying to downplay his wealth. She continued, "Instead of backing off the whole corporations are people thing, for example, the Romney campaign has decided to turn the corporations for people line into a campaign ad as if this may be a good slogan for him."[52]

Romney also was criticized for playing it safe, particularly during the July debt ceiling crisis, accused of "staying on the sidelines"[53] rather than taking a stand. During this period, this frame began to shift from "cautiousness" to "timidity," particularly when considered in relation to other, bolder candidates. While other candidates took the opportunity to actively promote Tea Party principles and took a hard line against the compromise deal, Romney was perceived to be ducking from making a strong statement. The *Wall Street Journal* quoted Pawlenty campaign manager Alex Conant as saying,

"The Romney campaign strategy is to not chase every ball, but there's a difference between chasing balls and staying out of the arena completely. . . . In [a] battle of ideas, Mitt Romney is a spectator."[54] This reinforced concerns that he was not authentically conservative enough to satisfy Tea Partiers' needs, concerns that some Tea Party members continually raised throughout this period. To help assuage this, "Romney has kept some of the pressure at bay by adopting some Tea Party positions. . . . Those efforts have helped him earn a plurality of support among Tea-Party-affiliated voters."[55] With Perry poised to enter the race, Romney's hard-earned progress with Tea Party voters was of heightened importance, and pundits expected Romney to move away from his conservative strategy: "His survival going forward . . . is dependent upon increasingly defending, and distinguishing, himself from the Republican field."[56]

PERRY: A CONSERVATIVE'S DREAM

While Romney had to fight for credibility and support among Tea Party and socially conservative voters, in this period Perry seemed to be their dream candidate. Authentically religious, fiscally conservative, and the governor of a Republican's fantasy state, Perry was considered someone who could realistically unite the GOP factions: "At a time when the Republican Party is being pulled between its establishment and insurgent forces, Perry has the potential to appeal to both."[57] He also was a gifted campaigner who intuitively knew how to engage with crowds: "If a presidential campaign could be won simply by kissing babies, high-fiving young boys and warmly embracing older women—all of which Mr. Perry did with an enthusiasm and ease that only the most gifted politicians can muster—then the transition from governor to candidate could be effortless."[58]

As one of the first Republicans to recognize the potential of and capitalize on the Tea Party movement, Perry laid claim to the same level of authenticity as Bachmann, but with actual executive experience. His campaign team was made up of seasoned professionals, including two of his longtime associates and advisers who were among the top aides to jump from the good ship Gingrich earlier in the campaign: Dave Carney and Rob Johnson. While the staffers' departure was not framed as leaving Gingrich to join up with Perry (in fact, Perry had not publicly considered his run when the decision was made to leave Gingrich's campaign), their joining Perry's campaign was a strong indicator that he was taking the process seriously.

During this period, considerable attention was paid to understanding Perry as a candidate. While others may have had the same level of exposition when they first decided to run, Perry was in the perhaps enviable position of having his "will he or won't he" process coincide with a time when the race was clearly gaining steam, yet nothing of particular import had yet happened. His declaration of intention offered media something new to talk about during an otherwise stagnant period, and thus his background, religion, and record dominated news coverage throughout the summer months. Across the media, coverage of his Boy Scouts experiences and football heroics as the good-looking son of cotton farmers in Paint Creek, Texas, were complemented by extensive coverage of his current religious beliefs.

The focus on the importance of prayer to Perry was reinforced by his decision to sponsor "The Response: A Call to Prayer for a Nation in Crisis," an early-August prayer rally held at Houston's Reliant Stadium attended by an estimated 30,000 people. As the primary figurehead, Perry was "criticized for spearheading an event that burnishes his conservative Christian credentials as he considers running for president, [although it] is only the latest instance—albeit the highest profile one—of the governor of the nation's second-largest state emphasizing his Christian beliefs and blurring the line between church and state." Notably, one of the groups sponsoring the event—the American Family Association—was characterized as "an evangelical group whose leadership has condemned pornography, abortion, homosexuality, and First Amendment rights for Muslims. The Southern Poverty Law Center classifies them as a hate group."[59]

Characterized as the "swashbuckling, gun-toting governor of Texas" frequently greeted by "raucous welcomes before adoring groups of conservatives across the country,"[60] Perry's tenure as the longest-serving governor of Texas gave reporters much to write about. Early coverage of him emphasized his masculine, aggressive style, both in terms of campaigning and governing, and reinforced his embodiment of the Texas cowboy. In fact, the associations between Perry and cowboy culture were so strong that a simple change in footwear revealed health concerns. While his uniform typically included cowboy boots, he began showing up to events wearing black orthopedic sneakers and a back brace.[61] When reporters started asking why, they eventually learned that Perry had undergone spinal fusion surgery in early July to correct a chronic back ailment.

Much was written about Perry's relationship with the Texas legislature and courts, including how his tenure allowed him much more influence with the state governing body than the executive office historically held. Journalists investigated and wrote about some of the more controversial elements of Perry's administration, including concerns about lobbyist impact, crystallized in his controversial decision to require millions of Texas girls to receive the Gardasil vaccine while his former chief-of-staff, Mike Toomey, was employed as a Merck lobbyist.[62] Reporters also wrote about his support for the death penalty, noting that "Perry . . . has overseen more executions than any governor in modern history: 234 and counting. That's more than the combined total in the next two states—Oklahoma and Virginia—since the death penalty was restored 35 years ago."[63]

Even stories on Perry's favorite talking points—the economic success of Texas under his governance—became fodder for discussion in the build-up to his candidacy. While reporters agreed that "Texas has created more jobs than any other state since the end of the recession in 2009, 37 percent of all new American jobs,"[64] others began to question how much of that Perry should take credit for. While Dallas Federal Reserve President Richard Fisher acknowledged, "conservative policymakers have made the Texas climate more attractive economically," he also "noted that the state has been blessed by abundant natural resources, wide-open spaces and good ports."[65] Others observed that many of the jobs created served the booming population, but the budget passed by the legislature in mid-2011 would slash funding for a number of those positions. Critics further "pointed to Texas' unemployment rate and low-wage jobs, noting that Texas ties Mississippi for the highest percentage of minimum wage workers."[66]

Once on a national stage and under a high-powered microscope, Perry found himself having to reverse course and/or revise his positions on important issues. When asked about New York's decision to allow same-sex marriage, Perry's initial response framed the decision as a states' rights issue and thus one he did not question. When religious conservatives recoiled at his response, Perry reconsidered and recanted—alarming the Tenth Amendment loyalists in his camp. He also notably shifted his language in relation to the immigration debate, moving to an increasingly strident anti-immigration policy more in line with the Tea Party's position. These questions, his responses, and the reactions from potential and actual supporters helped illustrate the conundrum faced by Perry in particular but all 2012 Republican candidates in general: How do you maintain your conservative credentials when your party is divided?

Horserace coverage was prominent in Perry coverage, with pundits speculating about the impact he would have on the other candidates. Particular attention was paid to how his candidacy would affect Bachmann, since it was presumed they would attract the same Tea Party base, and Romney, due to Perry's perceived appeal to establishment Republicans. By the end of July, before he was even officially a candidate, Perry was polling among the top contenders.

ALL EYES ON IOWA

As calendars turned to August, all eyes turned to Iowa. After "a slow-moving Republican presidential campaign"[67] thus far, the third candidate debate was scheduled for August 11 at the Iowa State University campus in Ames. While eight candidates prepared to meet on stage, a "brass-knuckle campaigner who has made an art of lighting bonfires on the political right"[68] stole their thunder. The announcement that Perry would officially declare his candidacy on Saturday—the same day as the Ames straw poll—became headline news and was the lead story for the cable news networks.[69]

Even with Perry's announcement monopolizing airtime, the Iowa debate went forward with "the fiercest face-to-face exchanges of the 2012 contest."[70] Considered "high stakes,"[71] the debate made pundits curious to see how the various candidate narratives would play out: Could Bachmann maintain the high level of performance she demonstrated in New Hampshire and make a national impression? Would Pawlenty land enough zingers to refute his weak persona? Would Huntsman, participating in his first debate, be able to connect with voters? Would Romney be able to escape unscathed once more despite his frontrunner status? What headline- (or punch line-) worthy claims would Paul, Cain, Gingrich, or Santorum offer?

When the debate was over, coverage focused on some of the pithier one-liners and catchier bits, including Pawlenty's pointed jabs about Romney's wealth and Bachmann's lack of experience. Gingrich accused the Fox News and *Washington Examiner* moderators of asking "gotcha questions,"[72] and audience members booed when Fox's Byron York asked Bachmann, based on her reliance on Biblical text as well as previous statements she made, whether or not she would be submissive to her husband as president. While the debate offered some fantastic sound bites and highlighted the "simmering animosity"[73] among the eight candidates on stage, it did little to shift perceptions going into Saturday's straw poll.

The Ames Straw Poll

While the debate generated considerable interest, it was but a prelude to what was considered the first real test of organizational strength for the candidates: the Ames Straw Poll, held on Saturday, August 13. This was the event that the socially conservative, Tea Party candidates had built toward throughout their campaigns so far. If things went well, this was their chance to prove their appeal to voters, generating much-needed buzz and momentum that would translate to donor support. For those who fell short of expectations, however, Ames could prove to be their Waterloo.

Long a tradition of the Iowa Republican Party, the Ames Straw Poll served as a lucrative fundraiser for the organization. Candidates paid tens of thousands of dollars to get prime tent locations; within these tents, they offered food, drink, and entertainment, including a concert from legendary country superstar Randy Travis in Bachmann's tent, all in an effort to grab the attention and interest of Iowa Republicans. In hopes that they will demonstrate support, voters are bused in, with most campaigns paying the entire $30 admission fee for potential backers to attend.

Despite the massive sums of money spent on the event, it has been a poor predictor of both the Iowa caucus winner and the eventual GOP nominee. In 2008, Romney spent millions to win the straw poll, only to see the conservative values candidate Mike Huckabee come in first during the caucuses and John McCain become the official nominee. Armed with this knowledge, some of the more establishment candidates, notably Romney and Huntsman, did not actively compete in the Ames Straw Poll.

Both the fallout from the previous debate in New Hampshire and the high stakes associated with the straw poll heightened the buildup to Ames. Pawlenty's campaign was derailed by his refusal to address Romney mano-a-mano with the "Obamneycare" accusation, reinforcing the narrative that he lacked the aggressiveness and fire needed to earn the GOP's nomination for president, and he had not yet figured out a way to stanch the bleeding. It was widely acknowledged that Pawlenty needed a strong showing in Ames to reinvigorate his stalled campaign: "Anything less than a second-place finish for Pawlenty may have a dire effect on his ability to woo contributors for a campaign having difficulty securing big-ticket donors."[74] Pawlenty was not the only candidate who found himself in a weakened position post–New Hampshire; a less-than-spectacular performance from Cain found him falling off the media's radar for much of the summer months, and he and other marginalized candidates needed their performances to offer new life to their candidacies.

When the day ended, Bachmann was declared winner with 28 percent of the vote, while Paul earned 27 percent. Pawlenty was a distant third. By the next day, he had officially dropped out of the race. The media framed his failure to connect with voters as being the wrong candidate at the wrong time, noting that this was not the year for Minnesota nice. Instead, voters seemed to be looking for a firebrand—someone with passion, authenticity, and conviction who would not be afraid to go toe-to-toe with President Obama to serve up the right's viewpoint. For all that he ran a textbook campaign and was, on paper, a top candidate, Pawlenty just could not meet the expectations of a "Republican electorate . . . looking for more fire and confrontation."[75]

PERRY "JOLTS" THE FIELD

As expected, Perry drew considerable attention away from Iowa when he officially announced his candidacy in South Carolina on the same day as the Ames Straw Poll. Observers anticipated that his candidacy would "reconfigure the dynamics of the race, offering Republicans a fiscal and social conservative who not only appeals to the party's base but can also challenge Mitt Romney . . . on jobs and the economy."[76] His impact was expected to be profound and immediate. As MSNBC senior political analyst Mark Halperin noted, "I think by most metrics we use to judge candidates, he becomes a first tier candidate. If he performs well in the first 15 days, I think for the time, it will be a two-person race between him and Governor Romney. That's a big if, though. He's never done this."[77]

As Halperin predicted, once Perry officially entered the race he quickly learned that a national campaign differed substantially from running for Texas governor. An off-the-cuff remark "at the end of a freewheeling and unscripted day of introducing himself to voters"[78] was interpreted as accusing Federal Reserve chair Ben Bernanke of treason. An immediate outcry followed, with both Democrats and Republicans taking Perry to task for his words. This experience "underscored the challenge facing Mr. Perry as he makes the transition from Texas governor to presidential candidate, where every phrase is parsed and ripe for criticism."[79] While he had never lost an election to this point and was known for his aggressive, tough campaigning, Perry quickly learned that he needed to be more disciplined on the presidential campaign trail. Within days of his Bernanke statement, a more focused Perry was staying on-message at campaign stops.

Despite Perry's early troubles, he almost immediately was considered a top-tier candidate, joining Romney and Bachmann in that much-vaunted group. According to some, however, that group should include a fourth candidate: Ron Paul.

PAUL'S PREDICAMENT

Although both Pawlenty and Huntsman had fallen from their lofty inclusion in the perceived top tier of candidates, Paul and his vociferous supporters regularly reiterated their belief that his name should be included in that list. Paul was second to only Romney in terms of fundraising, and his fan base was considerable—and vocal. Paul's performance during straw polls, including winning the Conservative Political Action Conference (CPAC) straw poll earlier in the summer and placing a close second in Ames, indicated more popular support than he had enjoyed in past presidential campaigns, and ultimately Paul decided to focus all of his energy on winning the nomination. In mid-July, he announced that he would not be running for reelection to the House of Representatives, declaring, "I will continue to do what I've been doing for 30 years: promoting individual liberty, sound economic policy and bringing our troops home."[80]

During this period, Paul finally began getting credit for being the forefather to the ideas that fueled the Tea Party; unfortunately, this also came with the recognition that other candidates, notably Bachmann and Perry, had appropriated them for maximum value. After all, Paul had "spent years sounding like a crackpot or a fringe case, spouting ideas that were outside the boundaries of mainstream Republican thinking. . . . The problem for Mr. Paul is that many of his ideas have been appropriated by the kinds of mainstream Republicans who used to snort when he talked."[81]

While Paul's libertarian positions had successfully entered the mainstream Republican conversation thanks to adoption by the Tea Party, Paul was still referred to as an "iconoclastic conservative,"[82] characterized as someone who advocated controversial ideas that were well outside of the accepted American political system. This perception that he was too far removed from mainstream American politics was thought to keep him out of top-tier candidate breakdowns; despite his success as a fundraiser, passionate supporters, and coming within 200 votes of Bachmann at the Ames Straw Poll, the media still did not perceive or present Paul as a legitimate candidate for president. Eventually, regular complaints about this led to the *Washington Post*'s ombudsman to write an article examining their coverage of the candidate. After opening with the question, "Has the *Post* Given Republican Presidential Candidate Ron Paul Short Shrift in Coverage?"[83] the article acknowledged that the *Post*'s "record on Paul coverage is sparse" and that coverage instead focused on Bachmann, Perry, and Romney.[84]

LIMITING THE POOL

Almost all of the candidates merited at least some coverage in the spring months, but that shifted during the summer. During this period, mainstream media emphasis clearly focused on "serious" candidates with a hook—those considered to have a realistic chance at winning the nomination, whether due to polling (Bachmann), fundraising (Romney), momentum (Perry), or agitating, vocal supporters (Paul). Even former top-tier candidate Huntsman found himself with a steadily declining media presence; as he failed to gain traction in the polls, his coverage correspondingly declined. There was very little attention to candidates Cain, Gingrich, or Santorum in newspapers; there was almost none for Johnson. While they fared better on cable news, their coverage paled in comparison to the other candidates. As Steve Kornacki, news editor at Salon, commented, "A few weeks ago there was this guy, Herman Cain who was getting all the attention, who's moving up in the polls, starting to raise money. He's been completely eclipsed now by Michele Bachmann."[85]

Fueling the volatility in the 2012 Republican contest was the overarching frame that the primary was a battle between the Tea Party and establishment GOP factions of the Republican Party. If Romney were to win, it would be a

victory for the traditional mainstream party. Any of the others, bar Huntsman, would offer support to arguments that these conservative voices were
the future of the GOP. The challenge faced in this period, however, was how
to reconcile what Rachel Maddow offered as "two truisms" about the race as
it stood in summer 2011: "Number one, Romney's going to win. Number
two: no one wins without the Tea Party on their side. The problem is that
those two facile, Beltway common wisdom axioms about Republican politics
right now cannot co-exist."[86] As Maddow explained, "To the extent that the
Tea Party faction is organized around Republican presidential politics at all
right now, they are organized to nominate anyone but Mitt Romney." They
just had to figure out who that "anyone but" would be.

This framing also was emphasized by the wildly disproportionate influence of Iowa—the home of social conservatives—and New Hampshire, a
state considered more amenable to mainstream Republicans. Very little was
discussed in terms of other states, in large part because candidates' resources—both time and money—were almost exclusively focused on the
"first in the nation" battlegrounds. With the Ames debate and Straw Poll,
Iowa held the attention of both media and candidates throughout the summer.
The overwhelming presence of values voters, evangelicals, and Tea Partiers
in Iowa characterized and shifted the debate in ways nothing else could,
pushing candidates further to the right in an effort to win these voters' affections, attention, and support.

Recognizing this and in some ways resentful of the exclusionary approach to campaigning experienced over summer, other states started making
noises about moving up their primary dates in order to get in on the summer
action. While the Republican Party protected Iowa and New Hampshire's
interests, the unsettled primary calendar added to the uncertainty of the field.
Ultimately, some looked to South Carolina; while it came behind both Iowa
and New Hampshire on the primary calendar, South Carolina often served as
the "firewall that snuffs out insurgent candidates" with campaigns "that re-
volved around guns, God, and gays."[87]

Moving into autumn, signs emerged that troubled times might be ahead
for candidates Bachmann and Perry. The latter's entrance into the race had
undermined the support and enthusiasm Bachmann had built, and his declaration of candidacy on the same day as the Ames Straw Poll did not allow
Bachmann to fully capitalize on her victory. By the end of the month, Paul
had passed her in some national polls. While he continued to poll well, Perry
too showed indicators that his early mistakes may come back to haunt him:
"But a few missteps by Mr. Perry reminded some in the GOP elite, including
Republican donors, of underlying concerns that, strong as his appeal is to
conservatives, it might not be broad enough to unseat an incumbent president."[88]

NOTES

1. Dan Balz, "August Could Be Make or Break for GOP Field," *Washington Post*, August 7, 2011, A-Section, Factiva.

2. Jonathan Weisman and Neil King Jr., "Calls Rise To Broaden GOP Field," *Wall Street Journal*, August 22, 2011, A1, Factiva.

3. Phillip Rucker and Perry Bacon Jr., "GOP Indecision on 2012 May Open Door for Perry," *Washington Post*, July 13, 2011, A-Section, Factiva.

4. Balz, "August Could."

5. T. J. Holmes, Chris Welch, Max Foster, Ray D'Alessio, and Shannon Travis, "Minnesota Government Shuts Down After Budget Talk Breakdown; Duke and Duchess of Cambridge Visit Canada; Michele Bachmann Campaigns in Iowa; Political Analysts Discuss Congress Debt Ceiling Negotiations; Michael Vick Signs Endorsement Deal With Nike; Georgia Experiencing Shortfall in Farm Labor Due to Anti-Illegal Immigration Bill," *CNN: CNN Newsroom*, July 2, 2011, LexisNexis Academic.

6. "Brooke Baldwin, Richard Roth, Jim Bittermann, David McKenzie, Sandra Endo, John Zarrella, and Wolf Blitzer, "Dominique Strauss-Kahn Case Falling Apart?; Hugo Chavez Has Cancer; The Duke and Duchess of Cambridge Visit Canada; NASA Prepares to End Shuttle Program; Financial Experts Give Advice; New Fundraising Numbers for Presidential Candidates," *CNN: CNN Newsroom*, July 1, 2011, LexisNexis Academic.

7. Ali Velshi, Anna Coren, Rob Marciano, Zain Verjee, Jeffrey Toobin, Jim Bitterman, and Shannon Travis, "Case Against Strauss-Kahn Shaky; Minnesota Government Shuts Down; Geithner Considers Leaving; Minnesota Government Out of Money; New Secretary of Defense," *CNN: American Morning: Wake Up Call*, July 1, 2011, LexisNexis Academic.

8. Dan Eggen and Perry Bacon Jr., "GOP Candidates' War Chests Mostly Empty," *Washington Post*, July 10, 2011, A-Section, Factiva.

9. Ibid.

10. Phillip Rucker, "Romney Visits Shuttered Pa. Plant to Attack Obama," *Washington Post*, July 1, 2011, A-Section, Factiva.

11. Suzanne Malveaux, Dan Rivers, Reza Sayah, Chris Welch, Alison Kosik, Brian Todd, Elizabeth Cohen, Paul Steinhauser, and John Zarrella, "British Parliament Calls Rupert Murdoch to Testify About Phone-Hacking Scandal; Pakistan Arrests Doctor who Helped CIA; Government Shutdown Hits Home; The Effects of Extreme Heat on Your Body; Final Spacewalk of Shuttle Era; Scandal Rocks Media Empire," *CNN: CNN Newsroom*, July 12, 2011, LexisNexis Academic.

12. Wolf Blitzer, Deborah Feyerick, Arwa Damon, Donna Brazile, Mary Matalin, Becky Anderson, Kate Bolduan, Jack Cafferty, and Chris Lawrence, "Interview with Pakistani Ambassador Husain Haqqani; Attack on U.S. Embassy in Damascus; Scandal Hits Two More Murdoch Papers; U.S. Cutting Aid to Pakistan; No Breakthrough in Debt Standoff; 'We Cannot Allow This to Happen,'" *CNN: The Situation Room*, July 11, 2011, LexisNexis Academic.

13. Kyra Phillips, Susan Candiotti, Mark McKay, Barbara Starr, David Mattingly, Zain Verjee, Kareen Wynter, Max Foster, Allan Chernoff, John Zarrella, and Jim Acosta, "Indefinite Recess in Anthony Trial; Los Alamos National Lab Closed; Case Against Former IMF Chief in Doubt; NBA Lockout Begins; Players Dispute Estimated Losses; Canada's Royal Reception; Minnesota's Government Shuts Down; Immigration Law Takes Effect Today; Golden Gate Ferry Service Canceled; Panetta Takes Control of Pentagon; Clinton Weighs In on 2012 Election; Hints of 'Sex and The City' Prequel," *CNN: CNN Newsroom*, July 1, 2011, LexisNexis Academic.

14. Wolf Blitzer, Brianna Keilar, Chris Lawrence, Arwa Damon, Jack Cafferty, Dan Rivers, Deborah Feyerick, Brian Todd, James Carville, Alex Castellanos, and Casey Wian, "Partisan Political Moves; A Plan B Without Spending Cuts?; Twists & Turns of Debt Ceiling Battle Continue; Lawmakers Summon Murdoch Over Scandal; Interview with Arab American Institute President James Zogby; Could President Obama Be Breaking the Law Amidst Efforts to Win Reelection?; 'Strategy Session,'" *CNN: The Situation Room*, July 12, 2011, LexisNexis Academic.

15. Kimberly Kindy, "Bachmann Benefited from Loan Programs She Decried," *Washington Post*, July 27, 2011, A-Section, Factiva.

16. Patrick O'Connor, "U.S. News—Election 2012: Bachmann's Tax Attorney Job was Collector for the IRS," *Wall Street Journal*, July 11, 2011, National Desk, Factiva.

17. Sheryl Gay Stolberg and Gardiner Harris, "Christian Counseling by Hopeful's Spouse Prompts Questions," *New York Times*, July 17, 2011, National Desk, Factiva.

18. Ibid.

19. Anderson Cooper, Jim Acosta, David Gergen, Gloria Borger, Gary Tuchman, Jill Dougherty, and Isha Sesay, "Controversial Clinic; Reparative Therapy, Pseudo-Science?; Deadly Crackdown; Mob Attacks U.S., French Embassies in Syria; Casey Anthony Juror Speaks Out," *CNN: Anderson Cooper 360 Degrees*, July 12, 2011, LexisNexis Academic.

20. Blitzer et al., "Interview with Pakistani Ambassador."

21. Brian Knowlton, "Criticizing Rivals, Huntsman Tries to Claim Middle Ground," *New York Times*, August 22, 2011, National Desk, Factiva.

22. Bill O'Reilly, "Talking Points Memo and Top Story," *Fox News Network: The O'Reilly Factor*, July 18, 2011, LexisNexis Academic.

23. Anderson Cooper, Isha Sesay, Gloria Borger, Gary Tuchman, and Drew Pinsky, "Rewriting History; Trillion-Dollar Showdown; Jaycee Dugard Breaks Her Silence," *CNN: Anderson Cooper 360 Degrees*, July 11, 2011, LexisNexis Academic.

24. Rachel Maddow, "The Rachel Maddow Show for July 7, 2011," *MSNBC: The Rachel Maddow Show*, July 7, 2011, LexisNexis Academic.

25. Patrick O'Connor, "U.S. News—Election 2012: Pawlenty Struggles to Gain A Foothold in Iowa Contest," *Wall Street Journal*, July 22, 2011, A6, Factiva.

26. Neil King Jr., "Pawlenty's Homespun Tale," *Wall Street Journal*, July 6, 2011, A1, Factiva.

27. Trip Gabriel, "Still in the Game, Underdog Says," *New York Times*, July 23, 2011, National Desk, Factiva.

28. Amy Gardner, "Pawlenty May Go For Broke in Iowa," *Washington Post*, July 9, 2011, A-Section, Factiva.

29. Michael Leahy, "As Iowa Poll Nears, Doubts About Pawlenty Grow," *Washington Post*, August 9, 2011, A-Section, Factiva.

30. Michael D. Shear, "Pawlenty Seeks Out Religious Voters in Iowa," *New York Times*, August 10, 2011, National Desk, Factiva.

31. Amy Gardner, "Not So Minnesota Nice," *Washington Post*, July 28, 2011, A-Section, Factiva.

32. Monica Langley and Patrick O'Connor, "Behind a GOP Contender's Iowa Surge," *Wall Street Journal*, August 5, 2011, A1, Factiva.

33. King, "Pawlenty's Homespun Tale."

34. Candy Crowley, Paul Begala, John Feehery, Kate Bolduan, Mary Snow, John Zarrella, Ed Lavandera, Ivan Watson, Jill Dougherty, John Zarrella, Paul Begala, and Brian Todd, "Republicans Pounce on Jobs Report; Countdown to Default: Debt Limit Drama; Men Outpace Women in Job Growth; Final Shuttle Mission Underway; Crushing Dissent in Syria; NASA's Next Frontier; 'Strategy Session,'" *CNN: The Situation Room*, July 8, 2011, LexisNexis Academic.

35. Nicholas Confessore, Griff Palmer, and Derek Willis, "Romney Seeing Smaller Pool for Donations in Second Run," *New York Times*, July 23, 2011, National Desk, Factiva.

36. Aaron Blake and Nia-Malika Henderson, "Struggling Huntsman Campaign Loses its Manager," *Washington Post*, July 22, 2011, A-Section, Factiva.

37. Nia-Malika Henderson and Perry Bacon Jr., "Huntsman Shifts Gears to Energize Campaign," *Washington Post*, July 24, 2011, A-Section, Factiva.

38. Ibid.

39. Howard Kurtz, Brooke Baldwin, Paul Steinhauser, Thelma Gutierrez, Joe Johns, Alison Kosik, Ed Lavandera, and Gustavo Valdes, "Debt Negotiations Continue; What Next for NASA?; No More Mr. Nice Guy?; Betty Ford Memorial; Cries for Help Go Unanswered; Hero Awarded Medal of Honor; Highest Honor for Army Ranger; Sherwood Schwartz Dead at 94; Michelle Obama's Shake Out," *CNN: CNN Newsroom*, July 12, 2011, LexisNexis Academic.

40. Knowlton, "Criticizing Rivals."

41. Michael D. Shear, "Huntsman Makes Bid To Step Out From Crowd," *New York Times*, August 19, 2011, National Desk, Factiva.

42. Phillip Rucker, "In Iowa, Mitt Romney Waging a Stealth Campaign," *Washington Post*, July 23, 2011, A-Section, Factiva.

43. Comment by Donna Brazile in Candy Crowley, Kate Bolduan, Mary Snow, Donna Brazile, Jack Cafferty, Chris Lawrence, Reza Sayah, David Mattingly, Jeffrey Toobin, and Dan Rivers, "President Obama: Debt Negotiations 'Far Apart'; Interview With Senator Tom Coburn; 'Strategy Session'; Terror Suspect Linked to Al-Awlaki," *CNN: The Situation Room*, July 7, 2011, LexisNexis Academic.

44. Bret Baier, William La Jeunesse, Wendell Goler, Catherine Herridge, Jennifer Griffin, John Roberts, and Carl Cameron, "Political Headlines," *Fox News Network: Fox Special Report with Bret Baier*, July 6, 2011, LexisNexis Academic.

45. Ibid.

46. Chris Cillizza, "Bachmann's Story Helps Her Connect with Voters," *Washington Post*, July 1, 2011, A-Section, Factiva.

47. Rucker, "Mitt Romney Waging."

48. Chuck Todd, Howard Fineman, Tyler Mathisen, Richard Wolffe, Eugene Robinson, and Bill Wolff, "Hardball for July 1, 2011," *MSNBC: Hardball*, July 1, 2011, LexisNexis Academic.

49. Philip Rucker and Peter Wallsten, "Democrats Join the Republican Fray," *Washington Post*, July 9, 2011, A-Section, Factiva.

50. Brooke Baldwin, Athena Jones, Paul Steinhauser, Shannon Travis, Elizabeth Cohen, Jim Acosta, and Soledad O'Brien, "President Obama Touts Jobs in Michigan; Who Will Win Iowa Straw Poll?; New Breakthrough May Cure Cancer; New Documentary Focuses on Mountaintop Removal Mining; Riots in London Dying Down; U.S. Stock Market Up on the Day," *CNN: CNN Newsroom*, August 11, 2011, LexisNexis Academic.

51. Carol Costello, Kristie Lu Stout, Jacqui Jeras, Fred Pleitgen, Christine Romans, Barbara Starr, and Carter Evans, "Hurricane Irene Gains Strength; Battle for Tripoli Not Over; Infant Falls from Parking Garage; Ex-Bengal OK after Getting Shot," *CNN: American Morning*, August 23, 2011, LexisNexis Academic.

52. Rachel Maddow, "For August 23, 2011," *MSNBC: The Rachel Maddow Show*, August 23, 2011, LexisNexis Academic.

53. Al Sharpton, "MSNBC Live with Cenk Uygur for July 14, 2011," *MSNBC: MSNBC Live with Cenk Uygur*, July 14, 2011, LexisNexis Academic.

54. Danny Yadron and Jonathan Weisman, "U.S. News—Election 2012: Romney, Back on the Trail, Hears Perry Rev His Engine," *Wall Street Journal*, August 9, 2011, A3, Factiva.

55. Amy Gardner, "Looking to Expand, the Tea Party Shifts its Focus," *Washington Post*, July 20, 2011, A-Section, Factiva.

56. Jeff Zeleny and Ashley Parker, "With Return to Iowa, Romney Heeds Call of G.O.P. Strategists," *New York Times*, August 11, 2011, National Desk, Factiva.

57. Tumulty, "Perry Weighs Options."

58. Jeff Zeleny, "A Confident Perry Lingers to Make Friends at the Fair," *New York Times*, August 16, 2011, National Desk, Factiva.

59. Lawrence O'Donnell, "The Last Word for August 3, 2011," *MSNBC: The Last Word with Lawrence O 'Donnell*, August 3, 2011, LexisNexis Academic.

60. Julian Aguilar, "Perry and Hispanics Coexist Uneasily in Politics," *New York Times*, July 1, 2011, National Desk, Factiva.

61. Manny Fernandez, "Recuperating From Surgery, Perry Persists In Campaign," *New York Times*, July 28, 2011, National Desk, Factiva.

62. Ross Ramsey, "Perry's Legion: The Folks Behind, Beside and Around the Man," *New York Times*, July 31, 2011, National Desk, Factiva.

63. Robert Barnes, "On Executions, Perry Easily Holds the Record," *Washington Post*, August 24, 2011, A-Section, Factiva.

64. Candy Crowley, Susan Candiotti, Sandra Endo, Martin Savidge, Martin Savidge, Nancy Grace, Hala Gorani, David Gergen, and Ed Lavandera, "Case Against Ex-IMF Chief in Sham-

bles; Casey Anthony Trial: Prosecutors Zero in on Home Computer," *CNN: John King, USA*, July 1, 2011, LexisNexis Academic.

65. Karen Tumulty, "Perry Weighs Options While the GOP Waits," *Washington Post*, July 3, 2011, A-Section, Factiva.

66. Becca Aaronson, "Private-Sector Jobs Are a Major Factor in Employment Growth," *New York Times*, August 28, 2011, National Desk, Factiva.

67. Neil King Jr. and Jonathan Weisman, "U.S. News—Election 2012: Debate Jolts Republican Race to Life—With Perry Set to Enter Race Saturday, Pawlenty Goes on the Offensive against Bachmann and Front-Runner Romney," *Wall Street Journal*, August 12, 2011, A5, Factiva.

68. Neil King Jr. and Leslie Eaton, "Texas Governor Upends GOP Race," *Wall Street Journal*, August 13, 2011, A1, Factiva.

69. Chris Matthews, Mark Halperin, Saijal Patel, Howard Fineman, Steve McMahon, and Pat Buchanan, "Perry and Palin Crash the Party; Iowa Fight Night; Dems Nervous About 2012; 2012 Political Strategy," *MSNBC: Hardball*, August 11, 2011, LexisNexis Academic.

70. King and Weisman, "Debate Jolts Republican Race to Life."

71. Leahy, "As Iowa Poll Nears."

72. Bret Baier, "GOP Presidential Debate," *Fox News Network: Live Event*, August 11, 2011, LexisNexis Academic.

73. Jeff Zeleny and Ashley Parker, "8 from G.O.P. Let Sparks Fly at Iowa Debate," *New York Times*, August 12, 2011, National Desk, Factiva.

74. Leahy, "As Iowa Poll Nears."

75. Jonathan Weisman and Neil King Jr., "Election 2012: GOP Race Gains Focus as Pawlenty Says Goodbye," *Wall Street Journal*, August 15, 2011, A1, Factiva.

76. Ashley Parker, Jeff Zeleny, and Matt Flegenheimer, "Shaking Up Republican Field, Perry Officially Enters the Race for President," *New York Times*, August 14, 2011, National Desk, Factiva.

77. Matthews et al., "Perry and Palin Crash the Party."

78. Jeff Zeleny and Jackie Calmes, "Perry Stands by Remarks on Fed Policy and Treason," *New York Times*, August 17, 2011, National Desk, Factiva.

79. Ibid.

80. Danny Yadron, "U.S. News: Ron Paul Opts to Give Up House Seat," *Wall Street Journal*, July 13, 2011, A3, Factiva.

81. Ross Ramsey, "A Texan in Washington Who Hasn't Gone Native," *New York Times*, July 17, 2011, National Desk, Factiva.

82. Amy Gardner and Dan Balz, "Ames, Iowa—On the day that T," *Washington Post*, August 14, 2011, A-Section, Factiva.

83. Patrick B. Pexton, "Desperately Seeking Ron Paul," *Washington Post*, August 28, 2011, A-Section, Factiva.

84. Ibid.

85. Tom Foreman, "Tensions Rise in Washington over Debt Ceiling; Time for a Truce in Washington?; The Murdoch Scandal," *CNN: In the Arena*, July 14, 2011, LexisNexis Academic.

86. Maddow, "For July 7, 2011."

87. Michael A. Fletcher, "S.C. Economy Trumps Other Concerns in GOP Primary," *Washington Post*, July 9, 2011, A-Section, Factiva.

88. Weisman and King, "Calls Rise To Broaden."

Chapter Four

The Rollercoaster Continues

September–October 2011

Perry's impact on the Republican nomination race was immediate and substantial, particularly impacting those candidates who had been best positioned heading into late summer. He had thwarted Bachmann's momentum and prevented her from capitalizing on her win in the Ames Straw Poll, drawing away the affections and support of Bachmann's Tea Party base. Despite his close-second result in Ames, Paul experienced a similar fate, finding himself polling in fourth place rather than enjoying a post–straw poll bump. With his expected appeal to both mainstream Republicans and values voters, Perry's entry had shifted the game. His approach was to consolidate support in a party moving quickly to the right. This was a potent message and one that threated Romney's electability claim.

The electability question became even more pronounced in September. Dire economic indicators continued to raise serious concerns about America's economic recovery. In the wake of an August jobs report that showed zero net job creation and predictions that unemployment would not decrease substantially before the election, Obama seemed more vulnerable than ever: "In both parties, there is now a sense that the president's political frailty . . . is even greater than it appeared at the start of the summer, injecting additional energy and urgency into the Republican primary race."[1] This elevated importance coincided with Labor Day, a holiday that was considered the "unofficial launch day of the 2012 presidential cycle."[2] Heading into this pivotal period, the declared candidates prepared themselves to face off at a series of debates intended to help voters learn about and differentiate among the potential nominees.

THE CANDIDATES DEBATE: SIMI VALLEY, CA AND TAMPA, FL

September was a busy month for debates and marked the beginning of an intensive—and debate-heavy—campaign season. For a pool of candidates who had limited previous experience on a national stage, this was an opportunity to get free exposure to Republican audiences. Earlier debates had served as springboards for widely unknown candidates Cain and Bachmann, and others hoped to enjoy the same fate. For media, the appeal was clear: these events gave them a hook—something new to talk about while they were months away from ballots being cast and still needed material to fill airtime and column inches.

On September 7, eight candidates assembled on stage at the Reagan Library in Simi Valley, California, for a debate sponsored by NBC News (MSNBC) and *Politico*. The powerful symbolism of this location was not lost on candidates fighting for prominence during a period when the Republican Party had elevated Reagan to demigod status, invoking his specter to add credibility to their conservative credentials. While seven of the candidates—Bachmann, Cain, Gingrich, Huntsman, Paul, Romney, and Santorum—had met before on similar stages around the country, this was Perry's first debate as a presidential candidate. Expectations were sky high and the candidates did not disappoint, at least in terms of creating controversy and spewing sound bites.

Coverage of this debate clearly framed the race as a two-man contest between Romney, the longtime frontrunner who lacked widespread support, versus Perry, the Texas governor whose "Lone Star bravado"[3] had injected excitement into the race. The two faced off during "an intense and ideological battle . . . sharply clashing over Social Security, health care, and each other's long-term prospect against President Obama."[4] Their contentious interactions and combative exchanges demonstrated that they "were willing to slug it out for the nomination,"[5] with each doing his best to land a knockout blow to his opponent.

The framing of the debate as a contest between Perry and Romney was not limited to media coverage; it was reinforced through the structure and conduct of the debate itself. The moderators returned repeatedly to the two men, offering them opportunities to engage with and respond to each other at the expense of other candidates. Perry sparked one of the debate's most memorable exchanges when he referred to Social Security as a "Ponzi scheme" and a "monstrous lie." Despite being within weeks of her Ames Straw Poll victory—a win that was supposed to cement her position in the top tier—Bachmann did not get the opportunity to answer a question until fourteen minutes into the event. Other candidates on the floor had even more difficulty getting their voices heard, resulting in perceptions of a two-man race leading to the reality of a two-man debate. Initial evaluations of Perry's debut debate performance were fairly positive, emphasizing the combative dynamic between Romney and him: "Although Perry has had relatively little experience in such a setting, he was at ease—and occasionally combative. The Texas governor appeared unflustered and unapologetic as he took fire on his record and on some of the more inflammatory statements he has made."[6]

The Reagan Library debate had barely faded from memory when a second event was held at the Florida State Fairgrounds in Tampa on September 12. Sponsored by CNN, the Tea Party Express, and more than 100 Tea Party groups, this contest had the feel of a "rollicking political game show," as candidates were "welcomed onto the neon-lit stage by Wolf Blitzer, the CNN anchor, as though they were contestants in a lightning round, complete with nicknames, including Mrs. Bachmann, 'The Firebrand'; former Speaker Newt Gingrich, 'The Big Thinker'; and Mr. Santorum, 'The Fighter.'"[7] These labels were part of an introduction that seemed inspired by the archetypes and style of reality television, as evidenced by the announcer's opening bit: "Tonight, eight Republicans, one goal: to win the White House and kick Barack Obama out. Cheering them on, their powerful allies and fierce critics, the grassroots movement putting a bold stamp on this election, the Tea Party."[8] There was no pretense of sophistication or presidential gravitas, no attempt to portray this as a civil discussion among competing candidates with a common objective. This was a set-up reminiscent of MTV's *Jersey Shore*. The tone was set and the intention was clear—this debate was pure entertainment.

With that tenor clearly established from the outset, the candidates emulated their reality show counterparts by coming out swinging. Newly minted frontrunner Perry was the recipient of most body blows, with his competitors recognizing that his momentum needed to be slowed before he ran away with the race. Seeds planted during the previous debate meant that Perry "found himself on the defensive in a Republican presidential debate here Monday night, pilloried for suggesting that states should take over Social Security, attacked for trying to mandate vaccinations for young girls and roundly criticized for immigration policies he has supported in his state."[9] Romney questioned Perry taking credit for job growth in Texas, noting that the southern state offered a number of incentives and advantages for potential employers including business-friendly laws and legislature and no state income tax. He noted, "If you're dealt four aces, that doesn't make you necessarily a great poker player."[10]

The previous debate had established Romney and Perry as the key competitors, but attacks this time were led by the other Tea Party candidates who hoped to curry favor with their audience while creating questions around Perry's credibility as a conservative. Bachmann particularly focused on Perry's support for mandatory HPV vaccinations, and she noted that Perry had received campaign donations from Merck, the manufacturer of the Gardasil vaccine. Bachmann also pointed out that Mike Toomey, Perry's former chief of staff, was a lobbyist for the pharmaceutical company at the time. Perry responded with the claim that Merck had donated only $5,000 to his coffers (a figure that would later be disproved as substantially lower than the company's actual contributions), prompting this exchange: "'If you're saying I can be bought for $5,000, I'm offended,' he said to Mrs. Bachmann, who snapped back, 'I'm offended for all the little girls and parents who didn't have a choice.'"[11]

Although Perry faltered under the almost nonstop attacks from his opponents during this battle royale/debate, he continued to perform strongly in polls. According to voters, establishment Republicans, and the media, the race at this time had crystallized: "Republican party leaders, who only a few weeks ago viewed the GOP presidential nomination race as wide open, now consider it a two-man contest between Rick Perry and Mitt Romney, and they are choosing sides in what many think could be a long and potentially divisive campaign."[12]

PERRY VERSUS ROMNEY

By mid-September, the two candidates were dominating media coverage of the race. Even Bachmann's campaign manager, Ed Rollins, publicly acknowledged that it had become a contest between those two candidates, a statement that was considered to have directly influenced his stepping down from her day-to-day campaign operations soon after. MSNBC's Lawrence O'Donnell characterized their dynamic as going all-out for a knockout: "But this is Perry versus Romney for the presidential nomination and neither one of them seems to be softening any punches so that they might preserve for themselves the possibility of the vice presidential nomination."[13] The discord between the two men was not surprising. During this period, stories began to emerge about the tensions that existed between the candidates when they were both governors. Furthermore, they demonstrated considerable differences in terms of campaigning and governing. Republican strategist Alex Castellanos characterized it as such: "Where Mitt Romney is obedient and cautious, Rick Perry is bombastic and spontaneous. You can see the playbook pretty clearly here: It's populist against patrician, it's rural Texas steel against unflappable Romney coolness, conservative versus center-right establishment, Texas strength versus Romney's imperturbability, Perry's simplicity versus Romney's flexibility."[14]

These polarizing differences shaped a compelling narrative for media coverage. Being able to paint the two as polar opposites helped support the frame that this nomination would unequivocally demonstrate the dominance of one of the warring factions within the splintered Republican Party. Based on this narrative, a Perry victory would reinforce the long-term and substantive influence of the Tea Party, reframing the movement from an insurgency to an established force. A Romney win, however, would put the Tea Party and its pitchfork populists back in their place while reasserting the supremacy of establishment Republicans. This was not just a choice between two candidates cut from the same conservative cloth. This was "a fundamental question for Republican voters as they seek a candidate to challenge Mr. Obama for the right to occupy the Oval Office: whether they want a Texas Republican or a Massachusetts one."[15]

PERRY UNDER A MICROSCOPE

Perry came into the nominating contest as the savior of the Tea Party voters, perceived as an authentic conservative who also had appeal for mainstream Republicans. His superhero status was reinforced in early September when Texas wildfires required he skip Senator Jay DeMint's Freedom Forum in South Carolina. Instead of trading barbed insults and sharing a stage with his competitors, Perry had the opportunity to be "crisis commander in chief" as the "brief suspension of his campaign was a made-for-TV moment in which Perry conveyed empathy by clutching the hands of a wildfire evacuee, clambered onto a helicopter for an aerial tour of the damage and pored over maps with his emergency management team."[16] During this period, Perry's team attempted to position him not only as the most authentic conservative on the ticket, but also as the only true conservative who had a chance to win against Obama.

As is often the case for politicians who had only experienced state elections, Perry was ill prepared for the scrutiny that comes with both the national stage and frontrunner status. With cameras tracking his every move, microphones picking up his every statement, and scores of reporters and researchers poring over his every decision, the spotlight on Perry shone brighter and hotter than the Texas sun as autumn wore on. His conservative positions on issues like skepticism about evolution and climate change and unequivocal support for the death penalty and abortion laws were popular with Tea Party and evangelical voters, but they raised concerns among more mainstream Republicans. A clear frame emerged: Could Perry play outside of Texas?

Ethics questions began to dog Perry, ranging from his use of a private jet from a donor under investigation for possible securities fraud to accusations of "crony capitalism," including "mounting criticism that his administration has rewarded large donors with favors that have enhanced their personal and business interests."[17] This frame and these accusations began to gain currency in the wake of the Tampa debate when reporters and critics began to look more closely at Perry's decision to require Texas schoolgirls to receive the Gardasil vaccine. While Perry attempted to frame the mandate as pro-life, "skeptics say the move was almost inexplicable, except for [former chief-of-staff] Toomey's influence, given that Perry has not been particularly aggressive on women's health issues in the past."[18] While questions about the influence Perry's donors wielded in the Texas governor's mansion concerned many mainstream Republicans and political observers, conservatives and evangelicals were treated as reacting more strongly to the ideological implications of his decision: How can a candidate claim to be anti-government and pro–individual liberty while mandating injections in children? Eventually the criticisms grew strong enough that Perry reversed course and said he had made a mistake.

This latter concern began to inform an emerging narrative as investigations into his positions and policies as governor of Texas began to raise concerns about how truly conservative he really was: While Perry the candidate was trying to lay claim to the mantle of "most authentic conservative," his record as governor did not support that. His claims on job creation in Texas were challenged and critiqued, and his efforts as governor to "strengthen his authority and centralize control"[19] inspired questions about his commitment to small government staying out of citizens' lives. A Texas job creation fund closely associated with him was cited by critics as "evidence Mr. Perry is not always the free-market fiscal conservative he claims to be,"[20] and the Club for Growth went so far as to characterize his record as indicating "Governor Perry is more pro-business than he is pro-free market."[21]

As these stories swirled, the Perry-as-savior narrative quickly ended and Perry found himself losing ground. Concerns quickly arose about his electability: "Yet the question that nags Republicans about Mr. Perry is a simple one: Is he too ideological, too conservative, or too extreme to win a general election?"[22] By the middle of September, polling indicated that he was losing favor quickly among Republican voters. Instead of rallying the GOP electorate, Perry was becoming a distraction, characterized as "an impossible blend of secession and treason and Ponzi schemes and monstrous lies. [The race] promises to be the sort of donnybrook the Republican Party hasn't seen in many years, keeping it feuding over forced vaccinations and immigration rather than attacking Obama for his stewardship of the economy."[23]

For a candidate who had never lost an election, this new political reality was daunting. Perry and his campaign did not seem equipped to deal with the criticisms, allowing damaging stories to continue longer than necessary. A subtle message seemed to permeate much of this coverage: You're not in Texas anymore. For Perry to escape the fate of the "flavor of the month" candidates before him, he had to find his footing during debates and figure out how to run a national campaign. Whether he and his team could do that was an open question.

ROMNEY: THE "EAT-YOUR-VEGETABLES" CANDIDATE

As Romney faced yet another candidate insurgency, his campaign recognized a need to shift ground. Their original strategy did not include prioritizing the Tea Party or evangelical voters, since his 2008 experience demonstrated the difficulty Romney would have making inroads with this group. Furthermore, the 2012 contest was chock full of Tea Party–friendly candidates; his team had counted on Bachmann, Cain, Gingrich, and Santorum splitting that vote, allowing Romney to own the mainstream GOP block. Instead of proactively courting voters who were not likely to be amenable to his message, Romney's campaign was fighting a war of attrition: His competitors could pick each other off while he stayed focused on Obama. Within the context of this strategy, the threat of flavor-of-the-month candidates was neutralized; he could focus on "the idea of being the last candidate standing, rather than the front-runner from wire to wire."[24]

The arrival of Perry into the race forced the former Massachusetts governor to reconsider this plan, however, since early on the Texas governor was thought to be the candidate best suited to unite the two factions and thus positioned to strip away some of Romney's support. The campaign had to balance Perry's threat against the risks of shifting strategy at this point in the contest. After all, "Mr. Romney is running this time as the unflappable former businessman and nonpolitician. Wading into the Tea-Party fray, GOP observers say, risks knocking Mr. Romney off his core message on job creation and tossing him into elbow-throwing among his rival candidates and their allies he has sought to avoid."[25]

With this new political reality in mind, Romney opened September with overtures to the Tea Party and its constituencies. While he had earlier indicated that he would not participate in South Carolina Senator Jim DeMint's candidate forum, an event designed to reach Tea Party voters, Romney changed his mind. He also began to speak at Tea Party rallies and offer to meet with their groups for the first time in his campaign. For some Tea Party leaders, this was perceived as a craven attempt to curry favor with the group, particularly since he had paid scant attention to them in the past.

To express their displeasure, Tea Party groups began to plan and execute protests in "an all-out effort to make sure the former Massachusetts governor does not win the Republican nomination."[26] Matt Kibbe, president of FreedomWorks, explained their decision to actively protest Romney to Fox News's Bill O'Reilly. According to Kibbe, this was not just about health care, but also Romney's "support of Wall Street bailouts, his support for ethanol. It's his unwillingness to stand with Paul Ryan on real balanced budget measures, real entitlement reform. It's his opposition to fundamental tax reform. There is a record here where Governor Romney has very consistently opposed the principles that Tea Partiers espouse."[27]

This strident opposition to Romney's candidacy marked a public disagreement in strategy among disparate Tea Party organizations, a stark reminder that it was not one monolithic group. Earlier in the nominating contest, some leaders had indicated that they would support a Romney candidacy in an "anyone but Obama" sign of solidarity. These September protests communicated a clear message that Romney could not count on that sensibility continuing. Instead, he would have to work for those votes in the face of active opposition. This also reiterated the importance of solidifying support among establishment Republicans who were more amenable to his candidacy. In his favor, Romney's campaign had substantial money in the bank, a formidable organization that far exceeded those of his competitors, solid business experience to highlight during tough economic times, and—perhaps most importantly of all—experience running for president that gave him the drive and vision to perform consistently across debates, stump speeches, and meet-and-greets with voters. While Romney had not yet set the world on fire, he had managed not to burn himself either.

During this autumnal period, media coverage of Romney continued to emphasize the frame that he was consciously constructing himself as a candidate. When he announced his jobs plan in early September, coverage of it often referred to how this fit into his business past: "Mr. Romney appeared to be trying to cast himself as the business conservative in the race."[28] The characterization does not reinforce or legitimize Romney's business experience; instead, the "appeared to be trying" calls attention to the constructive and deliberate nature of positioning. Rather than seeing the "real" Mitt when he was eating Carl's Jr. and Subway and flying on Southwest, this was framed as a blatant attempt to become more accessible: "Like the stars in *Us Weekly*, Mitt Romney wants voters to know that he is just like them."[29] Taken to its most extreme, this frame reminds audiences that candidate Romney is little more than a Hollywood-esque avatar, built for an election but not a true, authentic representation of the man.

Romney's attempts to construct an everyman image were repeatedly challenged, often due to coverage of his own financial reality. Discussions about his personal wealth and professional actions permeated coverage, coming to a head in mid-September when Romney filed paperwork to begin renovation on his $12 million beachfront home in La Jolla, California, because the existing house was too small. MSNBC's Al Sharpton called these contradictions out on his show: "He eats fast food, tweeting this picture eating Carl's Jr. That's definitely something we all do. And just like us, he talks about taking bargain flights on Southwest, tweeting his picture with the crew. Of course, we all take pictures on flights with the crew." Sharpton then highlights the absurdity of the everyman posturing: "And just like us, he's worth $200 million. And just like us, he's doubling the size of his $12 million California home."[30] Whether or not Romney really did eat fast food and fly coach in "real life" was immaterial; his vast wealth created evidence that contradicted his attempts to frame himself as an everyman, and this reinforced perceptions that he was artificially constructing a persona he hoped would appeal to voters. During this period, his opponents (including President Obama) also began to use this frame to characterize Romney as a candidate whose extreme wealth made him incapable of understanding the concerns and experiences of middle-class Americans.

The crystalization of this as a dominant frame corresponds with earlier perceptions that Romney was a shape-shifter, someone willing to become completely malleable in appearance, demeanor, and values in order to achieve his electoral dreams. In a race for votes among people who were committed to their candidate of choice being a true believer, these demonstrable instances of Romney making changes attributed to his desire to win reinforced that he was not worthy of their votes. His opponents did their best to reiterate and reinforce this frame, often through subtle allusions: "The criticism continued . . . as rival Rick Perry, the Texas governor, told an audience, 'I come by my conservatism authentically, not by convenience. . . . You won't hear a lot of shape-shifting nuance from me.'"[31]

Related but subtly different was the "Romney as flip-flopper" frame. While accusations of shape shifting spoke more to Romney's personal malleability to be a more appealing candidate, the flip-flopper frame focused more on his changeable policy positions. Favored by the Obama administration, Obama's senior strategist David Axelrod claimed, "I will give him this. . . . He is as vehement and as strong in his convictions when he takes one position as he is when he takes the diametrically opposite position."[32] The frame was echoed by his competition in an effort to "revive the image of the former Massachusetts governor as a flip-flopper who took conservative positions more out of political convenience than conviction, a criticism that dogged him in the 2008 campaign."[33] In October, Perry's team went to Twitter, asking supporters to use the hashtag #flipflopmitt. Perry spokesman Ray Sullivan said, "Voters need to consider the fact that Romney, in one week, changed positions on man-made global warming, capping carbon emissions, and Ohio's efforts to curb union powers."[34] In relation to this last point, *Washington Examiner*'s Byron York called it an "unforced error" to Fox News's Greta Van Susteren, noting, "It feeds the narrative of Mitt Romney either flip-flopping or trying to avoid taking a position on something that's important. And then after he just caught a lot of criticism in the conservative blogosphere, in the conservative world, he turns around the next day and supports it entirely."[35]

While earlier months had seen the kernels of the "Romney as robot" frame, during this period that frame developed to more clearly draw parallels between his seemingly unemotional, rigid nature and a difficulty engaging with or inspiring excitement among voters. Even when Romney tried to use humor, reporters conditioned that "from a politician sometimes ridiculed as robotic that qualified as a joke."[36] Observers noted that Romney was "overly polished or wooden on the campaign trail, [but] his defenders say that is just how he is, reserved yet caring."[37] His physical appearance played into this, with his "porcelain-perfect smile"[38] and "mannequin-like grin."[39] Despite improvements from 2008, Romney could "still be awkward and occasionally wooden, especially in face-to-face moments with voters that mean so much in Iowa and New Hampshire."[40] This disconnect between Romney and his audience often was pointed to in an effort to explain why he had not yet been able to solidify his position as frontrunner, despite staying at the top of the polls.

There was a positive counter to this frame, however; the same characteristics that made Romney robotic also were framed as consistency and discipline. His robotic nature offered a way to explain why Romney had not yet suffered the indignity of sliding down the polls and into oblivion and highlighted the professionalism that Romney and his team brought to the campaign. He was not dragged into dogfights he could not win, and he did not lose focus chasing after the latest stories. His authoritative demeanor during debates meant voters could see him being presidential, even if they did not want to vote for him to be their presidential nominee. Romney was focused on his goal, running a buttoned-up campaign almost flawlessly to this point. With his competitors operating as their own worst enemies, Romney looked good in comparison: "The time has long passed for Mr. Romney to be the first choice in the hearts of many Republicans. So his strategy, by necessity, has evolved into being the last choice, an eat-your-vegetables candidate who may only be seen as more appealing when he is matched up alongside his rivals."[41]

FOCUS ON FLORIDA

By the end of September, eyes turned to Florida for two major events: a debate on September 22 at Orlando's Orange County Convention Center, and then the Florida straw poll two days later. With cracks in Perry's campaign beginning to raise questions about his candidacy and Romney's failure to catch fire setting the backdrop, this period was considered pivotal for success. Criticism had mounted about Perry's previous debate performances, and he found himself losing ground to his rivals as he prepared for this meeting. With this window of opportunity now opened, others who hoped to be the "anti-Romney" candidate needed to shine. Bachmann and Cain wanted to reinvigorate their campaigns with dynamic, scene-stealing performances as they had enjoyed in the past. Santorum and Gingrich looked to continue a series of strong performances that were helping boost Santorum's name recognition and Gingrich's esteem. Huntsman needed to finally break through in a debate to garner attention. Paul had the opportunity to share his platform with fellow libertarian Johnson, who was joining the other nominees for only his second (and, it turns out, final) debate.

The set-up for the Orlando debate was designed to maximize audience engagement and involvement, including drawing questions from those submitted on YouTube. While unusual for a debate among presidential candidates, this embracing of the audience received plaudits from Florida blogger Craig Crawford on CNN, who said, "I actually think some of those questions, if they're carefully chosen, are—they're more from the heart. They're from the grassroots. Those are the kinds of questions I actually like best."[42] The questions and reactions from the audience contributed to a carnival atmosphere, a "freewheeling event in which virtually all the candidates played more visible roles than in the previous two debates."[43]

While more candidates were involved, the debate continued to focus on frontrunners Perry and Romney as "they engaged in a sometimes heated back and forth over immigration, health care, and entitlements, their rivalry dominating a stage that included seven other candidates struggling to catch up in the race for the Republican presidential nomination."[44] Perry took the brunt of most attacks, and he was considered ineffectual when he tried to go on the offensive against Romney. Evaluations of Perry's performance were dire. On Fox News, Jason Riley noted, "I still don't think he's given a debate performance that justifies his frontrunner status in the race. That's for sure. He can't seem to land a solid punch on Romney. . . . But as we saw in that piece, he's really struggling with the attack lines."[45] Analysis of and explanations for Perry's struggles in the debate featured prominently in post-debate coverage. During the same conversation on Fox News's *Journal Editorial Report*, *Wall Street Journal* editorial board member Dorothy Rabinowitz offered her perspective, outlining the difference when you see Perry in private versus publicly: "And the first impression you get is, not only does he look tough, he is tough. What happens when you put him in the public arena? He becomes an inhibited person, suppressing all of that arrogance because he thinks it wasn't necessary. And this makes him constrict [his] performance."[46]

Perry's post-debate coverage did not just focus on the limitations of his on-stage performance. During the debate, he was attacked for his support of a Texas program that allowed undocumented immigrants to pay in-state tuition rates to attend state universities. He responded to this criticism by saying: "But if you say that we should not educate children who have come into our state for no other reason than they've been brought there by no fault of their own, I don't think you have a heart."[47] This contention sent reverberations throughout Florida and the Republican electorate, reinforcing concerns about Perry being soft on immigration and lacking true conservative convictions. While Perry eventually backed off the statement and said the tone was inappropriate, he had little time to recover before the Florida straw poll two days later. As Fox News's senior political analyst Bill Hume put it, "Perry really did throw up all over himself in the debate at a time when he needed to raise his game. I mean, he did worse, it seems to me, than he had done in previous debates."[48]

Raising Cain: The Florida Straw Poll

While Perry had been expected to dominate the Florida straw poll, his debate performances and questions about his conservative credentials opened the door for a competitor to steal a victory. Herman Cain took advantage of that opportunity, winning almost 40 percent of the votes cast. Cain's victory stunned the media and his competitors. All of a sudden, a candidate whose days had seemed numbered was back in the race, and his victory explicitly was considered the voters' "rebuke to Texas Gov. Rick Perry."[49] Media observers credited Cain's success to his debate performance, noting that he had consistently stood out among his competitors. Faring less well was Bachmann, who had pinned her hopes on a strong performance reigniting her campaign; she attracted less than 2 percent of the vote.

Moving into October, the race had once again reset. Perry, considered a sure-fire frontrunner and the potential savior of the Tea Party at the beginning of the month, had almost completely imploded. Bachmann, a candidate who should have been riding a wave of momentum from the Ames straw poll, had sputtered out almost entirely. And Cain, a businessman running a nontraditional campaign who had already experienced (and lost) a marginal bump, suddenly was a force to be reckoned with. As the month began, the volatile nature of this race dominated headlines. No candidate had emerged as a strong challenger for Romney, yet Romney had not gained any traction outside of the solid 25–30 percent he had held for months. Establishment Republicans, voters, and pundits alike settled in for a potential long haul "amid signs that the fight for the GOP nomination could be protracted."[50]

This primary represented more than the selection of a candidate to be standard-bearer for a cohesive Republican Party. Instead, this person would give direction to what the party would be at its very core: a socially and fiscally conservative bastion of right-wing ideology or a more moderate and mainstream version of conservatism. After all, as CNN's John King posited, "The Tea Party is a new force in the Republican coalition. . . . There is a bit of sort of the new grassroots Tea Party struggle, tug-of-war with the establishment over who will win the heart and soul of the Republican Party. Which brand of candidate will lead the party against President Obama?"[51]

THE RISE (AND FALL) OF "ANTI-ROMNEY" CANDIDATES

Cain's emergence as a GOP frontrunner reiterated the rollercoaster nature of this campaign. With no dominant candidate emerging, voters seemed to be "trying on" new options in hopes of finding someone who was a good fit. Unfortunately, none of the current crop seemed up to the task.

Perry Falls Short

As discussed earlier, Perry's debate performances had opened him up to considerable criticism and critique, leaving him as an increasingly unappealing option for mainstream Republican and Tea Party voters alike. Veteran GOP operative Pete Wehner criticized him as coming across "as unprepared, sometimes, unsteady, and at times his answers border on being incoherent."[52] Republican strategist Mike Murphy was even harsher, tweeting that "Listening to Perry try to put a complicated policy sentence together is like watching a chimp play with a locked suitcase."[53] Perry attempted to assuage concerns by encouraging voters "not to pick 'the slickest candidate or smoothest debater,' but rather one 'with the best record' who will 'stick to principles.'"[54]

In the wake of Perry's campaign missteps and debate disasters, a new frame began to emerge strongly in Perry coverage: He just was not very smart. This was grounded in his failure to create coherent responses or cogent arguments in support of his positions: "His performances, in which he has at times struggled to answer questions or speak clearly in full sentences, have energized his rivals. Increasingly, they are questioning not only Perry's views but also his knowledge and intelligence."[55]

When Perry's smarts became part of his narrative, media coverage began to look back over his academic record. Stories reported that he had to switch to an easier major while at Texas A&M, dropping out of the veterinary science program to move into animal science. This corresponded with lists of classes in which he had done poorly (including grades of D and F) while at university. Even Perry's high school performance was covered, including his self-deprecating jest during a campaign speech: "He added that at high school in the town of Paint Creek, Tex, 'I graduated in the top 10 of my graduating class—of 13.' The crowd laughed and applauded."[56] While this material was often treated lightly, the frame was clear: Perry was not too bright.

In addition to questions about his intelligence, Perry's performance in the first weeks of his candidacy reinforced the frame questioning how much appeal he really would have outside of Texas. Concerns were raised that his "personal mix of aw-shucks conservatism and swashbuckling anti-Washington rhetoric"[57] would not play among mainstream Republicans and independents who would be needed to defeat Obama. His appeal to Wall Streeters, an important funding source for Republican candidates, was questionable as well: "The red meat Rick Perry is serving up to Republican primary voters is causing him problems with deep-pocketed Wall Street donors. . . . Some bankers say they would prefer a more moderate candidate, and worry the Texas governor's style and stances on social issues could sink him in the general election."[58]

These anxieties were warranted in early October when the *Washington Post* ran a damaging exposé centered on the name of Perry's hunting camp in Texas. The story began, "In the early years of his political career, Rick Perry began hosting fellow lawmakers, friends, and supporters at his family's secluded West Texas hunting camp, a place known by the name painted in block letters across a large, flat rock standing upright at its gated entrance. 'Niggerhead,' it read."[59] While there was debate about how long the name was visible and whether or not Perry should be held responsible for this, the story dominated news coverage in early October, particularly on cable news. On CNN, L.Z. Granderson commented, "I don't see how you can stand on the stage across from President Obama, the first African-American president, with nigger hanging over your head, which is essentially what this story will be for him." Later in the discussion, Will Cain noted to anchor Don Lemon, "So, this word is so powerful, Don. It's such an atomic bomb on a campaign that I just think we need to be very careful, and very responsible about how we treat this story."[60] While some debated the relevance of this story, it reinforced the frame that Perry would not be able to transition to a broader audience in a general election.

Perry's appeal problems were not limited to mainstream Republicans and independents. Encouraged by narratives promoted by his rivals, questions about Perry's true convictions began to gain currency among Tea Partiers and values voters. His speeches, once given to large, enthusiastic crowds that he could whip into a frenzy with a well-timed jab at Obama or Romney, began to weaken: "But Perry drew moderate crowds of 150 or so and only polite applause with his most pleasing lines."[61] Despite his best efforts, Perry was losing his grip on the election. By mid-October, he was down to fourth place in the polls. As Fox News's Neil Cavuto noted, "The governor, fairly or not, came out of the gate as a frontrunner, and that first impression stuck, and he disappointed people in the early debates, and he can't take that back. You don't get a second chance at a first impression."[62]

To counteract this, Perry tried to go on the offensive against Romney, drawing fire away by reminding Tea Party voters about the ties between Massachusetts health care and the much-despised Obamacare. These attempts to attack Romney reinforced the perception that Perry was a bareknuckle, cutthroat campaigner. While that had advantages in appealing to the red-meat voters who desperately wanted a bold, aggressive candidate, it also meant that he was easily brought under suspicion. In early October, Texas pastor Robert Jeffress introduced Perry at the Values Voters summit in Washington. After walking off stage, Jeffress sparked controversy when he "said in pretty strong, plain language what you think of Mormonism. You described it as a cult and you said that if a Republican votes for Mitt Romney, they're giving some credibility to a cult."[63] When asked if he stood by that comment by CNN's political correspondent Jim Acosta, Jeffress replied, "Oh, absolutely. . . . I think Mitt Romney's a good, moral man, but I think those of us who are born-again followers of Christ should always prefer a competent Christian to a competent—to a competent non-Christian like Mitt Romney. So that's why I'm enthusiastic about Perry."[64] When asked by Romney to repudiate this statement, Perry refused, saying only that he disagreed. While ostensibly Jeffress was not affiliated with the Perry campaign, "it raised immediate suspicions that the attack might have been a way for surrogates or supporters of Mr. Perry, the Texas governor, who has stumbled in recent weeks, to gain ground by raising religious concerns about Mr. Romney."[65]

The sole silver lining in the thunderclouds hanging over Perry's campaign came in mid-October with the announcement that his donations topped $17 million—more than any other candidate, including Romney. This money meant it was too early to write him off, giving him a bit of a resurgence: "And they say that ultimately Perry will emerge because the $15 million he has left in campaign funds . . . will allow him to wage the kind of campaign that Cain and other would-be challengers to Romney cannot."[66]

Bachmann's Lost Her Buzz

Perry was not the only former frontrunner struggling to maintain relevancy. Long gone was coverage of Bachmann's summer in the sun, where stories often focused on "the Elvis-blaring, megachurch-visiting, tea-partying campaign bus of Michele Bachmann"[67] and the enthusiastic crowds lapping up her brand of Christian conservatism. Her momentum crashed to a halt when Perry joined the race, and she had not yet been able to rekindle the same energy. Bachmann's previous political experience had indicated that she could benefit from making bold (and, at times, unfounded) statements to throw red meat to her base, and she attempted to do this again by illustrating the dangers of Perry's mandated HPV vaccination. Specifically, "Appearing on NBC's 'Today' show, [Bachmann] recounted that after the debate in Tampa, Fla. a tearful mother approached and said her daughter had suffered 'mental retardation' after being vaccinated against HPV. 'It can have very dangerous side effects,' Mrs. Bachmann said."[68] The backlash was immediate and impassioned, with reporters and pundits in both print and television condemning her statement. Clearly, her attempt to fight her way back into the mix by challenging Perry on the HPV vaccine had backfired, and she "ended up shifting the focus off Mr. Perry and on to her long-running penchant for exaggeration."[69]

The HPV vaccination controversy seemed to inspire an early death knell for Bachmann's campaign. Negative frames dominated her coverage during this period, including her aforementioned "penchant for exaggeration," discord that often arose between Bachmann and her staffers, and continued questioning of her performance as a congressional representative. Clearly, at this point Bachmann was considered unelectable and, without poll numbers offering a credible hook, she was losing the media's interest. A final nail in her coffin came with disappointing financial disclosures in October; although she had raised $4 million, mostly from small donors, the campaign had spent $6 million. This presented an interesting point for journalists who had listened to Bachmann's stump speeches throughout the summer: "But the campaign is also burning through cash faster than it is coming in, somewhat of an embarrassment for a candidate who has a stock moment in speeches when she turns out a pocket of her slacks to illustrate the government's profligate spending."[70] By October and the rise of Cain, she primarily was relegated to mentions in stories about the candidates as a whole.

Paul Beginning to Surge

While Paul had never enjoyed the same bounce to the top of the polls the aforementioned candidates did, he was proving himself a steady contender to challenge Romney. Paul was the only candidate to exceed his previous quarter fundraising, accumulating over $8 million, mostly in small donations. He was doing better than he had ever done before, consistently polling nationally in double digits. Finally, "After 35 years in politics and two unsuccessful runs for the top job, Paul is enjoying a surge in support and the most high-profile campaign of his life."[71]

Continuing his tradition of doing well in measures of voter enthusiasm, Paul won the Family Research Council's Value Voters straw poll in early October. Despite this victory, Paul could not break through into popular consciousness the same way other conservative candidates did. This was a challenge, since he clearly needed to expand his base in order to be seen as a legitimate top-tier candidate. While Paul's passionate supporters had buoyed him thus far, he would face challenges expanding his audience. Polling indicated that Paul "was viewed more negatively by likely Republican primary voters than any of eight GOP candidates tested, except Ms. Bachmann."[72]

The media's explanation for this shaped a recurring Paul frame: He had good ideas, but he could not communicate them very well. As one reporter noted when comparing Cain's 9-9-9 plan to Paul's economic proposals, "Mr. Paul's plan has no such catchy title. The 11-page document on his Web site is simply called 'Plan to Restore America.' And it was unclear whether it would be as successful in entering the campaign conversation, attention-grabbing as its proposed cuts may be."[73] Fundamentally, even in an electoral environment that was fertile ground for Paul's brand of libertarian fiscal policies, he had a branding problem.

Cain: The Latest Flavor-of-the-Month

Cain's stunning victory in the Florida straw poll catapulted him to the top of the Republican candidate pool in early October. His surprising emergence as a candidate was chalked up to three factors: his compelling personality, his unconventional campaign style, and buzz from his 9-9-9 economic plan (9 percent income tax, 9 percent corporate tax, and new 9 percent national sales tax). The latter, in particular, featured prominently in this coverage, with reporters noting, "He has uttered the triple digits repeatedly, metronome-like, in speeches and debates, until they have acquired the catchy power of a brand."[74] While the plan was criticized for being too simplistic and likely to transfer the tax burden to the poor, it resonated with Tea Partiers hungry for a strong candidate who would be willing to make bold fiscal policy decisions.

Cain's charm and humor were commonly referenced during this period. "No candidate today is as daring as Herman Cain when it comes to charming an audience with silky silliness. His humor has distinguished him from his rivals, lending an air of folksiness and authenticity, a visceral contrast to his cooler, more staid rivals, especially Mitt Romney and President Obama."[75] He was a particular favorite on cable news channels, with Fox News's Sean Hannity declaring "I love the guy" before Dana Perino lauded Cain's im-provement: "He had his best interview of the presidential election cycle . . . last night. I thought he was the most personable and success agrees with him. Every time he does a little bit better, a little more confidence, a little bit more relaxed and a little bit more able to explain his policies."[76] Cain's outsider status meant that he had time to learn and could make mistakes; his personal charm and charisma would make up the difference.

Rather than following a traditional campaign model, Cain opted instead to travel in support of his book, *This is Herman Cain! My Journey to the White House.* Facing accusations that he was running nationally as a vanity candi-date rather than embracing the retail politicking that presidential elections require, Cain likened his strategy to running a "lean and mean" start-up business.[77] At this point, his nontraditional style was working, but there was a growing concern that the lack of professionalism and experienced staffers in his campaign meant his time at the top likely would be brief.

Cain often found himself clarifying or playing down statements he made off the cuff, whether he was claiming that Sharia law was infiltrating the United States or calling for an electrified fence between the United States and Mexico. His casual remarks raised conservative eyebrows when he appeared to be inconsistent about abortion, indicating in an interview with Piers Morgan that it was a family's decision before insisting to Sean Hannity "I am pro-life from conception, end of story."[78] Cain almost celebrated his lack of knowledge about foreign policy. During an interview, he said he would learn the names of foreign leaders when he needed to, but until then he considered this outside the scope of what he needed to know: "I'm ready for the gotcha questions. And they're already starting to come. And when they ask me who's the president of Ubeki-beki-beki-beki-stan-stan, I'm going to say, 'You know, I don't know. Do you know?'"[79] While this was cited as an example of his humor, these statements, taken together, began to constitute a frame that Cain had neither the preparation nor the desire to take his candidacy seriously, explaining the lack of professionalism demonstrated during his campaign. In a late-October *New York Times* article by Trip Gabriel, this frame was articulated quite nicely: "But increasingly, Mr. Cain is becoming known for walking back provocative statements made in a shoot-from-the-hip speaking style, which raises questions about his grasp of issues and his readiness for office."[80]

During this period, occasional pieces would address the race issues surrounding Cain's candidacy. As "a black man in a party that has battled charges of racism,"[81] coverage of Cain often read as deliberate efforts on the part of the Republican Party in general and Tea Party in particular as proof that their objections to President Obama were because of his policies, not his skin: "Mr. Cain scanned his overwhelmingly white Tea Party audience, jammed into a hall at a rural fairgrounds, and offered his assessment. 'I see 3,000 patriots here tonight,' he boomed, the crowd leaping to its feet. 'I don't see any racists!'"[82] Cain himself often introduced racial discourse into his campaign. The candidate did not shy away from incorporating race into his speeches and statements, "relish[ing] the opportunity to provoke as a black conservative,"[83] although often in a manner that generated controversy and some negative reactions particularly among African-Americans: "And while his casual style of racially inflected humor works to ingratiate him with mostly white audiences at campaign rallies, it has angered some black critics, who believe he uses age-old stereotypes."[84]

Particularly controversial were Cain's statements that many blacks were "brainwashed" into supporting the Democratic Party and that he did not believe that racism in this country still "'holds anybody back in a big way.'"[85] This created tension among some commentators and voters who noted that Cain's claims would not be applied to other groups. As the *Washington Post*'s Nia-Malika Henderson commented on MSNBC, "He seems to play the race card when it comes to talking about African-Americans, talking about the ways in which they vote for Democrats. It's not something that he would, for instance, say about white evangelicals who vote in overwhelming numbers, for Bush . . . and for McCain."[86]

Despite Cain's popularity among voters and rise to the top of the polls, media coverage during this period indicated a clear skepticism about his ability to maintain that position. The *Washington Post*'s October 10 headline asked, "Cain Is the GOP Flavor of the Month. Who Will Be Next?" In that same article, Chris Cillizza wrote, "But if the arc of the 2012 presidential race tells us anything, it's that social conservatives—and conservatives more generally—will tire of the former Godfather's Pizza CEO at some point and once again search for the next big thing."[87] Others felt Cain had a bit more staying power: "This could be Mr. Cain's moment. With Gov. Chris Christie of New Jersey taking a pass and Gov. Rick Perry of Texas struggling, the yearning for a candidate who can combine fiery conservative populism with concrete policy proposals has led a growing section of Republican voters to embrace, or at least take a hard look at, Mr. Cain."[88]

OCTOBER DEBATES: HANOVER, NEW HAMPSHIRE, AND LAS VEGAS, NEVADA

The new pecking order within the Republican candidate list was made clear at the first October debate held at Dartmouth College in Hanover, N.H., on October 11. Perry's fall from the top was crystallized both visually and substantively; candidates were seated according to relative strength and Perry was relegated to the side. Unlike the previous debates, it was Cain in the middle of the platform with Romney. During the debate, Romney continued to present himself as the candidate best positioned to take on Obama, returning to that drumbeat with Perry's decline: "With a fresh air of confidence in his candidacy, Mr. Romney set out to diminish Gov. Rick Perry of Texas and all but ignored him."[89] Post-debate consensus was that Romney once more "solidified his frontrunner status . . . in the battle for the Republican presidential nomination."[90]

As was the case when Perry was in the lead to be the "anti-Romney" candidate, Romney was able to stay on strategy because Cain bore the brunt of attacks: "You know, it was another smooth night for Mitt Romney and that's because so much of the focus was on Herman Cain, the former Godfather's CEO, probably felt like one of those pizzas last night. That's because his rivals were turning up the heat."[91] Going into the debate, Cain's challenge was to escape the fate of Bachmann and Perry before him, maintaining his strong debate performances that had launched his candidacy rather than wilting under the increasingly hot spotlight. Cain defended his signature 9-9-

9 tax plan from attack, particularly from Santorum, who used the plan to accuse Cain of "giving Washington a huge, new tax opportunity to get money through a sales tax. Can we trust you that with your lack of experience that you won't continually give Washington the ability to take freedom away from freedom loving people here in the Live Free or Die State?"[92]

One week after the New Hampshire debate, the candidates met once more in Las Vegas for a debate characterized as a "series of attacks more intense and personal than any in their previous appearances together."[93] This combative tone was echoed on Fox News, where Bret Baier likened the event to a boxing match: "If the gloves had been on before, they certainly came off last night."[94] A feisty Santorum opened the attacks on Romney by linking him to Obamacare, but Perry was the first to deliver a stunning blow when he accused the frontrunner of hiring undocumented workers for lawn care. This was the aggressive campaigner Perry's team knew could come out, showing "a full-throated, no-holds-barred personal lashing of his chief opponent on a night when Romney momentarily looked on the defensive for the first time in the campaign."[95]

For all participants, however, the tensions continued to build: "It was the most acrimonious debate so far this year. Marked by raised voices, accusations of lying and acerbic and personal asides, it signaled the start of a tough new phase of the primary campaign a little more than two months before the first votes are cast."[96] Media coverage often characterized this shift in tone as a product of the race itself: "The vitriol onstage was the product of the far larger dynamic in the GOP race. . . . The normally orderly process by which Republicans select a presidential contender has this year turned into a frenzied and fickle courtship that has seen opinion polls swinging from one infatuation to the next."[97]

MOVING RIGHT

In their effort to capture the hearts and minds of this capricious electorate, the Republican candidates spent much of this period trying to out-conservative each other. They accused opponents of being liberal on key issues in order to reinforce their own conservative bona fides, each trying to position himself or herself as an "authentic conservative, not a conservative of convenience."[98] Cain wanted to build an electric fence to electrify border crossers? Bachmann would build a double fence. They both were more conservative than Perry, since he was soft on immigration. Perry engaged in this liberal tarring himself, saying about Romney, "'I knew when I got into this race that I'd have my hands full fighting President Obama's big-government agenda. I just didn't think it would be in the Republican primary.'"[99] Romney's response? "Gov. Perry is desperate to shift attention away from his liberal policies that encourage illegal immigration."[100] As candidates moved further to the right on immigration, pundits warned candidates of the risks faced if they moved too far to the right during these immigration speeches, particularly in terms of appealing to Hispanic voters in the general election. Republicans were "competing over who can talk the toughest about illegal immigration—who will erect the most impenetrable border defense; who will turn off 'magnets' like college tuition benefits. But . . . some party officials see a yellow light signaling danger. . . . Will Hispanic voters remember and punish the eventual Republican nominee?"[101]

To attract support from evangelical and conservative voters, the candidates found themselves moving farther and farther to the right. They were "under intense pressure from conservative activists to prove their ideological commitment, highlighting the tension between those who think the path to the White House lies in mobilizing the party's base and those who believe the eventual nominee will have to appeal to moderates and independents as well."[102] This frame of ideological commitment versus mainstream appeal was particularly prominent in coverage of Romney during mid to late October.

ROMNEY: ESTABLISHMENT'S CHOICE, BUT WHAT ABOUT VOTERS?

Despite Romney's struggle to connect with voters, October was a successful month for him overall. His fundraising total of $14 million exceeded all candidates except Perry, and "the campaign-finance data offer new evidence of Mr. Romney's staying power in the 2012 presidential campaign, despite the lukewarm response he has inspired among GOP primary voters."[103] He continued to lock down major endorsements, with New Jersey governor Chris Christie a particularly significant coup since the "pugnacious, fiscally conservative Mr. Christie has been a bridge between the Republican Party establishment and the grass roots, and his endorsement helped cement the perception that the establishment, including many big donors, has now lined up behind Mr. Romney."[104] By now, Romney was considered the "inevitable candidate" by party insiders: "Buoyed by a series of strong debate performances, Mitt Romney is suddenly attracting new support from major donors and elected officials, some of whom had resisted his previous entreaties, as people across the GOP grow more accepting of the presidential contender as the party's standard-bearer."[105] A growing list of endorsements included state and federal officials, providing the "latest sign of Mr. Romney's steady accumulation of support among party bigwigs, despite tepid enthusiasm for his candidacy at many levels of the Republican Party."[106]

This "tepid enthusiasm" could be (and usually was) explained through the frames delineated earlier, but pundits wondered when—and how—Romney would finally connect with the audience and break past the 25 percent barrier in terms of public support. Fox News's Greta Van Susteren noted that Romney was "rather constant or flat or there seems to be a ceiling. He got no bounce when Governor Christie got out of the race. He got no bounce when Governor Christie endorsed him. He got no bounce when everyone said that he did a really good job at a debate." She continued, "It's almost as though he's sort of stuck at a point, and it's, like, he can't seem to move upward."[107] According to this application of the frame, Romney needed to figure out some way to engage with and excite voters. His competitors had mastered the art of using rhetoric to electrify crowds, whipping audiences into frenzies with their verbal assaults on Obama and, at times, each other. As one New Hampshire voter put it, his ideal candidate would be "Romney with a little more pizzazz."[108] This frame continued to be clear: Romney just did not generate excitement among voters, even after all this time on the campaign trail.

With the establishment coalescing around him but the electorate still hesitant, Romney's team needed to reconsider their strategy. Iowa, a state that only a month or two ago seemed unwinnable, was back on the table. Romney's team had maintained much of its organization during the ensuing four years, and operatives were ready to be deployed. No one else had managed to dominate the Iowa polls, and the race there was wide open. The strategy had risks—if Romney were to make a play for Iowa and fail, it could derail his campaign again as it did in 2008. The idea had considerable upside, however. If he could do well in both Iowa and New Hampshire, "Such a one-two punch could consolidate GOP support behind Mr. Romney. No Republican dating to 1976 has won both states' nominating contests, except for sitting presidents. Even if he doesn't win, a strong finish could cripple other candidates."[109]

According to media explanations, the openness of Iowa was in part due to the constant shifting of fortunes among the values candidates. While coverage in the summer months had emphasized candidates' retail politicking in key early voting states, the steady barrage of debates during September and October shifted strategy. No longer were potential nominees required to follow the traditional Republican primary playbook, glad-handing voters and paying their dues on the ground. Instead, candidates were choosing to use the airwaves to focus on a national strategy, taking advantage of the frequent (and well-viewed) debates to make their case in living rooms around the nation. The debates were said to have "shaped the Republican race, perhaps as never before in a nomination battle,"[110] and cited as "by far the biggest influence on the Republican contest."[111]

THE INFLUENCE OF DEBATES

By mid-October, alarm bells were ringing about the impact debates were having on the race. The frequency of televised debates was credited with allowing second-tier candidates—those who might not have the resources to run television advertisements—an opportunity to be heard at a national level. In the past, "The battle for the Republican presidential nomination always moves first through Iowa, New Hampshire, South Carolina, and lately Nevada. But before the 2012 candidates ever get to those states, they have been forced to run through an unexpectedly significant proving ground: nationally televised debates."[112] In theory, this would counteract the alarming influence that money and special interests played in determining the candidate pool. As the debates progressed, however, there was an increasing realization that giving such a platform to "marginal candidates" can be problematic: "The marginal candidates have no incentive to drop out. Once the also-rans sign up for a debate, the stronger candidates are all but required to show up. . . . The also-rans and the cable people have them over a barrel."[113]

There seemed to be a sentiment, particularly notable among newspapers, that these second-tier candidates were disrupting the process—even though they would never be qualified to be president. Rather than substantive discussions among likely nominees, the debates in the build-up to 2012 were likened to the most base of reality shows: "Series like 'The Real World' and 'The Real Housewives of Beverly Hills' taught viewers to follow the antics of amateurs who couldn't act but would act out. And more than almost any others in recent memories, these debates pit candidates whose main qualifications rest on personality, not resumes."[114] Rather than perceived as being produced to help create an informed electorate, the debates instead were framed as creating entertainment: "With their often-glitzy sets, vocal audiences, and introductions that sometimes sound straight from the sporting world, the debates are infotainment for the politically interested. They have become a form of reality TV, competitions familiar to many Americans."[115] It worked—the September debates were viewed by millions of people, including 6.1 million watching the Fox debate in Orlando.[116]

The frequency and geographic spread of the debates forced candidates to disrupt their campaign schedules, traveling to locations near and far to get their time on television. That time itself carried risks, since "every debate offers the risk of a costly political mistake,"[117] something Pawlenty and Perry could speak to only too well, leading Perry to threaten in October that he would no longer participate in debates. After all, as he and his team continued to insist, there was more to being president than being a good debater. This much emphasis on only one component of candidates carried an inherent risk. Furthermore, there was a growing recognition that the debates were making the race "more combative than it might otherwise have been, at least this far ahead of election year. The media like conflict, encourage it, and have succeeded in generating it."[118]

Pundits expressed concerns that the negativity and aggression fostered in these debates would turn off the moderate Republicans and Independents needed to win a general election. This was not just because of what was happening on stage among the candidates; during these debates, the audience often became part of the story, whether for cheering during a hypothetical question about a dying thirty-year-old who did not have health insurance or booing a gay soldier who asked a question via YouTube. "The audience's outspokenness has in many ways served a positive purpose by illustrating the energy of the base, GOP strategists say. But it also has conveyed a somewhat unsavory image to less ideological people at home watching on television."[119] The question remained: Would these visceral representations of responses to red-meat issues have a lingering impact on the race?

GETTING READY FOR THE FINAL STRETCH

With the holiday season quickly approaching, Romney held steady, Perry attempted to resurrect his campaign by rebooting it, and Cain maintained his status as a campaign rock star. Candidates struggled to get their organizations and infrastructures sorted before it was too late. Perry in particular labored to overcome the hurdles introduced during the debates, bringing on a new team of advisers to professionalize his campaign and refine his message: "With time running short before the first votes are cast in the Republican presidential contest, Gov. Rick Perry of Texas is urgently trying to convince voters that his candidacy warrants a second look. He is retooling his campaign with a newly emphatic anti-Washington message and steering the race into a sharper ideological contest with Mitt Romney."[120]

Recognizing that he needed to take action to turn around his campaign, Perry launched his first television spots in Iowa, using his sizable campaign war chest to take his message to the airwaves, and put forward a "broad economic policy agenda . . . reintroducing himself as the 'bold' choice for the Republican nomination."[121] Even as he took these positive steps, however, Perry once again shot himself in the foot when he publicly offered support to the birther movement, questioning whether Obama was born in the States and thus could legitimately serve as president. This was perceived to be a distraction at a pivotal time in his campaign and was characterized as "the last vestige of a desperate candidate who hopes to survive."[122]

While Cain entered the last week of October riding high, enjoying massive donations estimated at the rate of approximately $1 million a week and playing to huge, enthusiastic crowds at his campaign stops, there were questions about how long he could maintain his frontrunner status. Negative coverage about Cain's lack of preparation and professionalism continued to gain traction; taken together, various incidents were framed as the campaign operated as its own worst enemy, "undermin[ing] itself with questionable decisions and a series of missteps which have led to the impression that the candidate lacks focus and preparation."[123]

Concerns that Cain's campaign might not go the distance intensified at the very end of the month when it was revealed that Cain had been accused of inappropriate sexual behavior while running the National Restaurant Association in the 1990s. *Politico*, the news organization that broke the story, alleged "at least two female employees of the group complained to colleagues and to senior officials there about Mr. Cain."[124] Moving into November, this raised serious questions about the viability of Cain's campaign, including whether he and his campaign were prepared to handle this October surprise.

NOTES

1. Jeff Zeleny, "G.O.P. Candidates Turn Attention to One Another," *New York Times*, September 4, 2011, National Desk, Factiva.

2. Jonathan Weisman and Naftali Bendavid, "U.S. News—Election 2012: Romney Stakes Out Centrist Ground," *Wall Street Journal*, September 6, 2011, A4, Factiva.

3. Neil King Jr. and Jonathan Weisman, "Perry, Romney Clash at Debate," *Wall Street Journal*, September 8, 2011, A1, Factiva.

4. Jeff Zeleny, Adam Nagourney, and Ashley Parker, "Perry and Romney Joust Over Direction of G.O.P.," *New York Times*, September 8, 2011, National Desk, Factiva.

5. Drew Griffin, Brianna Keilar, Carol Costello, Jim Acosta, Ted Rowlands, Karin Caifa, Rob Marciano, Paul Steinhauser, and John Zarrella, "Price Tag of President Obama's Jobs Plan; GOP Candidates Face Off; Jury Selection in Conrad Murray Case; Breaking Down the Obama Jobs Plan; NASA is Going Back to the Moon," *CNN: CNN Newsroom*, September 8, 2011, LexisNexis Academic.

6. Karen Tumulty and Philip Rucker, "Perry and Romney Spar in GOP debate," *Washington Post*, September 8, 2011, A-Section, Factiva.

7. Jeff Zeleny, Ashley Parker, and Jim Rutenberg, "At Debate, Perry Wears a Bull's-Eye as 7 Other G.O.P. Candidates Take Aim," *New York Times*, September 13, 2011, National Desk, Factiva.

8. Wolf Blitzer, "Full Transcript of CNN-Tea Party Republican Debate, 20:00–22:00," *CNN: CNN Live Event/Special*, September 12, 2011, LexisNexis Academic.

9. Dan Balz and Nia-Malika Henderson, "Perry is on Defensive during Tea Party Forum," *Washington Post*, September 13, 2011, A-Section, Factiva.

10. Jonathan Weisman and Neil King Jr., "U.S. News: Perry's the Man in the Middle—Fellow Republican Presidential Candidates Take Aim at Front-Runner in Debate," *Wall Street Journal*, September 13, 2011, A4, Factiva.

11. Ibid.

12. Phillip Rucker and Perry Bacon Jr., "Republicans Expect Long Battle between Perry, Romney," *Washington Post*, September 14, 2011, A-Section, Factiva.

13. Lawrence O'Donnell and Jonathan Alter, "The Last Word for September 16, 2011," *MSNBC: The Last Word with Lawrence O'Donnell*, September 16, 2011, LexisNexis Academic.

14. Philip Rucker, "Two GOP Rivals Are Worlds Apart," *Washington Post*, September 19, 2011, A-Section, Factiva.

15. Michael D. Shear and Ashley Parker, "A Preview of Strategies to Come," *New York Times*, September 9, 2011, National Desk, Factiva.

16. Amy Gardner, "Perry's Response to Crises Offers Glimpse of Leadership Type," *Washington Post*, September 7, 2011, A-Section, Factiva.

17. Carol D. Leonnig, "Perry's Donors Fare Well, Texas-style," *Washington Post*, September 4, 2011, A-Section, Factiva.

18. Karen Tumulty, "For Perry and Ex-aide, Mutually Beneficial Deep Ties," *Washington Post*, September 17, 2011, A-Section, Factiva.

19. Jonathan Weisman, "U.S. News: In Texas, A Weak Office Becomes Stronger," *Wall Street Journal*, September 12, 2011, A6, Factiva.

20. Leslie Eaton, "U.S. News: Perry's Job-Creation Funds Draw Flak from Left, Right," *Wall Street Journal*, September 2, 2011, A2, Factiva.

21. Ibid.

22. Gerald F. Seib, "U.S. News: Capitol Journal: Doubts about Electability Also Shadowed Reagan," *Wall Street Journal*, September 13, 2011, A4, Factiva.

23. Dana Milbank, "Democrats for Romney?" *Washington Post*, September 18, 2011, A-Section, Factiva.

24. Dan Balz, "With Perry in the Race, Romney Has to Run Another Way," *Washington Post*, September 2, 2011, A-Section, Factiva.

25. Neil King Jr. and Jonathan Weisman, "U.S. News—Election 2012: Romney, in Shift, to Court Tea Party," *Wall Street Journal*, September 1, 2011, A4, Factiva.

26. Amy Gardner, "Tea Party Splits as Some Wage War against Romney Campaign," *Washington Post*, September 4, 2011, A-Section, Factiva.

27. Bill O'Reilly, "Impact," *Fox News Network: The O'Reilly Factor*, September 1, 2011, LexisNexis Academic.

28. Jonathan Weisman, "U.S. News—Election 2012: Romney Unveils Pro-Business Economic Plan," *Wall Street Journal*, September 7, 2011, A5, Factiva.

29. Ashley Parker, "Mitt Romney Has Some Down-to-Earth Tastes, He'd Like You to Know," *New York Times*, September 22, 2011, National Desk, Factiva.

30. Al Sharpton, "Politics Nation for September 22, 2011," *MSNBC: Politics Nation*, September 22, 2011, LexisNexis Academic.

31. Patrick O'Connor and Neil King Jr., "U.S. News—Election 2012: Republican Rivals Put Focus on Shifts in Romney's Views," *Wall Street Journal*, October 20, 2011, A4, Factiva.

32. Jackie Calmes, "Obama Camp Attacks Romney as Flip-Flopper," *New York Times*, October 13, 2011, National Desk, Factiva.

33. O'Connor and King, "Republican Rivals Put Focus."

34. Jonathan Weisman, "U.S. News—Election 2012: Romney Rivals See Flip-Flop—Front-Runner Calls Talk About His Climate Views 'Hot Air from Career Politicians,'" *Wall Street Journal*, October 29, 2011, A4, Factiva.

35. Greta Van Susteren and Dennis Kneale, "Interview with Dick Morris; Group Plans Virtual 3rd Party Primary; Dow Jumps 339 Points," *Fox News Network: Fox on the Record with Greta Van Susteren*, October 27, 2011, LexisNexis.

36. Philip Rucker, "President's Words are Used against Him," *Washington Post*, October 19, 2011, A-Section, Factiva.

37. Sheryl Gay Stolberg and Kitty Bennett, "For Romney, a Role of Faith and Authority," *New York Times*, October 16, 2011, National Desk, Factiva.

38. Philip Rucker, "Up Close and Way Out of His Comfort Zone," *Washington Post*, October 23, 2011, A-Section, Factiva.

39. Michael D. Shear and Ashley Parker, "Lectern Gone, Romney Finds More Success," *New York Times*, October 25, 2011, National Desk, Factiva.

40. Ibid.

41. Jeff Zeleny and Ashley Parker, "Romney Waits as G.O.P. Flirts with Alternates," *New York Times*, September 29, 2011, National Desk, Factiva.

42. Howard Kurtz, Candy Crowley, Susan Candiotti, and Elise Labott, "Obama Administration Accuses Suskind of Distorting Facts; Coverage of GOP Debate; Interview with Connie

Schultz; Interview with Nate Silver," *CNN: CNN Reliable Sources*, September 25, 2011, Lexis-Nexis Academic.

43. Dan Balz and Perry Bacon Jr., "Perry and Romney Battle in GOP Debate," *Washington Post*, September 23, 2011, A-Section, Factiva.

44. Jim Rutenberg, Jeff Zeleny, and Ashley Parker, "Perry and Romney Rain Attacks at Republican Debate," *New York Times*, September 23, 2011, National Desk, Factiva.

45. Paul Gigot, James Freeman, Dan Henninger, Dorothy Rabinowitz, and Bret Stephens, "Journal Editorial Report for September 24, 2011," *Fox News Network: Journal Editorial Report*, September 24, 2011, LexisNexis Academic.

46. Ibid.

47. Lawrence O'Donnell, Howard Fineman, and Chris Hayes, "The Last Word 2300 for September 22, 2011," *MSNBC: The Last Word with Lawrence O'Donnell*, September 22, 2011, LexisNexis Academic.

48. Chris Wallace, "Fox News Sunday Roundtable," *Fox News Network: Fox News Sunday*, September 25, 2011, LexisNexis Academic.

49. Perry Bacon Jr., "Cain Comes Out on Top in Florida Straw Poll," *Washington Post*, September 25, 2011, A-Section, Factiva.

50. Patrick O'Connor and Jonathan Weisman, "U.S. News—Election 2012: Perry, Romney Go on Attack—Candidates Spar on Social Security, Health Care at Sixth GOP Debate This Year," *Wall Street Journal*, September 23, 2011, A6, Factiva.

51. Lisa Sylvester, Kate Bolduan, John King, Jim Acosta, Jack Cafferty, Wolf Blitzer, and Dana Loesch, "Republicans Prepare for Presidential Debate," *CNN: The Situation Room*, September 12, 2011, LexisNexis Academic.

52. Dan Balz, "Perry's Challenging Road Ahead," *Washington Post*, September 24, 2011, A-Section, Factiva.

53. Chris Matthews, David Corn, Chris Cillizza and Milissa Rehberger, "The GOP Debate; Audience Members Boo Gay Soldier; Pakistan's Spy Agency Linked to Attack on U.S. Embassy; Obama and Israel," *MSNBC: Hardball*, September 23, 2011, LexisNexis Academic.

54. Patrick O'Connor and Jonathan Weisman, "U.S. News: As Perry Slips, Lead Narrows," *Wall Street Journal,* September 13, 2011, A4, Factiva.

55. Phillip Rucker and Perry Bacon Jr., "Perry Moves to Reassure GOP Base," *Washington Post*, September 28, 2011, A-Section, Factiva.

56. Richard A. Oppel Jr., "Opposing Views on Perry as Job-Creating Master," *New York Times*, September 22, 2011, National Desk, Factiva.

57. Miguel Bustillo, "U.S. News: The Tao of Perry: Just Be an Aggie—To Decode the Candidate, Look to His Years as a Texas A&M Student; 'What You See Is What You Get,'" *Wall Street Journal*, October 1, 2011, A4, Factiva.

58. Brody Mullins and Steve Eder, "U.S. News: Wall Street Is Bearish on Perry's Electability," *Wall Street Journal*, September 30, 2011, A5, Factiva.

59. Stephanie McCrummen, "Perry's Roots, the Property, the Rock," *Washington Post*, October 2, 2011, A-Section, Factiva.

60. Don Lemon, Matthew Chance, Susan Candiotti, L.Z. Granderson, Will Cain, Tina Kim, Jacqui Jeras, Azadeh Ansari, Howard Kurtz, and Erin Burnett, "Amanda Knox Appeal Ruling; "Occupy Wall Street"; California Family Rescues Their Dad; Autopsy Reports the Drugs in Michael Jackson's Body; Controversial Book about Walter Payton is Released," *CNN: CNN Newsroom*, October 2, 2011, LexisNexis Academic.

61. Amy Gardner, "Perry Plays a Bit of Political Catch-up in New Hampshire," *Washington Post*, October 2, 2011, A-Section, Factiva.

62. Neil Cavuto, "Interview with Former Arkansas Governor Mike Huckabee," *Fox News Network: Your World with Neil Cavuto*, October 14, 2011, LexisNexis.

63. Jim Acosta, Chris Lawrence, Gloria Borger, Dan Lothian, Wolf Blitzer, Mary Snow, and James Carville, "Mitt Romney on the Attack; New Jobs Numbers Released; Battling Over Religion; Interview with Dr. Robert Jeffress of First Union Baptist; More Jobs, But Not Enough; Understanding the Jobs Report With Austan Goolsbee and Stephen Moore," *CNN: CNN The Situation Room*, October 7, 2011, LexisNexis Academic.

64. Ibid.

65. Richard A. Oppel Jr., Erik Eckholm, and Jeff Zeleny, "Prominent Pastor Calls Romney's Church a Cult," *New York Times*, October 8, 2011, National Desk, Factiva.

66. Perry Bacon, "Perry Urges More Oil, Energy Production to Boost Economy." *Washington Post*, October 15, 2011, A-section, Factiva.

67. Amy Gardner, "In Florida, Bachmann Eager to Broaden Appeal," *Washington Post*, September 2, 2011, A-Section, Factiva.

68. Trip Gabriel and Denise Grady, "In Republican Race, a Heated Battle Over the HPV Vaccine," *New York Times*, September 14, 2011, National Desk, Factiva.

69. Trip Gabriel, "With Stakes for Bachmann Higher Now, Her Words Get in the Way," *New York Times*, September 16, 2011, National Desk, Factiva.

70. Trip Gabriel, "For Bachmann, a Bid To Reconnect in Iowa," *New York Times*, October 18, 2011, National Desk, Factiva.

71. Shyamantha Asokan, "Paul Finds GOP Ideals Shifting His Way," *Washington Post*, October 9, 2011, A-Section, Factiva.

72. Elizabeth Williamson, "U.S. News: Paul's Policies Foreign to GOP," *Wall Street Journal*, October 24, 2011, A4, Factiva.

73. Jim Rutenberg, "Blueprint for Deep Cuts," *New York Times*, October 18, 2011, National Desk, Factiva.

74. Trip Gabriel and Susan Saulny, "With Three 9s, Cain Refigured Math for Taxes," *New York Times*, October 13, 2011, National Desk, Factiva.

75. Susan Saulny, "Behind Cain's Humor, a Question of Seriousness," *New York Times*, October 19, 2011, National Desk, Factiva.

76. Sean Hannity, "Governor Christie Will Not Run for President," *Fox News Network: Fox Hannity*, October 4, 2011, LexisNexis.

77. Susan Saulny and Michael D. Shear, "A Candidate Writing His Own Campaign Rules," *New York Times*, October 6, 2011, National Desk, Factiva.

78. Sean Hannity, "Interview with Herman Cain," *Fox News Network: Fox Hannity*, October 26, 2011, LexisNexis.

79. Ben Wedeman, John King, and James Carville, "Fast and Furious Controversy Escalates; Wall Street Protests Continue," *CNN: John King*, October 10, 2011, LexisNexis Academic.

80. Trip Gabriel, "For Cain, Reverse Becomes a Prominent Gear," *New York Times*, October 29, 2011, National Desk, Factiva.

81. Nia-Malika Henderson, "Cain: The GOP's Next Big Thing?" *Washington Post*, September 30, 2011, A-Section, Factiva.

82. Sandhya Somashekhar, "Cain Plays the Race Card and Plays it his Way," *Washington Post*, October 22, 2011, A01, Factiva.

83. Ibid.

84. Saulny, "Behind Cain's Humor."

85. Somashekhar, "Cain Plays the Race Card."

86. Chris Matthews, David Corn, and Julia Boorstin, "Herman Cain; Wall Street Protests; Mitt vs. the Tea Party; MLK Memorial This Weekend," *MSNBC: Hardball*, October 14, 2011, LexisNexis Academic.

87. Chris Cillizza, "Cain is the GOP Flavor of the Month. Who Will Be Next?" *Washington Post*, October 10, 2011, A-Section, Factiva.

88. Saulny and Shear, "A Candidate Writing His Own Campaign Rules."

89. Jeff Zeleny and Ashley Parker, "Romney Looks Past Perry as Debate Focuses on Economy," *New York Times*, October 12, 2011, National Desk, Factiva.

90. Philip Rucker and Amy Gardner, "Romney Keeps Solid Footing in GOP Race," *Washington Post*, October 12, 2011, A-Section, Factiva.

91. Carol Costello, Christine Romans, Ali Velshi, Jim Acosta, Rob Marciano, Barbara Starr, and Erick Erickson, "Alleged Iranian Terror Plot Foiled; GOP Candidates Debate the Economy; Does Romney's Changing Position on Health Care Matter to You?; Alleged Terror Plot Foiled; U.S. Foils Alleged Iranian Terror Plot; Cain In The Crosshairs; Fly To Japan For Free?" *CNN: American Morning*, October 12, 2011, LexisNexis Academic.

92. Sean Hannity, "Interview with Michele Bachmann," *Fox News Network: Fox Hannity*, October 12, 2011, LexisNexis.

93. Karen Tumulty and Amy Gardner, "A Fight in Vegas for GOP Hopefuls," *Washington Post*, October 19, 2011, A-Section, Factiva.

94. Bret Baier, Carl Cameron, Shannon Bream, Ed Henry, Mike Tobin, Jonathan Serrie, and Mike Emanuel, "Vice President Pushes President's Jobs Bill; GOP Presidential Candidate Rick Santorum Interviewed; Vice President Makes an Allusion to Political Opponents Involving Rape; Republican Presidential Candidates Mix It Up In Las Vegas," *Fox News Network: Fox Special Report with Brett Baier*, October 19, 2011, LexisNexis Academic.

95. Michael Leahy, "Perry Won Race, Lost a Friend in 1998," *Washington Post*, October 25, 2011, A-Section, Factiva.

96. Ibid.

97. Tumulty and Gardner, "A Fight in Vegas."

98. Ibid.

99. Jonathan Weisman, "U.S. News: Texan Gets Tough on Romney," *Wall Street Journal*, October 1, 2011, A4, Factiva.

100. Ibid.

101. Trip Gabriel, "Tough Immigration Talk Heats Up Debate, and Alienates Some Hispanics," *New York Times*, October 20, 2011, National Desk, Factiva.

102. Ashley Parker, Michael D. Shear, and Jeff Zeleny, "Christie Aligns With Romney, Bolstering Him on the Right," *New York Times*, October 12, 2011, National Desk, Factiva.

103. Brody Mullins and Danny Yadron, "U.S. News—Election 2012: Romney Is Mining Wall Street—His Finance-Sector Donations Top Perry, Who Outdraws Him from Energy Firms," *Wall Street Journal*, October 17, 2011, A4, Factiva.

104. Parker et al., "Christie Aligns."

105. Philip Rucker and Perry Bacon Jr., "GOP Views Romney as 'Inevitable' Nominee," *Washington Post*, October 13, 2011, A-Section, Factiva.

106. Brody Mullins and John D. McKinnon, "Romney Picks Up Bush Backers," *Wall Street Journal*, October 29, 2011, A1, Factiva.

107. Greta Van Susteren and Dennis Kneale, "Interview with Dick Morris; Group Plans Virtual 3rd Party Primary; Dow Jumps 339 Points," *Fox News Network: Fox on the Record with Greta Van Susteren*, October 27, 2011, LexisNexis.

108. Ashley Parker and Jeff Zeleny, "Their Hopes Rising, Republicans Seek a Winner," *New York Times*, September 5, 2011, National Desk, Factiva.

109. Patrick O'Connor, "U.S. News—Election 2012: Iowa Back on Romney's Map—Winning There and in New Hampshire Could Knock Out Rivals; State Activists Urge More Visibility," *Wall Street Journal*, October 21, 2011, A5, Factiva.

110. Dan Balz, "As GOP Race Shifts Into High Gear, Debaters are Throwing Plenty of Elbows," *Washington Post*, October 19, 2011, A-Section, Factiva.

111. Fred Barnes, "How TV Debates Have Changed the Race," *Wall Street Journal*, October 10, 2011, A9, Factiva.

112. The Take, "GOP Debates Become Key Proving Ground," *Washington Post*, October 18, 2011, A-Section, Factiva.

113. Barnes, "TV Debates."

114. Alessandra Stanley, "Viewers Get Latest Episode of 'Real Republicans of the Trail,'" *New York Times*, October 19, 2011, National Desk, Factiva.

115. Take, "GOP Debates Become."

116. Barnes, "TV Debates."

117. Michael D. Shear, Trip Gabriel, and Sarah Wheaton, "Perry Ignites Discussion Over Debates He May Skip," *New York Times*, October 28, 2011, National Desk, Factiva.

118. Barnes, "TV Debates."

119. Sandhya Somashekhar, "Boisterous Audiences Dominate GOP Debates," *Washington Post*, September 25, 2011, A-Section, Factiva.

120. Jeff Zeleny and Jim Rutenberg, "Perry Presses for Second Look from Early Voters," *New York Times*, October 31, 2011, National Desk, Factiva.

121. Philip Rucker, "Perry Raising 'Birther' Questions," *Washington Post*, October 26, 2011, A-Section, Factiva.

122. Chris Matthews, David Corn, and Brian Sullivan, "For October 24, 2011," *MSNBC: Hardball*, October 24, 2011, LexisNexis Academic.

123. Susan Saulny and Trip Gabriel, "As Cain Promotes His Management Skills, Ex-Aides Tell of Campaign in Chaos," *New York Times*, October 27, 2011, National Desk, Factiva.

124. Trip Gabriel and Michael D. Shear, "Tested Again and Again, Cain Takes Comfort in His Rise in the Polls," *New York Times*, October 31, 2011, National Desk, Factiva.

Chapter Five

The Final Stretch

November–December 2011

News and speculation about Cain's alleged sexual harassment of employees during his tenure as head of the National Restaurant Association in the 1990s dominated coverage as November began. In a race that had been defined by conservative "anti-Romney" candidates surging to the head of the pack before sputtering out (Bachmann) or falling spectacularly (Perry), this sort of revelation could be the political equivalent of an incendiary device—either fizzling out due to lack of oxygen or exploding spectacularly. At this point, no one knew how the Cain situation would play out. Were there more accusations? Was this chronic or a one-off? Was this a legitimate red flag about Cain's leadership and treatment of women, or was it a pay-off for a simple misunderstanding? Voters, pundits, politicians, and the media were waiting and watching, wondering how Cain would react and if his campaign could survive this type of story.

While most eyes were on the Cain camp, the administrative elements of nominating a candidate for president continued. November finally brought clarity about where and when voters would determine the candidate when the primary calendar was finalized. With early nominating contests spaced out over January and February, the calendar was thought to work in Romney's favor, making it difficult for candidates with weaker state-by-state organizations and smaller bank accounts to last until Super Tuesday. At the same time, rule changes about how delegates would be assigned could offer hope to well-organized and -funded second-tier candidates. In the wake of 2008, the GOP decided to shift from winner-take-all to proportional delegations, making an early slam-dunk victory much more difficult. Candidates and campaigns had to adjust their strategies accordingly, planning for nominating contests that were long down the road.

With the Iowa caucuses officially scheduled for January 3, the race suddenly felt like it was moving into hyperdrive. Candidates struggled to be everywhere at once, trying to build momentum in Iowa and New Hampshire while simultaneously making inroads in South Carolina and Florida. November was packed with events, ranging from the Iowa National Association of Manufacturers Forum to five debates in eighteen days. Pundits sensed that the field was not settled and the frontrunners could shift again. Each candidate who was not Romney or Cain wanted to facilitate that movement as much as possible. Cain, on the other hand, just wanted a respite from the barrage of revelations that threatened to end his candidacy.

CAIN: A CANDIDATE MIRED IN CONTROVERSY

At first, the lack of information about the scope and impact of what happened at the National Restaurant Association during the 1990s made it difficult to gauge the potential impact of *Politico*'s reveal. Cain and his surrogates tried to play off the sexual harassment allegations as simple misunderstandings due to his personal style; the same laughing, friendly, off-the-cuff humor that made him a hit on the campaign trail could be misconstrued as inappropriate behavior. This explanation made sense to his supporters, who rushed to show their support at campaign events and by pouring money into his coffers: "Ka-ching, ka-ching! Now, that is the sound of Herman Cain's campaign cash register. . . . It all started yesterday when presidential candidate Cain began facing questions about two allegations of sexual harassment. How busy is the cash register? Well, Mr. Cain made $300,000 on line yesterday, the biggest one-day haul of his campaign."[1]

Cain certainly did not dial back his enthusiasm or attitude during this period. When Cain appeared at an Americans for Prosperity event in Washington he received "a rousing welcome"[2] as he "strode onstage while exuberant supporters cheered, rose to their feet, and, in some cases, danced and mugged for cameras that were broadcasting the images onto two jumbo screens flanking the stage."[3] Before the speech was over, Cain referred to himself as the "brother from another mother" of Americans for Prosperity's controversial founder David Koch and his (actual) brother, Charles, clearly not afraid to celebrate his conservative connections nor inclined to lay low during this period despite the controversy surrounding him.

Regardless of Cain supporters' early acceptance of his denials, it was quickly apparent that the story was not going to just die down naturally. Information seemed to emerge every day, either about the known cases or from previously unknown accusers stepping forward. This meant new headlines and a renewed discussion about what Cain did or did not do. Reporters and pundits quickly recognized that Cain and his team were in over their heads and not handling this crisis well. Rather than having one carefully prepared and consistent response, Cain was perceived to be "stoking the fire rather than putting it out."[4] He offered various explanations, seeming at times to mix up his accusers and his actions, and these "shifting answers continued to raise questions about the capabilities of a campaign that seasoned party hands still view with skepticism."[5] Cain and his advisers' inability to tamp down this story reinforced the existing frame that they were unprofessional and out of their league. This perception was exacerbated when it was revealed that the candidate and his team had been informed about the story ten days before *Politico* ran it, but "inexplicably had no immediate response."[6]

In the wake of continued accusations, Cain and his surrogates went on the attack. The campaign's blame-game strategy chalked the story up to "a continued appalling smear campaign,"[7] pointing fingers at the accusers, Democrats, fellow Republican candidate Rick Perry, and eventually the political culture as a whole. Cain and his supporters insisted the accusations were untrue, proclaiming that this was an orchestrated attempt to stop his momentum and end his bid. On Fox News, Donald Trump mitigated Cain's responsibility by minimizing his actions, telling Greta Van Susteren, "I think it's a very ugly witch hunt and I think it's very unfair. You say, Oh, hello, darling, how are you? And you get sued because you've destroyed somebody's life. It's ridiculous. And I think it's very unfair to him."[8]

When accusers stepped forward and their names were publicly revealed, their backgrounds immediately became fodder for discussion, including any financial or legal issues they may have faced. Cain referred to one accuser as a "troubled woman,"[9] saying she was a tool of the Democratic machine out to end his nomination. Emboldened by support from conservative media stars like Rush Limbaugh and Andrea Peyser, Cain's lawyer "warned new accusers to 'think twice'" before coming forward with their complaints.[10] These continued and vicious attacks on the women Cain was accused of harassing worked for him by keeping others away from the press; despite efforts by the second woman to come forward to hold a joint press conference, the others refused to publicly reveal their identities.

Early on, the use of racialized language was apparent in this coverage, with both Ann Coulter and an ad produced by a Cain-affiliated super PAC referring to this as a "high tech lynching,"[11] a phrase that likely would not have been used—and certainly not with the same connotations—for a white man facing these same claims. Within the context of a self-made black southern man running for the highest office in the land, referring to accusations of sexual harassment against him as a "lynching" immediately framed the situation as one loaded with prejudice and racism. Rather than evaluating the allegations on their own merits, they now had to be considered within the context of the accusers' (or, in a different framing, victims') races as well as that of their alleged harasser. Whether consciously or not, this likely impacted the way media covered this story, perhaps making them more cautious than they might have otherwise been.

As Cain's shifting explanations and additional reveals continued to dominate the news coverage, the sexual harassment charges (or his ill-prepared response) began to impact his polling numbers. While the door had not completely closed on Cain's candidacy, other candidates recognized that this was an opportunity to become a frontrunner, with Bachmann, Santorum, and Perry "hoping they, too, might seize any momentum if Cain's supporters suddenly abandon him."[12]

VYING FOR SUPPORT

Former front-runner Bachmann entered the holiday period trying desperately to regain her footing after falling from the top of the polls. In an effort to attract interest once again from her Tea Party base, Bachmann went back to her political wheelhouse, formulating attacks on her opponents in an effort to paint herself as the only true conservative in a race full of pretenders. This sort of aggressive posturing had proved successful in the past, with each new attack generating massive online fundraising. As CNN's John Avalon noted, Bachmann had "built a political career off irresponsible statements, saying that President Obama is bringing tyranny to the nation, slaving the country, running a gangster government, a thugocracy."[13] While coverage of Bachmann's presidential campaign before and during the brief period she was a frontrunner had mostly stayed away from including her history of making false and often absurd declarations and accusations, this context became more common as it became increasingly unlikely that she would be able to successfully revive her campaign.

Unlike Bachmann and Perry, Santorum had not yet found his place in the sun. His campaign continued to slog along, framed as a one-man show emphasizing traditional retail politics, "hoping a better than expected showing in the Iowa caucuses January 3rd will give him momentum for the primary season."[14] During this period, Santorum completed his tour of all ninety-nine counties in Iowa, believed to be the first candidate to do so. He visited the state 187 times for campaign activities, which was almost half of the total visits made by 2012 candidates. While the media covered Santorum's shoe-leather campaigning in the Midwestern state, this was framed as likely futile: "Rick Santorum has spent more time in Iowa than any of the other Republicans running for president. He has attended church services, hunted pheasant, and even moved his family to the state for a few weeks during the summer. . . . So far, Iowa Republicans haven't rewarded that effort."[15]

Media coverage quietly framed Santorum as a curiosity rather than a legitimate candidate. He was doing everything he needed to do in Iowa, a state tailor-made for his brand of socially conservative populism, but he just was not connecting with voters. Despite his low polling numbers, Santorum refused to give up and go home. This was a higher calling. He was quoted in the *New York Times* as saying, "I prayed a lot about this and thought a lot about stepping out and putting my family through this, from the point of view of not being there. . . . But you've got to feel like your whole country is at stake . . . if that doesn't motivate you, you shouldn't be doing this."[16]

Only two short months after he had been lauded as a sure-fire contender and the potential savior of conservative Republicans, Rick Perry found himself spending early November trying desperately to make up ground. He took to the airwaves, explaining to Republican voters that his notable challenges in public speaking meant he was no Obama: "If you're looking for a slick politician or a guy with great teleprompter skills, we already have that, and he's destroying our economy. I'm a doer, not a talker."[17] His ads were designed to reassure voters that "he's genuine, not scripted and publicist-approved . . . which could be a dig at Romney and Obama."[18] As this quote indicates, Perry's attempt to reinvigorate his campaign often led to subtle frames that he was consciously constructed—just like Romney himself. Calling attention to and analyzing his message shift reinforced that Perry was, in fact, a candidate trying to find a way to appeal to voters. While his message might have been true (despite attempts from his competitors to undermine the credibility of Perry's "most conservative" position), reporting on the political decision-making motives helped shape the "consciously constructed" frame, inherently undermining any message of authenticity.

Perry's attempt to regain traction in the race was further complicated during the November 9 debate in Rochester, Michigan. Unfortunately for the candidate, this event marked a new low for his campaign: When trying to identify the three government agencies he would eliminate, Perry experienced "brain freeze" and could not remember the third. Despite other candidates offering suggestions, after 53 painful, seemingly endless seconds Perry finally acknowledged defeat: "I can't, the third one I can't. Sorry. Oops."[19] The fallout was immediate. As reporters and pundits noted at the time, "The lapse reinforced negative stereotypes about his candidacy,"[20] emphasizing the "lack of intelligence" frame that had emerged earlier in the fall. He attempted to mitigate the repercussions, appearing on late night talk shows in an effort to "neutralize an onslaught of ridicule with a dose of humor."[21] According to media coverage, however, this was likely not enough to recover.

CAIN'S FOREIGN POLICY DEBACLE

Throughout his campaign, Cain had made a number of statements indicating a questionable grasp on foreign policy, including admitting he did not know China had nuclear weapons and claiming that he would be open to war with Iran. In the wake of continued discussion around his sexual harassment charges, Cain had little room to create additional complications for his campaign on this front, since his previous reputation on foreign policy "makes Sarah Palin's foreign policy sound smart."[22] Because of this, the candidate had a lot riding on the November 12 debate in South Carolina, the first debate of the season to focus specifically on foreign policy. While none of the candidates had a stand-out performance at this event, Cain's performance was notable for how uncertain he seemed: "He had a lot to prove last night. And it became clear that he read his briefing book and he made all the right—made all the right points, he just appeared nervous at times, wading into territory that is beyond his catchy 9-9-9 economic plan."[23]

While Cain had managed to escape the debate without a major gaffe, his foreign policy luck ran out just a few days later. During an interview with reporters and editors from the *Milwaukee Journal Sentinel*, Cain was asked whether he agreed with President Obama on Libya. Rather than immediately offering an answer, Cain appeared to struggle as he attempted to come up with the correct sound bite memorized from his foreign policy primer. His "confused-looking pause, stares at the ceiling, and mangled response were captured on video . . . and reporters have been asking about the five-minute clip ever since."[24]

The clip was widely criticized and was used to support the frame that Cain was ill prepared to be president. After all, this was a basic policy question that directly related to a recent action taken by the president; it was not an absurd hypothetical situation. As CNN's chief political analyst Gloria Borger commented to Wolf Blitzer, "You know, Wolf, it wasn't a trick question. He was asked a direct question . . . and he seemed confused and flat-footed and unprepared to answer the question, then seemed to be running through in his mind what he was actually going to talk about."[25] For Borger and other media pundits, this was a real problem: "And you would think if you were a presidential candidate, it would be something that you could talk about immediately because you thought about it an awful lot."[26] If the media generally seemed hesitant to call Cain on the carpet for the sexual harassment allegations and payoffs, this Libya answer was fair game. It strongly supported the contention that Cain was not ready to run for president and offered additional questions about the seriousness of his candidacy.

ROMNEY: DISCIPLINED CAMPAIGNER

While Cain continued to face challenges to his credibility as a candidate, Romney worked to maintain his spot in the top tier. Despite his efforts, however, Romney still could not manage to convince conservative Republicans that he was authentic enough for them. When speaking at the Americans for Prosperity event in early November—the same event where beleaguered Cain received a standing ovation and enthusiastic response—Romney's reception was generally indifferent; the audience greeted him with a "lukewarm welcome with only tepid applause throughout, rising for an ovation only when he promised to repeal Obamacare."[27] This reinforced an earlier frame: While Romney was running a smart, long-term, calculated campaign, it was not one that inspired great excitement among Republican voters, particularly conservatives associated with the Tea Party and evangelical movements. His quandary was summed up in the *Wall Street Journal* as such: "Mr. Romney rarely says incendiary things, which is why many Republicans think he is the most electable candidate. But it is also why he can be less than inspiring. His challenge . . . is to persuade voters that the data-driven, economic-modeling, analytical manager can also be a leader."[28]

Interestingly, this frame had both positive and negative connotations. On the upside, Romney's consistency and planning was framed as being smart, professional, and completely buttoned up; he had built the strongest organization, had made the fewest mistakes, and was ready to capitalize on an extremely well-built foundation. The downside of this frame, however, was the perception that this level of preparation meant Romney was running to be manager-in-chief rather than offering the type of bold leadership that so many conservative Republicans wanted in a candidate. At its most extreme (and negative), this frame indicated a certain timidity in Romney; his insistence on data-driven decisions and following rules were considered indicators that he would not have the guts to really go after Obama in the general election—something that conservatives desperately craved.

To help counter this negative interpretation of Romney's "buttoned-up" frame, his campaign launched a new spot attacking Obama in late November. This advertisement was considered a sign that they were moving into a more aggressive phase of the campaign, ready to call the president out and make the case against him. Notably, however, the ad was criticized for being misleading; it used footage of Obama speaking about the economy without providing appropriate context: "The ad . . . left the impression that the president was saying he could not win if he talked about the economy, when in fact he was quoting something said by an associate of John McCain."[29] In response to criticisms that this tactic was manipulative and dishonest, Romney showed no regret for this decision, saying, "we obviously got under their skin, because the last thing they want to be doing is talking about the economy and the president's failure to get this economy turned around. And we're just going to take it to them, day in and day out."[30] Even within this new aggressive stance, however, Romney continued to demonstrate the discipline fundamental to this frame, keeping his sights set on Obama.

During this period, Obama's team likewise focused on Romney. Media speculated that the Obama team considered Romney their most likely nominee, and "they are really trying to define Mitt Romney from the get-go."[31] To do this, the team created an ad intended to re-raise and reinforce the perception that Romney was a flip-flopper, using a science fiction motif that featured two men trapped in one body. *Roll Call*'s Jonathan Strong continued this argument on Fox News, offering this analysis: "Well, the ad goes to his core weakness as a candidate, which is his inconsistency on issues over time. . . . it goes to the core of his character, of whether he really got into politics because he cares about changing the country, or if he was kind of a bored businessman."[32] This effort to continue raising and reinforcing the "flip-flopper" frame was partnered with statements from Obama staffers that also emphasized the related "shape-shifter" perception, including this statement from Ben LaBolt: "Mitt Romney will say and stand for anything to get elected—he was pro-choice until he was pro-life, pro-immigration reform until he was against it and he took action against climate change until he started pretending there was nothing we could do about it."[33]

The Obama campaign's belief that Romney was the most likely nominee was buttressed by his continued support from elected Republican officials, including prominent and popular Tea Partier, New Hampshire Senator Kelly Ayotte. While he had not yet won over a majority of the Republican base, these signs of support from prominent GOPers were framed as evidence of Romney's electability. Republican media figure Ann Coulter defended Romney's candidacy, noting that he was the "strongest candidate to beat Obama. And, you know, I'm a little tired of these Johnny-come-lately conservative purists . . . but let's just get a Republican in there and get Obama out."[34] The final element of that statement—get Obama out—was part of an important frame; while the base was not yet excited about Romney, they certainly were passionate about beating Obama and taking back the White House in 2012. Thus, electability mattered.

This electability argument was supported by Romney's steady performance despite the volatile race around him. Challengers competing to be the conservative choice rose and fell, yet Romney maintained his frontrunner status throughout. With the fall of Perry and increasing signs that Cain's time was up, Romney made the risky decision to go all-in for Iowa—the state widely credited with ending his 2008 bid. While his strategy up until this point emphasized New Hampshire, a place much more amenable to Romney's type of Republican, no one had managed to develop a substantial and consistent lead in this Midwestern early voting state. His religion, a stumbling block four years earlier, did not seem to generate as much concern; instead, voters were focused on fixing the economy and beating Obama, two areas where Romney polled at the head of the class. He had maintained much of the infrastructure built during his earlier campaign, and his organization had continued to work under the radar within the state. As such, his team now believed "he could try to steal a victory in a state that toppled his hopes of winning the party's nomination in 2008."[35] But as was the case throughout this turbulent period, Romney soon found himself facing a new—an unexpected—challenger at the top of the polls: Newt Gingrich.

THE REBIRTH OF GINGRICH

With a campaign left for dead just a few months earlier, Gingrich's emergence as a frontrunner in mid-November caught many observers by surprise. Long questioned for the seriousness of his candidacy with many accusing him of running a vanity campaign intended to sell more books, Gingrich had "tapped into an anti-Washington vein"[36] and was gaining traction among Republican voters. The Lazarus-like recovery was not lost on the same media who decried his candidacy. On Fox News, chief Washington correspondent James Rosen commented, "The same press corps that wrote his obituary last summer was glued to Newt Gingrich in Iowa today as the latest Fox News poll crowns him the new GOP primary frontrunner."[37] His resurgence was thought to be because he "cheered many conservatives with his combative debate performances and disdain for the news media."[38] By going after the moderators and media during each of the debates, Gingrich had managed to do what had previously been considered impossible: resurrect his campaign as the voice of the conservative right.

Almost immediately, however, Gingrich's time since leaving the House came under intense scrutiny: "The political hot water for Republican presidential hopeful Newt Gingrich who shortly after making his dramatic jump to the top of the polls is now facing some serious questions about his ties to a number of big companies."[39] Of particular concern were revelations that he had earned over $1.5 million between 1999 and 2008 consulting for the much-maligned Freddie Mac. Gingrich initially tried to play down his relationship with the company, claiming he had used his expertise as a historian to warn executives of the coming housing crisis. Those involved at the time were quick to contradict that characterization. While Gingrich declared that he offered strategic advice—a position he differentiated from being a lobbyist—these claims were widely refuted. Salon.com's Joan Walsh discussed the situation on MSNBC's *Hardball*, noting, "And in fact, what he did was trade on his relationships and trade on his status . . . to create these talking [points] and to create this campaign to say, Hands Off Freddie. And I think it's a ridiculous distinction to say that's not lobbying."[40] In the wake of these revelations, Gingrich—not someone associated with stringent principles during his time in the House—once again was framed as a candidate with questionable ethics.

Gingrich's post-House activity not only opened questions about his ethics; it also led to examinations of conflicting position and policy statements, leading to two tentative and competing frames used to examine and explain these contradictions. While his shifts were not yet characterized as flip-flopping (a frame veritably owned by Romney at this point in the race), they were at times characterized as further evidence of Gingrich's moral and ethical fluidity. At other points, however, media adopted Gingrich's preferred frame: These conflicting positions were evidence of the evolution of a man who had been in politics for decades, a charitable explanation that he did not extend to Romney. To help facilitate the use of the latter frame, Gingrich's team created a web page called "Answering the Attacks," offering varying explanations for issues his team felt could be problematic. It is worth noting the naming of the site; by characterizing the content as a required defense against being attacked, Gingrich could tap into voter perceptions that he was being unfairly judged by the media and his opponents—a victim frame that had proved successful for Cain at the beginning of the month.

Clearly recognizing that his time at the top of the polls could be limited, Gingrich immediately began trying to prove that he was not just another anti-Romney candidate. His campaign argued that Gingrich represented conservatives finally settling on a candidate; thus, he had more staying power than the previous flavors-of-the-month Bachmann, Perry, and now Cain. Gingrich claimed he was the sole conservative who could bring together the various camps; economic, social, and national security conservatives could all unite behind his candidacy. He went on the offensive against Romney by reengaging the frame questioning his opponent's conservative authenticity, cuttingly noting, "I don't claim to be the perfect candidate, I just claim to be a lot more conservative than Mitt Romney and a lot more electable than anybody else."[41] Gingrich's success rattled Romney; while his campaign had contingencies in place for the likes of Perry, Gingrich's rise was unexpected.

While Romney was thrown by these shifting fortunes, Gingrich's candidacy was by no means considered a sure bet. A clear frame quickly emerged that Gingrich was his own worst enemy. His charm was counterbalanced by perceptions of a petty focus on past slights. His oft-lauded intelligence could easily slip into being a know-it-all, particularly in terms of sprinkling historical references into otherwise irrelevant conversations, "[striking] some as evidence that Mr. Gingrich is the smartest candidate in the room—and others that he is a man determined to let you know how much he knows."[42]

Perhaps most problematically, Gingrich was seen as a hothead whose lack of discipline would ultimately undermine his candidacy. On CNN, Democratic strategist Maria Cardona linked two of the dominant Gingrich frames when she discussed the challenges he faced as frontrunner: "The issue . . . with Newt is that—and we saw this when he first came into the race, he has two issues for him. One of them is discipline. He is very undisciplined. And he is very—it's difficult, very difficult for him to stay on message."[43] She went on to note that despite Gingrich's claims to true conservative authenticity, that position would not hold up to scrutiny: "And the other one, and I think this is counterintuitive, is that he is actually too moderate for the primary process. And that has really come up to haunt him as well."[44] Both concerns—Gingrich's lack of discipline making it difficult for him to stay on message and more moderate positions on some issues—almost immediately were in evidence. During the November 22 debate, Gingrich indicated that he would support allowing some illegal immigrants to remain in the United States, saying "let's be humane in enforcing the law"[45] in order to keep families together. Although he stopped short of advocating for a path to citizenship, his opponents quickly characterized Gingrich's statement as indicative of his support for amnesty—a word known to incite strong negative reactions among Tea Partiers and conservative Republicans.

THE END OF CAIN

While Cain had managed to survive earlier allegations of sexual harassment and embarrassingly inept responses to questions of foreign policy, a final blow was dealt to his candidacy in late November when a new woman—Ginger White—came forward to claim she had a long-term affair with Cain over a thirteen-year period. While she insisted that their relationship was romantic, it was still framed as part and parcel of Cain's problematic sexual past. As in previous coverage, media often focused on White's own personal and financial history. Fox News's chief Washington correspondent James Rosen detailed White's background: "Ginger White is an unemployed single mother. . . . White once settled a sexual harassment claim against someone else and has a history of litigation."[46] Cain acknowledged that he knew her but said it was just friendship and that he was simply helping her out with money, once more unequivocally denying the claims of his accuser. By this point, Cain was losing support, and eventually he decided to pull the plug on his campaign. On December 3, Cain announced he was no longer running for president.

In his announcement that he was ending his bid, Cain went down the same way he had dealt with these allegations: blaming others. Characterized as "unapologetic and defiant," Cain said he was leaving the race "because of the continued distractions, the continued hurt caused on me and my family, not because we are not fighters. Not because I'm not a fighter."[47] Even in these parting words, Cain refused to acknowledge any agency in, ownership of, or responsibility for the various scandals that brought down his campaign. Instead, he once again embraced the victim persona and continued to play the blame game to explain his defeat.

CAMPAIGNING IN DECEMBER: THE FINAL SPRINT BEGINS

With only a month to go before voting commenced, stakes were higher than ever for the seven remaining major candidates. To help reach potential voters, four debates were scheduled for the month: the Mike Huckabee Presidential Forum on December 3; a debate at Drake University on December 10; the Gingrich-Huntsman Lincoln-Douglas Debate on December 12; and a final meeting at the Sioux City Convention Center in Sioux City, Iowa, on December 15. For Gingrich, this schedule could work to his advantage; debates had elevated his campaign into the top tier, and his rhetorical skill was legend. Romney, however, faced a more uncertain December.

Romney: Changing Strategy?

Gingrich's rise was an unexpected speed bump for Romney's carefully planned ascent to the Republican nomination. This was the first real surprise for his campaign and they needed to quickly decide how to proceed without a preapproved plan B. For a candidate reliant on data-driven and methodical analysis, this created uncomfortable uncertainty. The media noted Romney's difficulty rolling with this deviation from his carefully planned campaign. On MSNBC, Chris Matthews noted, "Mitt Romney's feeling the heat as Newt Gingrich does rise in the polls. He got a tad testy in an interview with Fox."[48] During this interview, Fox host Bret Baier asked Romney, "Your critics charge that you make decisions based on political expediency and not core conviction. You have been on both sides of some issues. . . . How can voters trust what they hear from you today is what you will believe if you win the White House?"[49] While this certainly was not the first time Romney had been asked to defend his varying positions or been accused of flip-flopping, he—as Matthews said—got testy. This crack in his otherwise carefully maintained persona showed just how rattled Romney was by Gingrich's ascendancy.

One decision his campaign had to make was whether Romney should directly attack Gingrich to help stop his momentum. At first, the team was content to let others do the dirty work for him, as was the case with other top-tier competitors. Eventually the attacks became more direct. In an effort to shift attention to Gingrich's multiple marriages and history of infidelity, Romney and his surrogates began to draw implicit comparisons by highlighting Romney's own happy (and long) marriage. During a discussion on CNN, political reporter Peter Hamby offered this analysis: "The Romney campaign is almost certainly putting Ann Romney out there to highlight the couple's forty-two-year marriage and her children and Romney as a family man, as opposed to Gingrich, who is right now on his third marriage."[50]

A Romney-affiliated super PAC, Restore Our Future, announced that it would spend \$3.1 million on advertising in Iowa; while one spot lauded Romney, the other called attention to Gingrich and his considerable baggage: "The announcer cites payments the former House speaker received from Freddie Mac and his \$300,000 fine for House ethics violations. And, perhaps worst of all in the eyes of many conservatives, 'Gingrich even teamed up with Nancy Pelosi and Al Gore on global warming.'" [51] By now, caution was no longer possible; with the Iowa caucuses less than a month away, Romney could not trust that his counterparts would pose an effective block to the Gingrich surge. Instead, he had to throw off his cautious mantle and fight back.

By December, Romney's frames were fairly consistent: He was consciously constructed; methodical and a stickler for rules and order; a flip-flopper and shape-shifter with a craven desire to be president; tremendously wealthy in a way that made him incapable of understanding the experiences and concerns of most Americans; and, in terms of demeanor, robotic. Each of these was evident in December coverage, offering little variation from earlier months. This was, perhaps, a result at least in part of Romney's tremendous discipline as a candidate and campaigner; because he so rarely made real mistakes and his foibles remained the same over time, there was little new to create or shape new frames. Romney seemed to take the "robot" frame most personally, working to shift this narrative by increasing face-to-face engagement with voters. As one reporter noted, "Romney has plenty of moments when he wins positive reactions and some when he seems to make a genuine link, undercutting his caricature as robotic. . . . He personally insisted on spending more hours talking to voters this election and fewer sequestered in his Boston headquarters."[52] He also began more actively involving his wife, Ann, in the campaign, since she could offer a more humanizing and compassionate portrait of her husband.

While Gingrich may have captured the hearts and imaginations of Republican voters, the "Romney machine built on establishment credibility keeps churning."[53] In mid-December, he "chucked up the coveted endorsement of Nikki Haley, the Tea Party darling and first-ever female governor of the first southern primary state of South Carolina."[54] Major Iowa daily the *Des Moines Register* also endorsed Romney, although Gingrich "dismissed the backing, saying it is from a liberal newspaper and won't count for much with Republican voters."[55] Former Republican standard bearers offered their support, with both presidential candidate Bob Dole and President George H. W. Bush publicly throwing their weight behind Romney. Bush cited Romney's "stability, experience, principles,"[56] commenting, "I just think he's mature and reasonable, not a bomb-thrower."[57] While some argued this was just the establishment rallying around their candidate of choice, others interpreted these statements as clear points of comparison to Gingrich.

Can Gingrich Maintain His Position in the Top Tier?

While Gingrich's extensive political experience made him road-ready as a candidate, his campaign was nowhere near prepared for the organizational demands of frontrunner status. He quickly began scrambling to put together the elements needed to succeed, including urgent fundraising appeals to supporters. Unfortunately, this desperate need for money meant Gingrich had to take time away from reaching voters to instead wine and dine those who could infuse much-needed cash into his accounts. Thus, "At a time when most of the Republican candidates are hustling for votes, Mr. Gingrich must, in a matter of weeks, build a fund-raising infrastructure that can finance last-minute campaign trips, advertising, and get-out-the-vote efforts in the early states and give him staying power to compete beyond them."[58]

While Gingrich worked to solidify his campaign organization, establishment Republicans began to coalesce against him. He faced serious backlash from some who worked with him during his tenure in the House, particularly as Speaker; his former colleagues cited his volatility, ego, and lack of discipline as fatal flaws that would make a Gingrich presidency untenable. Oklahoma Senator Tom Coburn stated, "I am not inclined to be a supporter of Newt Gingrich's, having served under him for four years and experienced personally his leadership."[59] Current New York Representative Peter King concurred: "As far as governing, as far as being a leader, he's too erratic, he's too self-centered. The time he was speaker, there was, like, one crisis after another, and they were almost all self-inflicted."[60] Senator Richard Burr from North Carolina added that Gingrich has "the attention span of a one-year-old."[61] Romney surrogate John Sununu, the former governor of New Hampshire, summed up these opinions by noting, "Tom Coburn, Susan Molinari, Mickey Edwards—all these folks that were part of his inner circle, who watched him on a daily basis, said 'Enough is enough, this man is not stable.'"[62]

These insider voices offered powerful ammunition to support several negative Gingrich frames, including his arrogance. They also provided evidence for the "unstable" frame, often used to articulate concern that Gingrich would be eliminated as a viable candidate *after* he had already won the nomination. In a worst-case scenario, this would be a drag on all down-ticket Republican candidates, potentially hurting the GOP far beyond the loss in the top race. These concerns were validated in early December when Gingrich "raised some eyebrows . . . when he declared that child labor laws are, quote, truly stupid. He suggested that low income students could take school janitorial jobs to learn about work."[63] When asked about the comments, Gingrich "doubled down, saying poor kids have no work habits because nobody around them works. It's not the first time that he's demonized the poor for political gain."[64] This example reflects how two frames can painfully intersect: Gingrich's inability to differentiate between good and bad ideas, combined with his lack of discipline on the campaign trail, could create disaster. The problems kept coming: "But as evidence that Mr. Gingrich still lacks discipline, his detractors point to recent controversial remarks about child janitors, Palestinians as an 'invented' people, and a call for federal judges to answer to Congress for 'anti-American' rulings, which legal experts on the right and left said could cause chaos."[65]

Romney took advantage of this opportunity to shore up his attacks on Gingrich, going after his opponent for being inconsistent, too volatile, and not an authentic conservative—other than volatility, the same accusations Gingrich made about him. While the media were not yet calling Gingrich a flip-flopper, Romney did not hesitate to evoke this frame, pointing out where Gingrich's consulting activities conflicted with his public statements and positions. Others agreed with this assessment, noting in particular how Gingrich's varying positions often meant that he was not on the side of true conservatives. Former candidate Cain went on CNN and said, "Newt Gingrich has stood on both sides of many issues. He sat on a couch with Nancy Pelosi and proclaimed the ills of manmade global warming and that we must do something about it. He championed the health care mandate that Mitt Romney is now crucified for."[66] Romney himself also contrasted his own demeanor "'as one of sobriety, care, stability,' [and] accused Mr. Gingrich recently of being 'a bomb-thrower,' rhetorically and perhaps literally, and in an interview Wednesday with the *New York Times* he sharpened that criticism, saying, 'Zany is not what we need in a president.'"[67]

During this period, Gingrich did his level best to demonstrate that concerns about his discipline and volatility were overstated. Even under a barrage of accusations from his competitors, "He's been very cool under the attack. He's been smiling. He hasn't been expansive. He stuck to a message. He's met with conservatives."[68] This last point was essential, since Gingrich still had work to do to gain the confidence of conservative leaders who still questioned his bona fides. While his fiery rhetoric and media attacks during debates appealed to voters, those who were looking a bit more closely at his record felt that there was room to question whether or not Gingrich was a truly conservative candidate in a meaningful way. To help assuage these concerns, in mid-December Gingrich endorsed the conservative Family Leader's "marriage pledge," a document that opposes marriage equality, adultery, and women in combat, although he stopped short of signing it outright. Steve Deace, an influential Iowa radio talk show host, talked about what this meant with MSNBC's Ed Schultz: "Ed, I think that people are very impressed with the brains and bravado that Newt has shown, especially in the debates. But I think they'd still like to hear a little bit more about his background and what specifically happened with him . . . to cause this change of heart."[69]

Gingrich's personal characterizations were not the only stumbling blocks he experienced during the holiday months; his campaign's lack of organization kept him distracted and often drove him off-message. After a scramble to collect signatures and get on the Virginia primary ballot—his adopted home state where he stood a good chance at victory—Gingrich learned late in the month that he would not qualify. This was a particularly embarrassing setback for the candidate since he reassured voters at the deadline that he had met the requirements. Larry J. Sabato, a political scientist at the University of Virginia, offered this assessment of the situation: "It's a disaster for him. . . . This sends yet another signal to Republicans that Gingrich is not able to organize."[70] During this period the press also realized that his team never purchased the "NewtGingrich.com" URL. Liz Marlantes from the *Christian Science Monitor* noted on Fox News, "And even organization matters. . . . It's really, really hurt him. I mean, even the NewtGingrich.com thing, the fact that he doesn't own the domain NewtGingrich.com, and this week we found out it's a Democratic group that owns it and they direct it to Freddie Mac or Tiffany's . . . little things like that do matter."[71]

Gingrich was particularly vulnerable during this period because of the seemingly endless stream of attack ads being directed his way toward the end of the month. His efforts to maintain a positive demeanor in the face of these adversarial assaults began to take its toll, and Gingrich found himself dropping in the polls as December wore on. Campaigning across Iowa "in the final days of an increasingly bitter campaign, he is wielding Nice Newt—or trying to—as a kind of last defense against a shelling of attack ads, ridicule from opponents, and a drip-drip-drip of tough news coverage that has clearly blunted his surge to near-front-runner status."[72] There was recognition among the media that the other candidates likely were trying to poke holes in this new "Nice Newt" persona. Charles Lane, editorial writer for the *Washington Post*, said on Fox News, "There is a lot to work with there . . . the things that Gingrich has done and thing[s] he said and money he has taken, and so forth. I think what they probably also have in mind here is to provoke him, to provoke Newt into doing something to be counterproductive."[73] Ultimately, "A two-week barrage of attack ads on television and radio appears to be damping enthusiasm for Mr. Gingrich in Iowa. That has created an opening for other candidates to leapfrog the former House speaker . . . before Republicans caucus on Jan. 3."[74] During this same period, Gingrich and his opponents were facing off at the final debates before voting began.

Five Days, Three Debates

Three debates were held in mid-December, each with varying permutations of candidates. The first, held at Drake University in Des Moines on December 10, did not include Huntsman because he did not meet the minimum-polling threshold to qualify. Described as a spirited debate, Gingrich was under fire for most of the night, with other candidates calling him on the carpet for controversial statements on Palestine, his post-House career as a consultant, and his scandal-ridden personal life. While Gingrich broadly was able to keep his cool, he went red-faced when Paul accused him of being an "inconsistent conservative."[75] Other than that, however, Gingrich "seemed to withstand the barrage of criticism that he faced during much of the debate, often using humor or a smile to deflect the attacks."[76]

The most notable misstep of the evening came from Romney who, in the course of a disagreement about his past positions on individual mandates, offered Perry a $10,000 bet. His opponents seized on this as an opportunity to reinforce the frame that Romney's vast wealth meant he was out of touch with the concerns of everyday Americans. The next morning, Perry was on Fox News Sunday. When asked about the bet, he replied, "I was a little taken aback. I'm driving out to the station this morning. I'm sure I didn't drive by a house that anyone in Iowa would even think about that a $10,000 bet was possible. So, a little out of touch with the normal Iowa citizen."[77] While it was likely just an unplanned throwaway line, Romney's $10,000 bet made headlines. As DNC Communications Director Brad Woodhouse said on MSNBC's *The Ed Show*, "I mean, look, in the same debate where he offered to bet Rick Perry $10,000 casually, as if he does it every time he plays golf . . . I mean he doesn't understand what $10,000 is to [the] middle class. He doesn't understand what $1,500 is to the middle class."[78]

Just two days later, Gingrich and Huntsman met in New Hampshire for the second Lincoln-Douglas–style debate. The three-hour debate focused on foreign policy and national security was substantive, if not particularly riveting; at one point, Huntsman, "when asked if he had more to add, said, 'I see my daughter nodding off, so let's move on.'"[79] While this was not a high point in the extensive number of primary season debates, it did offer Huntsman one more chance to make his case to the Republican electorate. During a period when almost all attention was focused on either national polls or Iowa, a state Huntsman had opted to bypass in favor of the more amenable New Hampshire, he had few opportunities to gain the momentum he needed to survive.

Much of the Huntsman-specific coverage during this period focused on the disconnect between his campaign's dire financial straits and his billionaire industrialist father's fortune. Despite earlier declarations that he wanted to do this without tapping into his father's bank accounts, the Our Destiny super PAC was created to help Huntsman gain traction in New Hampshire. His team ran a major ad campaign in the Granite State, hoping to generate some momentum. As had been the case throughout Huntsman's campaign, the rabble-rousers and dynamic speakers who made up the competition drowned out his quiet approach. Romney's remarkable consistency and discipline so far meant that Huntsman never had an opportunity to rise to the top as the mainstream Republican candidate; instead, the shifting sands of the campaign were limited to those focused on appealing to the right. At this point, media framed Huntsman as a candidate who was running out of time to save a campaign with almost no momentum; only a surprisingly strong performance in New Hampshire could salvage his campaign.

The final debate before the holidays—and voting—began was held on December 15 at the Sioux City Convention Center in Sioux Center, Iowa. The candidates were characterized as "going deep into the playbook during the last critical debate before the Iowa caucuses, the frontrunner, Newt Gingrich playing defense on his conservative values and his electability. Mitt Romney stood by his business background playing it safe and Texas Governor Rick Perry realizing it may be the fourth down."[80] Buoyed by Gingrich's declining poll numbers, Romney reverted back to his focus on Obama and let his opponents attack each other; his counterparts took Gingrich to task for his record and electability. Ultimately, this debate was thought to do little to shake up the race, instead cementing the status quo. On Fox News, Juan Williams suggested, "the consensus in Washington political circles today is that there were three people who have come off this looking like they have a chance to win the Iowa caucus, and that would be Romney, Gingrich, and Paul. Rick Perry I think is in the middle."[81] He went on to describe the remaining three candidates as "also-rans. . . . But the people who lost out were Santorum, Bachmann, and Huntsman."[82] Williams's reason for keeping Perry in the middle? He had much more money at his disposal than the three "also-rans."

At this point in the campaign, having sufficient resources at their disposal was essential to candidate success. No longer were goodwill and perceived momentum sufficient to maintain a candidacy. With the opening votes drawing close, candidates had to refocus their energies to deal with the realities of this campaign: the return of retail politicking, the Fox Effect, and the rise of super PACs.

REALITIES OF THE WINTER CAMPAIGNS

While autumn coverage often noted the increased emphasis on national campaigning, this late stage required candidates go back to the basics and return to retail politicking: glad-handing, kissing babies, and giving hugs in an effort to cajole, charm, and convince voters to caucus or cast ballots in their favor. This type of personal campaigning was particularly important due to the incredibly tight nature of the race (with multiple candidates polling within statistical margins of error) and the fluidity of favorites. Because the race had primarily been televised up until now, it had been characterized as high on entertainment value, low on gravitas, defined by embarrassing gaffes and controversial quips. Spending quality time in pizza parlors, community centers, and churches was a good way to show Iowa and New Hampshire voters that the candidates were more than their televised personae, and these experiences were foregrounded in December.

This does not mean that candidates stopped turning to television, however. They regularly showed up on various channels for interviews, particularly Fox News. This relationship became so close that even politicians outside of the race commented on it, including Kansas Governor Sam Brownback: "It's like a town hall every day on Fox News. You hear people talking back to you what you saw yesterday on Fox. I like Fox, and I'm glad we have an outlet, but it is having a major, major effect on what happens."[83] Their regular appearances on Fox also meant campaigns had less need to advertise; after all, their base—the voters they want to reach—are already seeing their message on Fox, so there was no need to start advertising too early. According to the *New York Times*'s Jeremy W. Peters, Fox hosted the candidates twenty-one times in the opening week of December, a remarkable opportunity for these campaigns to reach their voters.[84] This did not mean that all candidates received equal treatment on Fox, however. MSNBC reported the liberal Media Matters finding that "In the last six months, Newt Gingrich has made nearly three times as many appearances on Fox as Mitt Romney has."[85] It was not lost on commentators that Gingrich had been a Fox News employee in the past. Interestingly, Santorum—the candidate with the fewest minutes appearing on Fox News from October through mid-December—had spent time on the Fox payroll as well.

While the Fox Effect allowed for campaigns to delay purchasing high-cost television spots, their paid media budgets also were helped by the emergence of super PACs. While technically unaffiliated with candidates, these organizations often had vast coffers filled by limitless donations from wealthy supporters. Perhaps more importantly, the super PACs also helped candidates by taking care of the dirty work for them. Rather than getting their own hands covered in mud, candidates could let their affiliated PACs go negative without the same threat of backlash. While questions emerged about the legalities of candidate and super PACs colluding—a practice that was not allowed—media coverage strongly suggested that in reality they worked as shields to help their candidate of choice take down opponents.

Within this complex campaign environment, Iowa conservatives still had not settled on a candidate around whom to coalesce. There was increasing recognition that this lack of cohesiveness could lead to a repeat of 2008, when conservatives failed to rally around Huckabee and let a candidate they considered deeply flawed—John McCain—to win the nomination. In an effort to prevent this, prominent evangelical leaders began to discuss publicly uniting behind a single (non-Romney) candidate, but they could not agree on which candidate that would be. In the vacuum left by their lack of endorsement, the race continued to be volatile. Paul started getting another look from Iowa voters; by mid-November, he had moved into second place in Iowa state polls.

RALLYING BEHIND A CONSERVATIVE CANDIDATE

After decades of fighting to have his voice heard, Paul found himself in the unusual position of being considered a viable presidential candidate—at least in Iowa. Toward the end of December, Paul had "become a serious force with the potential to upend the nomination fight and remain a factor throughout next year's general-election campaign."[86] Over the years, Paul had built a considerable organization in Iowa, staffed with an enthusiastic volunteer corps made up of true believers. Now that his libertarian message was resonating with conservative voters, Paul was "the wild card in the Republican presidential deck—and that makes him one of the most important cards of all."[87]

A new frame emerged during this period: Paul as credible candidate. His well-funded war chest meant that he could run an aggressive television campaign, and his consistency as a politician—holding fast to the same basic libertarian principles over time—meant that he could escape the accusations of flip-flopping that had dogged his rivals. Those same positions, however, could prove to be his Achilles heel, particularly his rigid anti-war stance. The more voters initially enamored with his economic principles learned about his foreign policy, the less likely they were to support him: "I'd say the big loser is Ron Paul. He started out fine. Fiscal issues, great. Criticizing Newt Gingrich on the judiciary reform plan, great. Foreign policy, a big huge problem, and he doubled down."[88] While Paul was a newly credible candidate, previous frames remained consistent in his coverage—unlike others, there was no possibility that he would change his positions in order to be more electable, even if some of these positions would create an insurmountable barrier to his election.

As was the case with Bachmann, Perry, Cain, and Gingrich, Paul's rise in the polls led to increased scrutiny into his past. His decades in public office meant most was known about Paul's history, but he quickly learned that even an issue that had come to light in previous elections could haunt him once more: "Emerging as a real Republican contender in Iowa, Representative

Ron Paul of Texas is receiving new focus for decades-old unbylined columns in his political newsletters that included racist, anti-gay, and anti-Israel passages that he has since disavowed."[89] Paul claimed that the newsletter content was written by supporters and that he had not been part of its creation, but he could not make this same claim about his 1987 book called "Freedom Under Siege." In it, Paul writes, "Every year, new groups organize to demand their rights. White people who organize and expect the same attention as other groups are quickly and viciously condemned as dangerous bigots. Hispanic, black, and Jewish caucuses can exist in the U.S. Congress, but not a white caucus."[90]

It was notable, however, that while Paul attempted to distance himself from the statements and political views from his past, he did not try to refuse the support of the white supremacists who strongly supported him. From Paul's perspective, they were endorsing him; he was not endorsing them, their beliefs, or their actions. While this is a logical (and solidly libertarian) perspective, his support from this group combined with the reemergence of controversial newsletter content created an awkward coalition of Paul's supporters. CNN contributor David Frum posited that Paul's surge "is a reflection of this ability to organize and attack enthusiasm. He has this strange coalition of college students who like the drug legalization and anti-war message, but this terrible history of having spent most of the past 10, 20 years actually appealing to some of the racially exclusive far right elements of American life."[91]

While Paul was enjoying a surge toward the end of December, Perry was still fighting to regain the enthusiasm he had engendered in early autumn. He attempted to use humor to offset his numerous gaffes, including using his infamous "oops" debate moment to make fun of himself in a new television spot: "The ad begins by replaying that cringe-inducing clip, and then Mr. Perry appears on the screen. 'We've all lost our train of thought before, but not many have done it on national TV,' he says. 'If you want a slick debater, I'm obviously not your guy.'"[92] He finished the ad on a similar light note, subverting the now-rote candidate approval message: "He then says, 'I'm Rick Perry, and . . . ' He looks for help off camera, then says, 'What's that line again? I'm Rick Perry, and I approve this message.'"[93]

At this point in the campaign, Perry was in better shape than his counterparts at the bottom of the polls for one reason only: money. He still had enough in his coffers to run heavy television advertising before voting began, and he soon created another ad to position himself as the "true Christian conservative." Intended to appeal to the social conservative and evangelical voters in Iowa, this ad emphasized Perry's right-wing positions:

> I'm not ashamed to admit that I'm a Christian, but you don't need to be in the
> pew every Sunday to know that there's something wrong in this country when

gays can serve openly in the military, but our kids can't openly celebrate
Christmas and pray in school. As president I will end Obama's war on religion
and I will fight against liberal attacks on our religious heritage. [94]

The spot immediately generated controversy. It "sparked backlash from people on both sides of the political divide and even garnered close to 500,000 dislikes on the campaign's YouTube channel."[95]

When asked to defend his accusation about Obama's war on religion, Perry once again unwittingly triggered the "lack of intelligence" frame. During an editorial board meeting with the *Des Moines Register*, Perry "said there were eight Supreme Court judges. There are nine Supreme Court justices. And he was searching for one recently appointed, Sonia Sotomayor. And here is what he said."[96] The Fox News anchors then played the clip, featuring Perry saying, "When you see his appointment of two from my perspective inarguably activist judges, whether it was, um, not Motamayor."[97] Soon after, Perry "intended to draw attention to his military service by unveiling a 'Veterans for Perry Coalition,' [but] he mixed up the nations of Iran and Iraq in public comments."[98]

While Perry wanted to be seen as a true conservative, stories continued to emerge from Texas that challenged that frame, particularly in terms of fiscal conservatism. During this period it was revealed that while still serving as governor, Perry "officially" retired—a move that gave himself a 60 percent pay increase: "Mr. Perry—who isn't stepping down as governor—nevertheless was able to officially 'retire' this year for benefits purposes, a move that gives him about $90,000 more in annual retirement compensation on top of his $150,000 salary as governor."[99]

While Perry's considerable funds meant he was still considered a candidate with at least some potential to surge once more, Bachmann's candidacy was all but ignored. Recognizing that a strong performance in Iowa was her only shot at moving forward, she visited all ninety-nine counties in ten days. Her efforts to rally momentum and be perceived as a credible candidate were undermined in late December, however, when her Iowa state chair, State Senator Kent Sorenson, abruptly quit to offer his support to Paul. Bachmann issued a statement on the defection that included accusations of improper ethics on the part of both Paul and Sorenson, saying, "It is clear that this is a deliberate move by the Ron Paul campaign to discredit our campaign and our growing momentum. . . . Sorenson personally told me he was offered a large sum of money to go to work for the Paul campaign."[100] Both Sorenson and the Paul campaign immediately denied the charges. In the wake of this, Bachmann's Iowa political director, Wes Enos, came to Sorenson's defense: "I cannot in good conscience, watch a good man like Kent Sorenson be attacked as a 'sell-out.' That is simply not the case and it was not the basis of the decision."[101] Within days, Enos was no longer part of Bachmann's Iowa campaign team. Increasingly it looked clear that Bachmann would not be the candidate around whom Iowa conservatives rallied.

As late as December 19, Santorum was thought to be with Bachmann in the basement bin—no-hopers who were encouraged to drop out to avoid splitting the conservative vote. His fortunes began to change, however, on December 20: "He spent more time in Iowa than any other GOP presidential candidate, and today, that investment paid off when Rick Santorum, the campaign's staunchest critic of gay marriage, won the endorsement of Bob Vander Plaats, president and CEO of the Family Leader."[102] Considered "an Iowa kingmaker,"[103] Vander Plaats's support could be just what Santorum needed to spark a surge in his campaign. Even with this prominent endorsement, however, some pundits and reporters doubted Santorum's ability to make a late move to the top: "In a deeper sense, Mr. Santorum has what one top Iowa Republican described as a 'minivan' problem, which he himself admits: he does not have the political equivalent of sex appeal. And it does matter, even to social conservatives, who have flirted with a string of more charismatic candidates,"[104] including (in chronological order) Bachmann, Perry, Cain, and Gingrich.

As the 2011 calendar drew to a close, with voting only a few short days away, open questions remained: Would Santorum be able to surge at the optimum time, eking out an Iowa victory that could propel his campaign into the big time? Would one of the other social conservative candidates be able to generate enough concentrated support to win? After years of campaigning and months of being a frontrunner with only tepid support, could Romney somehow win often and quickly enough to wrap up the nomination without a protracted (and expensive) primary? As 2012 commenced, the time for questions ended. It was finally time for voters to make their voices heard.

NOTES

1. Greta Van Susteren and Brit Hume, "Herman Cain Reaps Campaign Cash on Sexual Harassment Allegations; Interview with House Majority Whip Rep. Dennis McCarthy," *Fox News Network: Fox on the Record with Greta Van Susteren*, November 1, 2011, LexisNexis.

2. Alicia Mundy, "U.S. News—Election 2012: Accuser Releases Statement—Woman's Lawyer Says She Alleged 'Inappropriate Behaviors' by Cain in Late '90s," *Wall Street Journal*, November 5, 2011, A5, Factiva.

3. Amy Gardner and James V. Grimaldi, "Accuser's Attorney Takes Aim at Cain," *Washington Post*, November 5, 2011, A-Section, Factiva.

4. Kyra Phillips, Paul Steinhauser, Christine Romans, Jill Dougherty, Shannon Travis, Patrick Oppman, A. J. Hammer, and Mark Preston, "Cain: 'I Was Falsely Accused'; Former Cain Employee Doubts Allegations; Greek Vote Shocks Wall Street; Europe's Youth Jobless Crisis; 'Occupy' Targets Iowa Caucuses; Halloween Shootings in New Orleans; 250 Spend Night in Shelter; JetBlue: 'We Are Truly Sorry'; Breaking Up a Spy Ring; Inside 'Occupy Seattle'; Bank's Firm Pokes Fun at Poor; Cain: 'This is a Smear Campaign'; Rick Perry Video Goes Viral; Jet Makes Emergency Landing in Warsaw; Hillary Clinton's Mother Dies; Kim

Kardashian Files for Divorce," *CNN: CNN Newsroom*, November 1, 2011, LexisNexis Academic.

5. Jim Rutenberg, Jeff Zeleny, Mike McIntire, and Michael D. Shear, "Cain Accuser Got a Year's Salary in Severance Pay," *New York Times*, November 2, 2011, National Desk, Factiva.

6. Dan Balz, "Cain's Missteps Show an Unsteady Candidacy," *Washington Post*, November 4, 2011, A-Section, Factiva.

7. Karen Tumulty and Aaron Blake, "Candidate's Maverick Style Guides Scandal Response, Too," *Washington Post*, November 4, 2011, A-Section, Factiva.

8. Greta Van Susteren, "Interview With Donald Trump; Cain Camp Says Perry Campaign Source of Harassment Allegations," *Fox News Network: Fox on the Record with Greta Van Susteren*, November 2, 2011, LexisNexis.

9. Lawrence O'Donnell and Toure, "The Last Word for November 8, 2011," *MSNBC: The Last Word with Lawrence O'Donnell*, November 8, 2011, LexisNexis Academic.

10. Jim Rutenberg, Susan Saulny, Richard A. Oppel Jr., and Jeremy W. Peters, "Cain Lawyer Warns Any Accusers: 'Think Twice,'" *New York Times*, November 10, 2011, National Desk, Factiva.

11. Jim Rutenberg, Michael D. Shear, Jeff Zeleny, Susan Saulny, Mike McIntire, Matt Flegenheimer, and Trip Gabriel, "Cain Confronts Claim From '90s of Harassment," *New York Times*, November 1, 2011, National Desk, Factiva.

12. Phillip Rucker and Perry Bacon Jr., "Campaigning in N.H., Romney Lays Out Deficit-Reduction Plan," *Washington Post*, November 4, 2011, A-Section, Factiva.

13. Erin Burnett, Jeffrey Toobin, Mike Galanos, John Avlon, Erick Erickson, Ben Wedeman, Matthew Chance, and Max Foster, "Penn State Sex Abuse Case; Second Mile Charity," *CNN: Erin Burnett OutFront*, November 11, 2011, LexisNexis Academic.

14. Bret Baier, Wendell Goler, Peter Barnes, Doug McKelway, John Roberts, Alicia Acuna, Claudia Cowan, and James Rosen, "Political Headlines," *Fox News Network: Fox Special Report with Bret Baier*, November 3, 2011, LexisNexis Academic.

15. Patrick O'Connor, "U.S. News: Santorum Makes Stand in Iowa," *Wall Street Journal*, November 3, 2011, A6, Factiva.

16. Richard A. Oppel Jr., "Meeting Iowans, County by County, Table by Table," *New York Times*, November 3, 2011, National Desk, Factiva.

17. Wolf Blitzer, Brian Todd, Mary Snow, Gloria Borger, Ivan Watson, David Gergen, Jill Dougherty, Lisa Sylvester, Jessica Yellin, Brianna Keilar, Kate Bolduan, and Athena Jones, "Penn State Child Sex Abuse Scandal Continues to Unfold; Major League Baseball Player Kidnapped in Venezuela; Aftershock Hit Eastern Turkey; GOP Presidential Candidates Propose Dramatic Cuts to Government Programs; Calm Urged at Penn State Amid Scandal; Controversial Oil Pipeline Project; White House Releases E-Mails on Solyndra Loans," *CNN: The Situation Room*, November 11, 2011, LexisNexis Academic.

18. Jeremy W. Peters, "Portraying the Face of Job Growth," *New York Times*, November 1, 2011, National Desk, Factiva.

19. Ali Velshi, Carol Costello, Christine Romans, Paul Callan, Soledad O'Brien, and Kyra Phillips, "New Greek Prime Minister Named; Joe Paterno Fired; Alabama County Files Largest Municipal Bankruptcy; Reports of Sluggish Blackberry Mail; Rick Perry Makes Gaffe at GOP Debate; USAA Posts Map of Best Places for Veterans to Find Employment; Where's the 'Black Mark Zuckerberg'?" *CNN: American Morning*, November 10, 2011, LexisNexis Academic.

20. John Harwood, "'Oops' Moment Takes on a Life of Its Own," *New York Times*, November 14, 2011, National Desk, Factiva.

21. Jeff Zeleny, Nicholas Confessore, and Richard A. Oppel Jr., "Perry Goes on TV to Regain Footing after Debate," *New York Times*, November 11, 2011, National Desk, Factiva.

22. Ed Schultz and Martin Bashir, "For November 2, 2011," *MSNBC: The Ed Show with Ed Schultz*, November 2, 2011, LexisNexis Academic.

23. Fredricka Whitfield, Wolf Blitzer, Candy Crowley, and Shawna Shepherd, "Gingrich Rising in Polls; Review of the Latest Republican Debate; Obama to Expand U.S. Trade; Perry Flubbed Debate; Bachmann Accuses CBS of Bias," *CNN: CNN Newsroom*, November 13, 2011, LexisNexis Academic.

24. Susan Saulny, "From Cain, More on Libya," *New York Times*, November 19, 2011, National Desk, Factiva.

25. Wolf Blitzer, Jack Cafferty, Mary Snow, Lisa Sylvester, Gloria Borger, Brian Todd, Jeanne Moos, Dan Lothian, and Jessica Yellin, "CEO of Charity Founded by Penn State Coach Accused of Child Abuse Resigns; NBA Players Reject Owners' Latest Offer; Herman Cain Has Trouble Answering Question on Libya; Russian May Have Aided Iran's Nuke Quest; 'Let Me Just Say . . . They're Wrong'; Poll: Gingrich Surges to Front of Pack; Obama Health Care Law Lands At Supreme Court," *CNN: The Situation Room*, November 14, 2011, LexisNexis Academic.

26. Ibid.

27. Ashley Parker, "Romney Debt Plan Includes Medicare Overhaul and Social Security Changes," *New York Times*, November 5, 2011, National Desk, Factiva.

28. Joseph Rago and Paul A. Gigot, "The Weekend Interview with Mitt Romney: On Taxes, 'Modeling,' and the Vision Thing," *Wall Street Journal*, December 24, 2011, A13, Factiva.

29. Jeremy W. Peters, "Portraying the Face of Job Growth," *New York Times*, November 1, 2011, National Desk, Factiva.

30. Lawrence O'Donnell, Melissa Harris-Perry, and Ezra Klein, "The Last Word for November 23, 2011," *MSNBC: The Last Word with Lawrence O'Donnell*, November 23, 2011, LexisNexis Academic.

31. Greta Van Susteren and Mike Huckabee, "Woman Alleges 13-Year Affair With Herman Cain; DNC Ad Attacks Romney Flip-Flops; Massachusetts Rep. Barney Frank Announces Retirement; Congress Neglects Medicare Doc Fix," *Fox News Network: Fox on the Record with Greta Van Susteren*, November 28, 2011, LexisNexis.

32. Ibid.

33. Ashley Parker and Jim Rutenberg, "Romney Heats Up Campaign in New Hampshire with an Ad Attacking Obama," *New York Times*, November 22, 2011, National Desk, Factiva.

34. Sean Hannity, "Interview with Ann Coulter," *Fox News Network: Hannity*, November 15, 2011, LexisNexis.

35. Dan Balz, "Iowa Has its Hawkeye on Romney—and He's Looking Back," *Washington Post*, November 22, 2011, A-Section, Factiva.

36. Brody Mullins, "U.S. News—Election 2012: Chamber of Commerce Paid Gingrich as a Consultant," *Wall Street Journal*, November 18, 2011, A6, Factiva.

37. Bret Baier, James Rosen, Jim Angle, Mike Emanuel, Doug McKelway, and Peter Barnes, "Political Headlines," *Fox News Network: Fox Special Report with Bret Baier*, November 16, 2011, LexisNexis Academic.

38. Trip Gabriel, "As Foes Flounder, Gingrich Gets Bump in Poll," *New York Times*, November 12, 2011, National Desk, Factiva.

39. Don Lemon, Wolf Blitzer, Barbara Starr, Brian Todd, Lisa Sylvester, Deborah Feyerick, Gloria Borger, Ron Brownstein, Nick Paton Walsh, Jessica Yellin, and Jeanne Moos, "Countdown to GOP Presidential Debate; Loose Lips on Iran?; Sources Say Gingrich's Paid by Freddie Mac; Who's on Freddie Mac's Payroll?; Giffords' Amazing Recovery Revealed; 'I'm Getting Stronger, Better'; Candidates to Debate National Security; Clock Ticking on Debt Super Committee; Energy Secretary: No Apology for Solyndra; Putin's Sexy 'Get Out The Vote' Ad," *CNN: The Situation Room*, November 19, 2011, LexisNexis Academic.

40. Chris Matthews, Michael Isikoff, Hampton Pearson, David Corn, and Ed Rendell, "For November 16, 2011," *MSNBC: Hardball*, November 16, 2011LexisNexis Academic.

41. Jeff Zeleny, "Gingrich Takes a Poke or Two at Romney," *New York Times*, November 29, 2011, National Desk, Factiva.

42. Trip Gabriel, "Gingrich Wields History, Seeking to Add Chapter," *New York Times*, November 29, 2011, National Desk, Factiva.

43. T. J. Holmes, Reynolds Wolf, Joe Johns, Joe Carter, and Elizabeth Cohen, "Major Fire Burning in Reno; Republican Presidential Candidates Attend Events in Iowa; Newt Gingrich Surges in Polls; Deadline Looms for Congressional Deficit Super Committee; National Adoption Day Celebrated; Kidnapped and Rescued MLB Player Returns to U.S. from Venezuela," *CNN: CNN Saturday Morning News*, November 19, 2011, LexisNexis Academic.

44. Ibid.

45. Martha MacCallum and Brit Hume, "Interview with Jon Huntsman," *Fox News Network: Fox on the Record with Greta Van Susteren*, November 22, 2011, LexisNexis.

46. Chris Wallace, James Rosen, Doug McKelway, Connor Powell, Ed Henry, and Bret Baier, "Political Headlines," *Fox News Network: Fox Special Report with Bret Baier*, November 28, 2011, LexisNexis Academic.

47. Susan Saulny, Robbie Brown, Ashley Parker, Jeff Zeleny, Nicholas Confessore, and Trip Gabriel, "A Defiant Cain Suspends His Bid For Presidency," *New York Times*, December 4, 2011, National Desk, Factiva.

48. Chris Matthews, Ed Rendell, Hampton Pearson, and David Corn, "For November 30, 2011," *MSNBC: Hardball*, November 30, 2011, LexisNexis Academic.

49. Bret Baier, Ed Henry, and Mike Emanuel, "Interview with Mitt Romney," *Fox News Network: Fox Special Report with Bret Baier*, November 29, 2011, LexisNexis Academic.

50. Wolf Blitzer, Dan Lothian, Joe Johns, Jack Cafferty, John King, Lisa Sylvester, Mary Snow, Stan Grant, and Jeanne Moos, "President to GOP: No Holiday for You; Battle Between the GOP Wives; Putin: John McCain Is 'Nuts'; Interview with Yochi Dreazen; U.S. Declares Iraq War Over; Ruling against Iran in 9/11 Case; Actor Christian Bale Finds Drama in China," *CNN: The Situation Room*, December 15, 2011, LexisNexis Academic.

51. Jeremy W. Peters, "PAC for Romney Takes a Big Swipe at Gingrich," *New York Times*, December 9, 2011, National Desk, Factiva.

52. Ashley Parker and Michael Barbaro, "The Retooled, Loose Romney, Guessing Voters' Age and Ethnicity," *New York Times*, December 28, 2011, National Desk, Factiva.

53. John Harwood, "In One Rival, Romney Now Sees A Grave Threat," *New York Times*, December 5, 2011, National Desk, Factiva.

54. Bret Baier, Carl Cameron, Steve Brown, Mike Emanuel, Ed Henry, Jim Angle, and Catherine Herridge, "Political Headlines," *Fox News Network: Fox Special Report with Bret Baier*, December 16, 2011, LexisNexis Academic.

55. Dan Balz, "Romney Hoping for a Win Sooner Rather Than Later," *Washington Post*, December 22, 2011, A-Section, Factiva.

56. Beth Marlowe and Chris Cillizza, "George H. W. Bush Says Romney 'Is the Best Choice for Us,'" *Washington Post*, December 23, 2011, A-Section, Factiva.

57. Greta Van Susteren, "Interview with Dick Morris," *Fox News Network: Fox on the Record with Greta Van Susteren*, December 22, 2011, LexisNexis.

58. Nicholas Confessore, "Fund-Raising Is Now Urgent in Gingrich Bid," *New York Times*, December 6, 2011, National Desk, Factiva.

59. Eric Bolling, Kimberly Guilfoyle, Bob Beckel, Greg Gutfeld, and Dana Perino, "The Five for December 5, 2011," *Fox News Network: The Five, Sunday*, December 5, 2011, LexisNexis Academic.

60. Chris Matthews, Chuck Todd, John Heilemann, Amanda Drury, Mark Halperin, and Michael Steele, "For December 9, 2011," *MSNBC: Hardball*, December 9, 2011, LexisNexis Academic.

61. Sara Murray and Patrick O'Connor, "U.S. News—Election 2012: Romney Keeps His Attacks Muted," *Wall Street Journal*, December 10, 2011, A5, Factiva.

62. Ashley Parker and Trip Gabriel, "Increasing Hostilities between Two Campaigns," *New York Times*, December 10, 2011, National Desk, Factiva.

63. Candy Crowley, "Interview with Ron Paul; Interview with Michele Bachmann; Interview with John McCain," *CNN: State of the Union with Candy Crowley*, December 4, 2011, LexisNexis Academic.

64. Michael Smerconish, Richard Wolffe, Jane Wells, Howard Fineman, Chris Cillizza, and Michelle Bernard, "For December 2, 2011," *MSNBC: Hardball*, December 2, 2011, LexisNexis Academic.

65. Trip Gabriel, "As New Gingrich Takes Center Stage, Old Reputation Lurks in Wings," *New York Times*, December 23, 2011, National Desk, Factiva.

66. Wolf Blitzer, Joe Johns, Gloria Borger, Will Cain, Mary Snow, Jack Cafferty, Chris Lawrence, Lisa Sylvester, Kate Bolduan, Roland Martin, Brian Todd, and Jeanne Moos, "Romney's Fight Back to Top; Dan Quayle to Endorse Romney; Gingrich Meets with Donald

Trump; Iran Claims It Shot Down U.S. Drone; Obama Pushes to Extend Tax Cuts; Is '9-9-9' Dead?" *CNN: The Situation Room*, December 5, 2011, LexisNexis Academic.

67. Trip Gabriel, "Gingrich's Foreign Policy Words Summon the Cold War, but Enemy Is Iran," *New York Times*, December 15, 2011, National Desk, Factiva.

68. Joe Johns, Kate Bolduan, Jim Acosta, Brian Todd, Wolf Blitzer, Brianna Keilar, Lisa Sylvester, Maria Cardona, Alex Castellanos, and Chris Lawrence, "Virginia Tech Shooting; DNC Chair Debbie Wasserman Schultz Interview; Mitt Romney Targets Newt Gingrich; Perry Ad Reality Check; Uproar over 'Morning After Pill' Decision; Obama Fires Back At Critics; Virginia Tech Lockdown Lifted; Markets Sharply Down on Eurozone Worries," *CNN: CNN The Situation Room*, December 8, 2011, LexisNexis Academic.

69. Ed Schultz, "The Ed Show for December 12, 2011," *MSNBC: The Ed Show with Ed Schultz*, December 12, 2011, LexisNexis Academic.

70. Katharine Q. Seelye and Michael Barbaro, "Gingrich Falls Short of Signatures Needed to Get on the Primary Ballot in Virginia," *New York Times*, December 25, 2011, National Desk, Factiva.

71. Chris Wallace, "Fox News Sunday Roundtable," *Fox News Network: Fox News Sunday*, December 25, 2011, LexisNexis Academic.

72. Mark Leibovich, "On Trail, Gingrich Strains to Show Nice-Guy Side," *New York Times*, December 29, 2011, National Desk, Factiva.

73. Bret Baier, Charles Krauthammer, Liz Marlantes, and Charles Lane, "Fox News All-Stars," *Fox News Network: Fox Special Report with Bret Baier*, December 9, 2011, LexisNexis Academic.

74. Danny Yadron and Jonathan Weisman, "U.S. News—Election 2012: Rivals Jockey to Overtake Slowing Gingrich," *Wall Street Journal*, December 20, 2011, A4, Factiva.

75. Jeff Zeleny and Jim Rutenberg, "G.O.P. Debate Sets All Eyes on Gingrich," *New York Times*, December 11, 2011, National Desk, Factiva.

76. Ibid.

77. Chris Wallace, "Interview with Rick Perry," *Fox News Network: Fox News Sunday*, December 11, 2011, LexisNexis Academic.

78. Schultz, "The Ed Show for December 12, 2011."

79. Trip Gabriel, "More Graduate Seminar Than Political Debate," *New York Times*, December 13, 2011, National Desk, Factiva.

80. Alina Cho, Carol Costello, Jim Acosta, Ron Brownstein, Susan Candiotti, Casey Wian, Joe Johns, Ted Rowlands, and Paula Hancocks, "Last Debate Before Iowa; With Friends Like These; Congress May Avoid Government Shutdown; Star Quarterback to Star Witness; Crashed Drone was Looking for Nuke Sites; Arizona Sheriff Accused of Racial Profiling; Deal to Prevent Govt. Shutdown; Wisconsin Governor Facing Recall; 'Cold Shutdown' Achieved in Fukushima," *CNN: American Morning*, December 16, 2011, LexisNexis Academic.

81. Bret Baier and James Rosen, "Fox News All-Stars," *Fox News Network: Fox Special Report with Bret Baier*, December 16, 2011, LexisNexis Academic.

82. Ibid.

83. Jeff Zeleny, "The Up-Close-and-Personal Candidate? A Thing of the Past," *New York Times*, December 1, National Desk, Factiva.

84. Jeremy W. Peters, "Campaigns Take Ad War to TV After Months of Holding Fire," *New York Times*, December 6, 2011, National Desk, Factiva.

85. Rachel Maddow, "The Rachel Maddow Show for December 1, 2011," *MSNBC: The Rachel Maddow Show*, December 1, 2011, LexisNexis Academic.

86. Peter Wallsten, "With Rise, Paul Could be Spoiler, or Kingmaker," *Washington Post*, December 21, 2011, A-Section, Factiva.

87. Gerald F. Seib, "U.S. News—Capital Journal: Paul Could Lead from Behind," *Wall Street Journal*, December 13, 2011, A4, Factiva.

88. Baier and Rosen, "Fox News All-Stars—December 16."

89. Jim Rutenberg and Richard A. Oppel Jr., "New Focus on Bias in Articles Paul Printed," *New York Times*, December 20, 2011, National Desk, Factiva.

90. Jim Acosta, Candy Crowley, Peter Hamby, Wolf Blitzer, Mohammed Jamjoom, Lisa Sylvester, Will Cain, Donna Brazile, Jill Dougherty, and Jessica Yellin, "Final Iowa Push for

Republicans; Unrest in Syria; How Ad Attacks Deflated Gingrich; Romney Slammed in Attack Ads; North Korea Nixes Thaw with South; Officials Hunting California Arsonist; Wall Street Ends 2011 Mixed; Verizon Flips on $2 Charge; Panetta Calls Egypt on Rights Groups Raids," *CNN: The Situation Room*, December 30, 2011, LexisNexis Academic.

91. Alina Cho, Deborah Feyerick, Joe Johns, David Frum, Reynolds Wolf, Jay Jackson, Mohammed Jamjoom, and Rafael Romo, "Crunch Time in Iowa; Cosmetic Surgery New Year's Rush; Stratfor Website Hacked; Arab League Monitors Arrive in Syria; Woman Suing Honda for False Advertising; Heather vs. Honda; Memorial for Kim Jong Il; Violence Greets Observers in Syria; U.S. Responds to Iran Oil Threat; Santorum Surging in Iowa; Atlanta Hostage Situation," *CNN: American Morning*, December 29, 2011, LexisNexis Academic.

92. Richard A. Oppel Jr., "Perry Ad Lampoons Perry," *New York Times*, December 2, 2011, National Desk, Factiva.

93. Ibid.

94. Sean Hannity, "Interview with Sarah Palin; Interview with Rudy Giuliani; President's Kansas Economic Speech Critiqued; Interview with Michelle Malkin; Donald Trump to Moderate GOP Debate," *Fox News Network: Hannity*, December 7, 2011, LexisNexis.

95. Chris Matthews, Chuck Todd, John Heilemann, Amanda Drury, Mark Halperin, and Michael Steele, "For December 9, 2011," *MSNBC: Hardball*, December 9, 2011, LexisNexis Academic.

96. Baier et al., "Fox News All-Stars-December 9."

97. Ibid.

98. "Election 2012—On the Stump: The Adventures of Rick Perry; Re-Re-Redistricting," *Wall Street Journal*, December 10, 2011, A6, Factiva.

99. Jay Root and Trip Gabriel, "State Still Footing the Bill for Perry Security Detail," *New York Times*, December 25, 2011, National Desk, Factiva.

100. Kimberly Guilfoyle and Griff Jenkins, "Interview with Gov. Rick Perry; Interview with Rep. Michele Bachmann." Fox on the Record with Greta Van Sustern, December 28, 2011. LexisNexis Academic.

101. Anderson Cooper, Candy Crowley, Jeffrey Toobin, and Isha Sesay, "Recent Poll Shows Mitt Romney Leading in Iowa; Bachmann's Iowa Campaign Manager Jumps Ship," *CNN: Anderson Cooper 360 Degrees*, December 29, 2011, LexisNexis Academic.

102. Bret Baier, Mike Emanuel, Ed Henry, James Rosen, Shannon Bream, Greg Palkot, and Jennifer Griffin, "Political Headlines," *Fox News Network: Fox Special Report with Bret Baier*, December 20, 2011, LexisNexis Academic.

103. Rachel Maddow, "The Rachel Maddow Show for December 19, 2011," *MSNBC: The Rachel Maddow Show*, December 19, 2011, LexisNexis Academic.

104. Richard A. Oppel Jr., "For Santorum in His Iowa Bid, Never Finding That Moment in the Sun," *New York Times*, December 24, 2011, National Desk, Factiva.

Chapter Six

Voting Begins

January–February 2012

After months of debates, events, polls, stump speeches, and seemingly endless shifts in fortunes among candidates, the build-up was finally over: Voting was about to begin. Only three days into the New Year, Iowa Republicans would head out in the cold to caucus for their candidate of choice. Pundits and observers were far from able to predict what that outcome would be: "Once again, the Iowa caucuses are coming right down to the wire and the volatility is everywhere. Anybody could pull out a victory here."[1] As voting officially kicked off, the party was mired in an increasingly nasty battle to determine its future and define its character by nominating a standard bearer who would lead the Grand Old Party in its fight to make Obama a one-term president. The stakes were unmistakably high, and frontrunner Romney characterized the nomination as no less than "an election to save the soul of America."[2]

In the waning days before the caucuses officially opened primary season, each of the remaining candidates making a play for Iowa[3] —Michele Bachmann, Newt Gingrich, Rick Perry, Ron Paul, Mitt Romney, and Rick Santorum—raced across the state in an effort to recruit precinct captains to make their final cases and persuade voters to consider their candidacies once more. For Bachmann and Perry, mired at the bottom of the polls, this was their last chance to relaunch their campaigns and reinvigorate voters and donors in other states, and each tried to position himself or herself as the true conservative in the race. A constant barrage of negative advertising targeting Gingrich meant his December momentum had stalled, so he needed to try to use his personal charm and appeal to convince voters to take up his mantle. Paul's passionate and committed supporters were expected to turn out en masse, and conventional wisdom held that bad weather would work in his favor since Paul's true believers would not be deterred by snow. Romney, on the other hand, hoped his aura of inevitability coupled with strong establishment support would tip the scales in his favor among voters who doubted his conservative credentials. Finally, after months of slogging across Iowa and persisting in the face of dire polling numbers, Santorum might just have peaked at the right time. Inspired by endorsements from leading conservatives, voters were looking at Santorum in a new light, just in time to cast their ballots. As MSNBC's Andrea Mitchell put it, "Rick Santorum has all the momentum coming out of the last couple of days."[4]

THE IOWA CAUCUSES BEGIN

As Republican voters headed to their caucus locations, no one knew how the night would pan out. In the days leading up to the event, polling indicated that 41 percent of expected participants said they could still change their minds. With four candidates boasting realistic hopes of winning, reporters and media commentators settled in for a long night. The race proved too close to call for hours, and instead the television commenters focused on how the race was netting out in terms of the horse race. On Fox News, anchor Megyn Kelly shared this analysis: "The decision desk had told us earlier that it appears that the candidates have broken out into . . . two different tiers. Three candidates per tier. Romney, Santorum, and Paul in the top tier; Gingrich, Perry, and Bachmann in the bottom tier."[5] Late in the night, the race was called for Romney, winning by the smallest of margins: eight votes, out of the tens of thousands cast. The initial reports indicated that Romney and Santorum were in a virtual tie, both earning approximately a quarter of the vote; Paul was a close third with 21 percent. While Romney and Santorum were close in terms of votes, their appeals to voters could not be further apart. On caucus night, MSNBC's Chris Matthews noted that the candidates' end-of-night speeches offered "a wonderful contrast between the politics of spirit, which you got from Rick Santorum . . . it was all about spirit and heart and belief and family. . . . Then you had sort of a merchandiser coming on there selling product. I mean, Romney was just showing one product after another." He concluded, "It was the politics of merchandising. No spirit. No heart."[6]

The top three candidates in Iowa clearly articulated the divided factions of the Republican Party: Romney, the establishment candidate; Santorum, the social conservative; and Paul, the fiscal libertarian. Perhaps as importantly for understanding the character and implications of this nominating contest, exit poll data also indicated that voters were divided on what motivated them to cast their support to the candidate of their choice: Did they want someone they believed could beat Obama, or the candidate who best reflected their conservative beliefs and values? In other words, were votes cast based on pragmatism or ideology? Fundamentally, the caucus results reinforced that "The deep ideological divisions among Republicans continue to complicate their ability to focus wholly on defeating President Obama, and to impede Mr. Romney's efforts to overcome the internal strains and win the consent if not the heart of the party."[7]

For former frontrunners Bachmann and Perry, two candidates who had banked on ideological purity being prioritized, the night's results were disappointing at best. This was particularly true for Bachmann, an Iowa native who came in last place despite winning the Ames Straw Poll only a few short months before. On the night of January 3, Bachmann reassured supporters that she would battle on in the primaries. She changed her mind, however; the very next day, Bachmann announced that she would no longer be running for president, declaring: "Last night, the people of Iowa spoke with a very clear voice. And so I have decided to stand aside."[8]

While Perry initially indicated that he planned to go back to Texas to reconsider and reflect, he surprised observers when he announced he was continuing. CNN's Wolf Blitzer shared the news: "He sent out a Tweet. Let me quote it. 'The next leg of the marathon is in the Palmetto State.' And then he said, 'Here we come, South Carolina.' I assume that means he's in."[9] While his electoral odds looked bleak, Perry still brought much to the table. He had never lost an election, and a robust bank account that still had $3–5 million after Iowa meant Perry could still run a viable campaign. He also had some advantages in southern states, so upcoming primaries in South Carolina and Florida might provide a more fertile ground for his candidacy. First, though, he had to face yet another potential Waterloo when he joined the other candidates in a pre-primary debate.

MOVING ON TO NEW HAMPSHIRE

Because Romney had thoroughly dominated the state polls for so long, New Hampshire was not considered much of a contest. While Huntsman had staked his campaign on a strong performance in the Granite State, some of the conservative values candidates competing to be the alternative to Romney bypassed New Hampshire and instead focused their energy and efforts in South Carolina. All candidates were present, however, for back-to-back debates held in the week between the first two nominating contests. The first, sponsored by ABC News, was held the evening of January 7; the second was on NBC's *Meet the Press* the next morning.

The debates were highly anticipated, particularly since previous meetings had inspired some of the most memorable moments, lines, and exchanges of the entire season. The first was fairly even-keeled, primarily notable for offering the first opportunity for Santorum to join Romney at center stage as frontrunner. Sparks flew at the Sunday morning debate, however. When Romney claimed that he was not a career politician, "Santorum was incredulous. Gingrich, dropping his let's-be-nice posture, told Romney to stop with the 'pious baloney.'"[10] The attacks on Romney continued in an effort to shake his position as frontrunner, with Gingrich in particular going after him to provide a boost to his own campaign.

On January 10, voters turned out to cast their ballots. Unsurprisingly, Romney won, garnering almost 40 percent of the vote. Paul came in second, followed closely by Huntsman. Neither Gingrich nor Santorum broke into double digits. While Huntsman enjoyed a late mini-surge in the state, it was not enough to catapult his campaign into the later primaries. He officially dropped out on January 16, throwing his support to Romney. While Huntsman's candidacy was eagerly anticipated, he never caught fire among voters. According to Republican strategist Alex Castellanos, "We never quite figured out which playoff game he wanted to play in. Is he competing for the anti-Romney conservatives? He is a conservative governor from Utah. Is he competing to be the Romney space in New Hampshire? Sometimes being everything to everyone is the same thing as being nothing to everyone."[11] With Huntsman out of the race, the contest moved to South Carolina.

SOUTH CAROLINA: THE FIRST SOUTHERN PRIMARY

Coming into South Carolina, it looked increasingly like the race was Romney's to lose. He was lauded as the first non-incumbent Republican to win both Iowa and New Hampshire, and South Carolina—a state with a perfect track record for supporting the eventual nominee—was considered an important test of Romney's appeal and electability in the conservative southern states. He had hoped the endorsement of Governor Nikki Haley, a Tea Party favorite, would help boost his appeal among these voters, and she actively campaigned with him during this period. This was taken as evidence that "the Romney campaign is really stepping up its efforts in South Carolina. . . . They're on the air all across the state. . . . So they're really competing hard. They'd like to win there and win in Florida and try to lock this thing up by the end of the month."[12] To facilitate this, establishment Republicans began to make noises that the time had come for challengers to step aside; with Romney the victor in the first two states and the frontrunner in South Carolina polls, his nomination seemed assured. As CNN contributor Jack Cafferty said, "And the saying is this . . . Democrats fall in love, Republicans fall in line. And it looks like it's about time for the remaining Republican candidates to fall in line behind the dominant frontrunner, Mitt Romney."[13]

Not everyone was on board with a default Romney victory, however. For evangelicals, Tea Partiers, and values voters, "South Carolina becomes the Super Bowl for the conservative candidate, the anti-Mitt Romney candidate, and that is where all these candidates who hope to be the person . . . that is where they fight."[14] While early money was on Santorum becoming that candidate, Gingrich was not willing to give up on becoming the conservative of choice. Trying to capitalize on his southern connections, the former Congressman from Georgia went after the state with gusto. Some speculated that Gingrich's fire was fueled by ire over Romney's nonstop barrage of attacks in Iowa. As Fox News's Bill O'Reilly noted, "But obviously, Newt Gingrich is royally teed off and it looks like he will go after the governor in South Carolina big time."[15]

Worried that the conservative vote would split, evangelical Christian leaders met in Texas to see if they could decide on a candidate to support. If consensus could be reached, the group could then try to work with candidates to ensure victory. While it was difficult for any one group to directly influence the primaries, the social conservatives arguably were the best suited to do so: "And if they get together and if they have a sit-down with Gingrich and they say, please, step out, if they say to Perry, please stop doing this, and if they say to Gingrich—or to Santorum, you're our guy—if they do something like that, it could get interesting."[16] Regardless of who they selected, their intention was clear: "to deal with the Romney matter. And they are not real keen on the governor."[17] While the group eventually settled on Santorum during the third ballot, divisions emerged almost immediately.

After mostly staying off the airwaves in New Hampshire, television stations were inundated. South Carolina Republicans were subjected to a deluge of negative ads designed to frame the remaining candidates in the worst possible light: Romney was a soulless "vulture capitalist," Santorum has not always been a true conservative, and Gingrich was a desperate politician. Record money poured into the state, with both campaigns and their affiliated super PACs working overtime to negatively define the opposition.

Perhaps the most surprising line of attack during this period was the aforementioned framing of Romney as a "vulture capitalist," a narrative first offered by Perry but quickly adopted by both Gingrich and Santorum. Attempting to subvert Romney's argument that his business experience gave him a unique ability to fix American economic woes, this alternate frame characterized Romney as caring more about corporations than people. Trying to tap into the public's anger about the economy, Wall Street, and government bailouts, Romney's rivals attacked him "as a predatory capitalist who destroyed jobs and communities, a full-scale Republican assault on Mr. Romney's business background."[18] Almost immediately, prominent Republicans leapt to Romney's defense, noting that this line of attack was at odds with the GOP's traditional business- and capitalism-friendly perspective. In the *Wall Street Journal*, this was characterized as "opening philosophical and tactical divides within the GOP. Some Republicans see the attacks on Mr. Romney as undermining the party's traditional defense of markets and rugged capitalism, as well as their likely nominee, while also playing into the hands of Democrats."[19]

Political advertisements were not the only way voters were exposed to the three remaining candidates. A candidate forum sponsored by popular evangelical conservative Mike Huckabee was held on January 14, and two debates were held during the eleven days between New Hampshire and South Carolina: the first in Myrtle Beach on January 16; the second in Charleston on January 19. While Romney managed to survive the events without sustaining major damage, his mantle of inevitability cracked on January 19 when it was revealed that the originally reported Iowa results—an eight-vote victory for Romney—actually were incorrect. When the official tallies were revealed, Santorum was declared the winner. Further complicating his efforts to be considered the likely nominee were new polls indicating that South Carolina was no longer a sure bet; Gingrich had once again pulled off a phoenix-like rebirth and surged in the polls after being left for dead post-Iowa. The threat of Gingrich taking control of the race was highlighted by Perry's decision to drop out; while he was no longer direct competition, Perry made clear in his withdrawal speech that his decision was intended to ensure conservative voters would coalesce around one of the remaining non-Romney candidates. With Perry out, his supporters likely would turn to either Gingrich or Santorum, strengthening their campaigns and adding to any potential momentum.

On January 21, voters went to the polls. Gingrich's comeback was complete: He had eviscerated the competition, winning 40 percent of the vote to Romney's 28. In just a week, the race looked completely new: "The rebirth of Newt Gingrich, a notion that seemed far-fetched only weeks ago, has upended a litany of assumptions about this turbulent race."[20] Coming into South Carolina undefeated, Romney left with just one state in his pocket—New Hampshire. No longer could Romney be considered a sure bet to win the nomination; this was now a real competition. In his concession speech, Romney struck a positive tone: "There were notes of humility, but not defiance. Instead, he was upbeat and passionate, saying he 'will keep fighting for every single vote . . . in every single state' as he put in sharp focus the party's choice between himself and the former House speaker."[21]

In the wake of South Carolina, Romney clearly had to rethink his strategy. While his team had successfully stemmed Gingrich's momentum in Iowa just a few weeks before, the former Speaker had managed to shift the tides almost completely. As the intense first month of primaries and caucuses continued, the stakes were suddenly much higher. By this point it was clear there would not be one knockout candidate who would be able to wrap up the nomination quickly. Instead, the race was becoming one that would require copious attention to delegate math: finding the right combination of states and doing just well enough to collect a sufficient number of delegates to win at the convention. In an effort to maximize their appeal to key Republican constituencies, some candidates were causing controversy.

CREATING RACIAL TENSIONS

During this period, Republican candidates made several controversial racially tinged statements that elicited questions about both intent and judgment. During a speech in early January, Santorum was accused of being "insensitive and offensive . . . [when] he singled out black people, while saying the best way to fight poverty is to help people to find jobs, not give them taxpayer money." During his Sioux City speech, Santorum was thought to have said: "I don't want to make black people's lives better by giving them somebody else's money. I want to give them the opportunity to go out and earn their money."[22] According to Santorum, he just stumbled over words: "I've looked at it several times, I was starting to say one word, and I sort of came up with a different word and moved on, and it—and it sounded like 'black.'"[23] Instead, he claimed he said "blah." While some supporters accepted this explanation, critics refused to let him off the hook. MSNBC's Ed Schultz clearly stated, "I'm not buying Santorum's excuse. And neither is Reverend Jesse Jackson. Today he released the following statement: 'Santorum's comments are not accidental. They are a calculation to target immigrants and now blacks. He is appealing to the fear vote that will take us backward, not the hope vote that will take us forward.'"[24]

Santorum was not alone in generating race-based controversy throughout this period. Gingrich continued "making increasingly provocative statements on matters of race and poverty, repeating his refrain this week that President Obama is the 'food stamp president' and reiterating his view that poor children lack a strong work ethic."[25] He also proposed speaking at the NAACP convention to "talk about why the African-American community should demand paychecks and not be satisfied with food stamps."[26]

Observers noted that these comments were intensifying as campaigns attempted to reach white working-class voters, and some pundits speculated that the candidates were taking calculated risks to use coded language that would motivate their base. Marc Morial, president of the National Urban League, went on CNN to discuss Santorum's statement with John King. Morial opined, "And what he said was not only insensitive, it was pandering, I think, to the worst interests of the American people, and divisive. . . . And I think what he did was deliberate. I think it was divisive."[27] Later that month, Dr. James Peterson of Lehigh University went on MSNBC's *The Ed Show* to discuss the continued use of racial language and connotations in the Republican dialogue, specifically in relation to Gingrich's NAACP remark. According to Dr. Peterson, "I think when we put it in the context of like Michele Bachmann's comments about slavery or Herman Cain's comments about this place not being racial, or Rick Santorum's black-to-blah comments—within that framework, it seems clear to me that there is a problem with race on the Republican side of things."[28]

FLORIDA: ROMNEY FIGHTS BACK

Almost before the last votes were counted in South Carolina, the candidates and their teams had already moved south to Florida. While the Palmetto State was considered a test of Romney's ability to connect with southern voters, Florida was much more complicated with a diverse audience, multiple major media markets, and diluted influence of evangelical and values voters. The latter two factors played to Romney's strengths, since he had the money and organization to reach and turn out voters in a state primed for his economic message and business background.

There were only two days between the South Carolina primary and the first of two Florida debates, but in that period Romney obviously had decided to change his approach. Rather than focusing his energy on Obama as he had done in the past, Romney used the January 23 debate in Tampa to launch a "searing attack against Newt Gingrich's character and raised pointed questions about his ability to lead."[29] He lambasted Gingrich for being an influence peddler, implying that he had abused the relationships and cachet that come with the role of Speaker for his own financial gain. The debate clearly was a battle between Gingrich and Romney, with the other two remaining candidates—Santorum and Paul—watching the fireworks from the side.

While Gingrich had found great success during previous debates, Romney's aptitude for planning and anticipation paid off during the second Florida meeting on January 26. Gingrich followed a line of attack he used in the past, attempting to link Romney to Florida's housing crisis because of his investments in Freddie Mac and Fannie Mae. When Gingrich finished, Romney responded by pointing out that Gingrich himself had mutual funds that invested in those same companies. When moderator Wolf Blitzer from CNN asked Gingrich to talk about accusations he had made about Romney outside the debates, Gingrich tried to deflect the question by once more blaming the media. Romney would not let him escape unscathed, however, rhetorically asking, "Wouldn't it be nice if people didn't make accusations somewhere else that they weren't willing to defend here?" Gingrich responded meekly, "Okay. All right."[30] In the battle for Florida, Romney was proving himself a formidable competitor. In post-debate analysis, Blitzer offered this: "And in the end, [Gingrich] had to back down, especially after Mitt Romney did not back down. . . . He didn't back down at all and I think that's . . . being reflected out in the polls right now."[31]

Much as Gingrich's negative attacks on Romney's business ethics helped him topple the frontrunner in South Carolina, Romney recognized that he needed to actively go after his top competitors in Florida to save his candidacy. They viciously attacked each other on the airwaves, and 92 percent of the spots that ran in the week before the Florida primary were negative.[32] One of the most notable and controversial was an attack on Gingrich run by Romney that used original footage of an NBC News report on Gingrich's ethics violations. In the wake of this spot running, Gingrich responded on MSNBC: "NBC is asking to take down the ad of Tom Brokaw in it. The fact is Romney knows that ad is misleading. . . . I never paid a fine. . . . I did not resign at the time. I served two more years." He concludes, "Romney knows all these things are true. He's running an ad that's factually false."[33]

With much of the focus on Gingrich and Romney's battle, Paul and Santorum continued to try to win over voters. Santorum's time on the campaign trail was cut short, however, when he had to rush to the side of his three-year-old daughter, Isabella, who had been hospitalized with pneumonia. Isabella was born with Trisomy 18, a rare fatal genetic disorder. As Santorum recounted to Fox News's Bill O'Reilly, "It was sort of miraculous, Bill. I haven't been home since Christmas Day and the one day I was home was the day that she—she really started to have a lot of problems and we ended up [going to the hospital] for the first time in three years."[34] Santorum's emotional references to his daughter and family were part of his campaign, offering evidence for why abortion should be outlawed and the ways Obamacare would hurt families. In the same interview with O'Reilly, Santorum pointed to Bella and other children like her as inspiration for his campaign: "[I'm] fighting for little kids like Bella who in many respects are, I think are going to be left behind whether its Obamacare or whether it's a system where government is going to start to evaluate people not based on who they are or what they are but what they can do."[35]

While Romney's resurgence offered him hope for winning Florida, his chances also were buoyed by his campaign's organizational dominance. His team had begun encouraging supporters to cast their ballots by mail in December, and by primary day more than 280,000 voters had already voiced their preference. Not content to sit back and wait, Romney continued to hammer at Gingrich, showing an aggressive side that he hoped resonated with primary voters looking for some passion in their candidate: "He drinks milk, not beer, and his vocabulary includes 'gee' and 'darn,' but Mitt Romney is being forced by increasingly tenuous political circumstances to show his mean guy."[36] His strategy worked: "Bolstered by superior resources and a relentlessly aggressive style, Mitt Romney won a decisive victory in the

Florida primary Tuesday night, dealing a major setback to principal rival
Newt Gingrich while putting himself back into a commanding position in the
race for the Republican presidential nomination."[37] When voting closed on
January 31, Romney had won 46 percent of the vote to Gingrich's 32. Despite Romney's attempt to position this victory as evidence of the inevitability of his nomination, others believed that this really just marked the end of
the first phase in the race. No knockout candidate meant nothing had been
decided; in February, the campaigns would go national.

SANTORUM'S RESURGENCE

Early February offered no break from the nonstop campaigning of January.
With four contests in the first week, candidates first turned their attention to
Nevada. Going in, Romney had new company in his camp; he was the first
candidate to be offered Secret Service protection. While this made logistics
more difficult at times, it offered the benefit of helping him look presidential.
Gingrich, on the other hand, began to show evidence of suffering from his
campaign's lack of organization; spokesman R. C. Hammond acknowledged
after his Florida loss that "Newt hasn't started thinking about Nevada yet."[38]
While it was mostly a symbolic triumph, Romney won 50 percent of the
Nevada vote. He hoped this would bolster confidence in his candidacy
among Republicans questioning his viability and that this would be the first
of a series of victories launching him to the nomination.

Romney's plans were thwarted, however, when voters met in Missouri,
Colorado, and Minnesota just three days later. Santorum convincingly swept
all three states, winning by double-digit margins across the board. While the
Missouri primary was only a beauty contest and thus no delegates were
earned, Santorum's wins were framed as a decisive rebuke to Romney. Since
his Iowa victory, Santorum had not placed above third or earned more than
17 percent of the vote. With his candidacy considered dead in the water, his
three victories were "an unexpected trifecta that raised fresh questions about
Mitt Romney's ability to corral conservative support."[39] Santorum had won,
and won decisively, and he could no longer be discounted a no-hoper. The
implications were clear. So far, the nominating contests demonstrated Romney's "limitations as a candidate. [They have] raised questions about his
consistency and highlighted his tendency to say things that get him in trouble. It also has drawn attention to his challenge in connecting with voters in a
party that is coursing with populist activism."[40] While Romney came back to
win the Maine caucus on February 11, the month clearly had not gone as
planned.

ROMNEY'S UNCERTAIN TERRAIN

In the beginning of January, when Romney was looking like his eventual nomination was practically a done deal, his frames remained consistent from past months. He was characterized as a tepid frontrunner who had not yet managed to break through the 25 percent barrier in polling. His competitors framed him as timid and themselves as bold. Stories emphasized the methodical, meticulous nature of his campaign, continually noting that his team's organization far exceeded that of his rivals. When Romney's electability argument was undermined by his losses in Iowa and South Carolina, these same frames were used to try to make sense of and explain his sudden fall. Voters were just not excited by his candidacy.

In the wake of a bruising South Carolina loss, Romney did what he does best: sit down, sift through data, and strategize how to revive his campaign. While others might go by gut or emotion (a la Gingrich), Romney returned time and again to the lessons he learned doing case studies at Harvard Business School. Decisions would be driven by data, and risk management ruled the day. The resulting decision: Destroy the competition through a series of concentrated attacks. While this was framed as a continuation of the "methodical" frame, it also reinforced perceptions that the candidate was either incapable of or just not interested in relating to everyday people. Instead of finding opportunities and avenues to better reach and engage voters, Romney went on the attack. Romney did not give voters a reason to vote *for* him; instead, his strategy was to give them reasons to vote *against* his opponents. This was simply the next stage of his war of attrition.

During this period, more connections seemed to be drawn between Romney's campaign and his personal robotic campaign style, highlighting the work he had to do on the campaign trail to inject sentiment or humor into his campaign speeches. For example, the *New York Times* included an anecdote about Romney perfecting a particular bit in his stump speech. When he first tried out this line, connecting corn and the amber waves of grain, the crowd did not react at all. Eventually, he elicited "polite laughter." Finally, he "perfected his delivery. 'If corn qualifies as an amber wave of grain, we have it right here,' Mr. Romney said as the crowd applauded and cheered. Mr. Romney exulted: 'It does! It does!'"[41] While most public speakers work out the kinks of their material on the road, figuring out what works and what does not based on audience reaction, Romney was the rare candidate for whom this was newsworthy. Why? Because it fit into his extant frames: a candidate who was robotic and thus had to practice connecting with voters.

The risk of being framed as a candidate whose campaign is meticulously organized and managed is that it is especially notable when things go awry. For Team Romney, this often manifested in the candidate going off script and saying something that would immediately go viral—and not in a good way. In an early February interview with CNN, "'I'm not concerned about the very poor, because they have a safety net,' he said citing food stamps, housing vouchers, and Medicaid. He pledged to repair holes in that safety net 'if it needs repair.'"[42] This statement sparked a wave of criticism, with both Santorum and Gingrich regularly referring to this as evidence of Romney's limitations as a candidate. Commentators echoed this refrain, including CNN contributor Jack Cafferty: "For many, the bottom line is Romney just hasn't been able to connect. He's seen as out of touch, too scripted, even aloof. Think about the infamous $10,000 bet he tried to make during one of the debates or his recent comment he's not worried about the nation's very poor."[43] As this quote demonstrates, several of Romney's negative frames were now conflating into one overarching narrative: He was just too out of touch to be able to connect with voters. Romney continued to make statements that inadvertently reinforced this, reiterating he had no idea what it was like to really worry about money or employment: "Mitt Romney said today he likes firing people. He also tried to say that he somehow empathizes with people who have been fired because he worried about a pink slip at some point."[44]

This frame was reinforced by continual reminders of just how spectacularly wealthy the Romneys were, including revelations about their Swiss bank account and complex tax shelters that were legal, but not necessarily fair. Of particular note was the revelation that Romney only paid a tax rate of approximately 15 percent, far lower than what would be expected of someone with his healthy bank accounts. Unfortunately for Romney, this meant he put a face to arguments that the American tax system unfairly favored the wealthy. His continued refusal to release his tax returns meant each new revelation about his money engendered further speculation about what exactly he did not want the public to know. According to Republican strategist Ed Rogers, "He looks guilty. It's just going to be untenable for Romney to keep it up. . . . This new tax return issue is a new bumper sticker: 'Release them.' And a bumper sticker always beats an essay."[45] In part because of these issues and Romney's inability (or refusal) to deal with them, his opponents were able to make the "vulture capitalist" frame stick in South Carolina and, perhaps, beyond.

While Romney had attempted to keep a laser-like focus on the economy, the extended primary found him increasingly talking about social hot-button issues. Because Romney was perceived to be increasingly conservative to appeal to the evangelical and values voters, these often were used to reinforce the "flip-flopper" frame. For example, Romney's current and past positions on illegal immigration seemed to be at odds: "But this year does represent a hard right turn for Mitt Romney. . . . Mitt Romney used to speak favorably about the John McCain/Ted Kennedy bill to give a path to citizenship for undocumented immigrants. But now, no mercy—papers for the whole nation. Self-deportation."[46] The media consistently framed these shifts as driven by the need to beat back Gingrich and Santorum. Romney needed to attract conservative voters, and he was willing to go to the right to do so. While this raised concerns about Romney's ability to attract independent and moderate voters in the general election, it was perceived as necessary to win the nomination.

At the same time as Romney was thought to be moving to the right, Gingrich and Santorum busily were painting him as the "Massachusetts moderate." Beginning almost immediately after the Iowa caucuses ended, Gingrich attempted to paint himself as the "bold Reagan conservative versus Mitt Romney, whom he calls the timid Massachusetts moderate. This is clearly going to be the way that Newt Gingrich is going to wage the rest of this campaign. And I believe he can actually do Mitt Romney some damage with this."[47] As Gingrich carried on this line of attack, he soon "made a case against the 'radical' President Obama and the 'moderate' Mr. Romney, sometimes scarcely distinguishing between the two."[48] Even Huntsman questioned Romney's conservative credibility while he was still in the race. When asked by CNN's John King to pick an issue on which he could differentiate himself from Romney, Huntsman responded: "What is your core? You run for the Senate as a liberal. You run for governor as a moderate. You run for president as a conservative. People want to know who you were yesterday and what you're going to be tomorrow."[49]

To bolster his conservative credentials, Romney spent time in February meeting with evangelical and conservative thought leaders and influencers, hoping to sell them on his candidacy. He referred to himself as being "severely conservative" during the Conservative Political Action Conference (CPAC), a label that raised some eyebrows. Conservative activist Richard A. Viguerie, a Santorum supporter, "scoffed" at this, saying, "Romney has shown, once again, that he can mouth the words conservatives use, but he has no gut-level emotional connection with the conservative movement and its ideas and policies."[50] Romney's fight to be seen as a truly conservative candidate was framed as evidence of the GOP's shift to the right due to the influence of the Tea Party, particularly since he was considered the conservative alternative to moderate McCain in 2008.

While Romney continued to have difficulty connecting with conservative voters, he simultaneously continued to build up his endorsements from establishment Republicans. In just January and February, Romney racked up support from 2008 Republican nominee (and sitting senator) John McCain, Bush's ambassador to the United Nations John Bolton, and, in early February, Donald Trump. He also received support from five former U.S. ambassadors to the Vatican, a particularly notable endorsement because Romney, a Mormon, was running against two practicing Catholics. For these endorsers,

Romney still represented the party's best chance to defeat Obama. Much like the candidate himself, they opted for pragmatism over ideology.

This dynamic—pragmatism over ideology—began to even more clearly emerge during the January and February coverage. Romney was the pragmatic choice; even if he did not reflect core conservative values, he was the most electable in a general election when compared to ideologues like Gingrich and Santorum. Even prominent Tea Partiers, including former Delaware senatorial candidate Christine O'Donnell, used this line of argument. In a conversation with CNN's Suzanne Malveaux, O'Donnell made the pitch that Romney had the economic experience needed in a candidate. Malveaux responded, "I'm wondering if that actually trumps what a lot of people are talking about, this debate within your own party about conservatism here, because you've praised Michele Bachmann, Rick Santorum. . . . But in the end you went for the pragmatic choice of Romney here."[51]

This "pragmatism" frame also was useful as an alternate way to understand and explain Romney's policy shifts, as opposed to flip-flops indicative of a lack of conservative credibility. As governor of Massachusetts, Romney had to find ways to work with liberals in the Statehouse. According to Salon.com's Steve Kornacki, Romney's efforts against gay marriage when governor represented a turning point in his career: "What he tried to do for the first two years of his tenure was to be sort of the pragmatic Massachusetts governor. . . . That forced him to choose between being a national conservative and Massachusetts moderate."[52] While this frame did not clearly emerge until voting began, seeds were planted in an earlier discussion of Romney's time at Harvard Business School: "Nearly four decades ago at Harvard, Mr. Romney embraced an analytical, nonideological way of thinking, say former classmates and professors, one that both matched his own instincts and helped him succeed."[53]

For voters in the early part of 2012, the reasons for Romney's positions while governor of Massachusetts were immaterial. While Romney's pragmatism and ensuing electability made him appealing to some voters, others hungered for a candidate who best represented their own passionate conservatism. For many, this man was Rick Santorum.

SANTORUM: THE CONSERVATIVE ALTERNATIVE?

Santorum's momentum going into the Iowa caucuses was credited to both his hard work and the support of prominent evangelical leaders. When the race was (incorrectly) called for Romney, however, Santorum did not enjoy the bounce an Iowa victor might expect. Instead, he went on to perform poorly in New Hampshire and South Carolina, then missing Florida due to his daughter's illness. Santorum's surprising resurgence in Colorado, Missouri, and

Minnesota, however, launched him back into the spotlight. While his campaign was hindered by a lack of organization, including to get on ballots in some states or not qualifying for all delegate districts in others, this generally was framed as a result of his very late surge: He just did not have time to carefully build an infrastructure like Romney's, especially since Romney had been running for president for years.

As was the case with other conservative candidates, what Santorum lacked in preparation he more than made up for in energy. On Fox News, the *Washington Post*'s Nia-Malika Henderson pointed out that Santorum's statements are "red meat for the base. You go to these campaign events and you see people holding up signs that say, 'Don't believe the liberal media.' So he's very much being able to gin up some excitement in the base, and that's an edge that he, in fact, has and Romney doesn't."[54] His personal story and emotional retellings also appealed to conservatives, particularly tales of his daughter Isabella, "who has a fatal chromosomal disorder called Trisomy 18. Bella's struggle is the emotional undercurrent of his campaign and, for his supporters, has become inseparable from Mr. Santorum's appeal as a Christian conservative who opposes abortion."[55]

Wearing his trademark sweater vest, at this point Santorum was perceived to be a reasonable, measured alternative to the other firebrand conservatives, a shift from earlier frames. His Red, White & Blue super PAC ran a new television spot "calling him 'the one principled' Republican to stop President Barack Obama. The ad . . . comes as the former senator makes a push to re-establish himself as the conservative alternative to front-runner Mitt Romney."[56] This media honeymoon, however, quickly ended as Santorum's candidacy proved to have legs. Santorum's trifecta of victories in early February put a spotlight on him and his campaign.

Conservative media voices anticipated the difficulties Santorum would face once he underwent full-scale scrutiny. On Fox News's *O'Reilly Report*, Bill O'Reilly and guest Laura Ingraham discussed the challenges Santorum would face. According to O'Reilly, "Look, all I'm saying is what the prevailing wisdom is but you know the media is going to brand him as a troglodyte. . . . Here's Santorum, he's against women, he's against blacks, he's against everybody." Ingraham responded, "Well yes, well, if you buy into that narrative, then you pretty much can run—can run no mainstream conservative ever again."[57] To that point, the *Washington Post* noted, "Despite Santorum's momentum, Democrats see him as a significantly flawed candidate in a general election. They believe his politics, particularly on social issues, are too conservative for most swing voters."[58] Others, however, argued that Santorum was the candidate best suited to beat Obama since he could draw the clearest distinctions. As this argument went, Santorum "was the most electable Republican—the reason being as Ronald Reagan said . . .

conservatives win when they draw bright contrasts in bold . . . contrasts in bright pastels, bright colors. They don't win if they muddle the difference."[59]

True to O'Reilly's predictions, Santorum coverage often was framed "too conservative to get elected"; while values voters and evangelicals responded positively to his positions and rhetoric, Santorum was considered too conservative for mainstream America: "Privately, strategists in both parties predict huge problems for Santorum. A GOP strategist . . . predicted that Santorum would be 'eviscerated' by the Democrats in a general election. A Democrat who knows Santorum's record intimately . . . said Santorum would be 'a Martian to women in the suburbs.'"[60]

As coverage of Santorum grew, he increasingly was framed as an aggressive candidate—a campaign brawler who was not afraid of bareknuckle battles against his opponents. Looking back over his career, reporters noted, "People in both parties over the years have accused him of hotheaded name-calling, reliance on immature antics, and attempts to reduce politics to steel-cage matches between people cast as heroes or heels."[61] At varying times calling him brash, blunt, and belligerent, coverage of Santorum during this period evolved from fairly harmless to an aggressive campaign style befitting "a testy and self-righteous 'culture warrior,' cultivated over 16 years in Congress."[62] As the election wore on, this frame began to allude to Santorum as a bully, often noting his mocking tone and aggressive stances in relation to his competition.

Stories of his time as part of the House's "Gang of Seven," a group that included 2012 Speaker of the House John Boehner, began to be rehashed in an effort to reinforce his conservative credentials. Santorum's press secretary, Alice Stewart, claimed Santorum has always fought for these values: "He was a Tea Party before there even was a Tea Party. . . . He was one of the original—the Gang of Seven that fought excessive taxpayer abuses, doing away with the fraud that we saw with the congressional—the post office."[63] While Santorum and his team attempted to highlight his cutting waste and conservative activism while in Congress, Romney and others tried to frame him as the consummate Washington insider. Television spots from the Romney-affiliated super PAC Restore Our Future branded Santorum as "'a big spender' and 'Washington insider' for designating projects to win taxpayer funding through lawmakers' earmarks."[64] They also highlighted Santorum's post-Congress work with organizations for which he advocated while in office, often noting his close ties with lobbyists: "In 2006, Mr. Santorum led all federal candidates in contributions from lobbyists and their family members, taking in roughly $500,000, nearly 40 percent more than the next closest candidate."[65]

As Santorum and his positions became better known, he began to generate controversy. Comments comparing public schools to factories raised eyebrows, as did his position that he "favored income inequality because some people contribute more to society than others."[66] He had to spend days backtracking from a comment saying John F. Kennedy's speech advocating for a strict separation of church and state "made him want to 'throw up.'"[67] When asked about prenatal testing, Santorum claimed it "does, in fact, result more often than not, in this country, in abortion. That is a fact."[68] By February, a substantial gender gap had emerged among Santorum's supporters, indicating that some of Santorum's more controversial views might be pushing women voters away. Comments from his 2005 book "It Takes a Family" were raised, including the charge that "Radical feminists succeeded in undermining the traditional family and convincing women that professional accomplishments are the key to happiness."[69] While Santorum later claimed that his wife wrote this line (apparently in a noncredited coauthor role), he doubled down when George Stephanopolous asked who those radical feminists are: "It comes from an elite culture, dictated, again, from academia, dictated, again, from the Hollywood culture and the news media, that says, 'The only thing that's affirming, the only thing that really counts is what you do at work.'"[70]

As these quotes indicate, Santorum took pains to differentiate himself from the elite during this period, encompassing political, media, and academic elites. This criticism extended to the highest office: "President Obama once said, he wants everybody in America to go to college. What a snob. There are good, decent, men and women who go out and work hard every day and put their skills to task that aren't taught by some liberal college professor and trying to indoctrinate them."[71]

GINGRICH: HIS OWN WORST ENEMY

If Santorum was suspicious of college professors, Gingrich continued to channel his inner academic during this period. He peppered his speeches and appearances with historical references intended to add credibility to his campaign. Unfortunately, he also was framed as embodying the downside of academic life: the absent-minded professor. Gingrich's campaign was thought to be in disarray, often characterized as being the product of last-minute decisions and insufficient planning: "A few days before the Iowa caucuses, Newt Gingrich's campaign headquarters just outside the city is a spectacle of pre-computer-age disorder, with volunteers rushing voter updates across the room on yellow Post-It notes."[72] This characterization often was compared negatively to Romney's methodical, efficient, focused campaign machine.

Framing him as a candidate flying by the seat of his pants, media were quick to note when Gingrich's team suffered a mishap, including a missed meeting with "wildly popular" Nevada governor Brian Sandoval in early

February. Coverage noted that Gingrich often was late to arrive, keeping supporters—and journalists—waiting: "But as you can see, there has been a lot of confusion, quite frankly, within the campaign tonight in terms of what he is going to be talking about and . . . where he is going to be appearing. . . . It's been a bit of a rocky road."[73] This lack of organization reinforced the frame that Gingrich lacked discipline.

Gingrich continued to be his own worst enemy in the campaign process. Poorly stated positions dominated headlines and generated controversy. His battle to keep "Nice Newt" in the forefront crumbled when goaded by his competitors. Instead of spending his limited time between primaries, caucuses, and debates giving speeches and meeting with voters, Gingrich had to step off the campaign trail at this pivotal point to raise funds instead. Even when his campaign was going well in South Carolina, Gingrich's personal life threatened to stop his candidacy in its tracks when his second ex-wife, Marianne, brought back up her accusations that Gingrich had asked for an open marriage. While Gingrich strenuously denied this, it reminded the evangelical voters he needed that he had a checkered personal past.

Gingrich's difficulties often were chalked up to his decision to run his own campaign, his own way. Gingrich made most of his own decisions, and served as his own strategist and media-messaging expert. This reinforced that Gingrich often demonstrated brilliant political instincts. While his campaign was on a rollercoaster adventure, his seemingly endless ability to get off the mat after being considered down for the count was laudable. Clearly, Gingrich knew how to connect with voters; the open question was whether he could maintain control of his ego and temper long enough to build his campaign. Based on coverage during this period, this seemed unlikely—but he would provide good theater: "But even as Mr. Gingrich becomes something of a bit player, he remains arguably the most provocative personality in the race, one whose flights of bombast, vitriol, and cutting wit regularly inject some psychodrama into the contest."[74]

After sizable losses in almost all of the January voting states, media and political observers questioned why Gingrich remained in the race. He had little money and even less chance of winning the nomination through the popular vote. As Santorum began to gain momentum after his three-state victory, calls rang out for Gingrich to step away from the race to help a non-Romney candidate succeed. While some were subtle, others were not; the conservative National Review Online said it would be "a mistake for Republican voters to nominate someone with 'such poor judgment and persistent unpopularity' to be the party's standard bearer."[75] As *New York Daily News* columnist Andrea Tantaros noted on Fox News, "I can see why the conservative media is making the argument. The longer Gingrich stays in, that helps Romney's chances who has not been a favorite of conservative media."[76]

While Gingrich himself was short on cash, he had a super PAC sugar daddy in Las Vegas casino owner Sheldon Adelson, who donated a massive sum to the coffers of Winning Our Future, the Gingrich-affiliated super PAC. This donation was used to spark discussion about the undue influence of super PACs during this primary season, particularly as the funds were used to create and air overwhelmingly negative advertising: "Then as you point out, Mr. Adelson gives Newt Gingrich $5 million—gives his super PAC $5 million. What does the super PAC do? It buys this really vicious 27-minute documentary that was created by someone solely for the purpose of selling it to a super PAC."[77] As media noted, Adelson's donation was 1,000 times the $5,000 he could legally give to Gingrich himself. By the end of this period, Adelson and his wife had donated $15 million to Gingrich's super PAC.

PAUL: LOOKING FOR LEVERAGE

If Gingrich relied on donations from one massive donor to stay afloat, Paul embraced the polar opposite by relying on dedicated, passionate supporters to keep him in the mix. While Paul had finished a relatively close third in Iowa, he had not managed to parlay that support into any real momentum. By the end of the opening electoral period, it seemed clear that Paul was no longer seeking the White House; instead, he wanted to gain leverage in order to better inform and influence the Republican platform: "At stake for Mr. Paul in these caucuses and primaries is not the Republican nomination but whether his support structure will finally grow . . . to a movement with the leverage to dictate policy and platform changes to the national Republican Party and its nominee."[78]

To do this, Paul took advantage of the new Republican delegate allocation system to focus on winning at least some delegates in each state; as long as he stayed in, Paul had a chance to become an influencer at the GOP's August convention. This also allowed him to demonstrate his pull among his voters—something many Republicans found a bit threatening: "Ron Paul has drawn continual speculation he'll run as a third-party candidate should he fail to win the Republican presidential nomination. The Texas congressman has said repeatedly he has no interest in doing so, but pundits note that he hasn't flatly ruled it out."[79]

As pundits questioned Paul's endgame, a new line of speculation emerged: He was staying in to help Romney. After years on the campaign trail together their families had become friendly, and their friendly banter at first seemed innocuous. In late February, however, Santorum accused the two of collusion. As Katharine Q. Seelye wrote in the *New York Times*, "Rumors of an alliance between Mr. Romney and Mr. Paul have simmered since it became evident that they were not attacking each other at the debates and that Mr. Paul was aiming his fire at whatever candidate had been threatening Mr. Romney."[80]

While Romney's advisers wrote this off as nothing more than "whining silliness" from the Santorum campaign, the story took hold. When Romney went on Fox News to address the accusations, Neil Cavuto addressed the suspected "subterfuge": "The latest that gets tongues wagging is the relationship you [have] with Congressman Ron Paul. Many make a big deal of the fact that you two don't throw too many darts at one another."[81] Romney explained that the two were friendly, but pointed out: "No one is going to tell Ron Paul what to say. This is a guy who says whatever he wants to say."[82] Others, however, believed there was more going on, and speculation abounded that the two candidates had struck a deal that Paul's help in the nominating contest would result in his son, Senator Rand Paul of Kentucky, being named to the Romney ticket as vice-president. While Paul's honesty generally was considered above reproach, this fit nicely into the frame that Romney would do anything it took to win.

ARIZONA AND MICHIGAN: ROMNEY'S RESURGENCE?

In the wake of this chaotic period, a slow middle of February offered a welcome respite from the election. The campaigns regrouped before meeting once more in Mesa, Arizona, for a debate hosted by CNN and the Arizona Republican Party. In the wake of a tumultuous January and early February, a lot was riding on this event: "It's fair to say it's make or break for everybody. And it is, of course, just six days before Michigan and Arizona's primary."[83] Romney and Santorum dueled throughout, with Romney attempting to define Santorum as a Washington insider who had been part of the problem and thus could not be part of the solution. No longer would he allow Santorum to carve out ground as a true conservative unchecked; instead, Santorum would experience the heightened attention and scrutiny that went part and parcel with being a frontrunner. Unwilling to concede the spotlight without a fight, Gingrich went back to his wheelhouse and attacked the media.

The Mesa debate was a prelude to the last two primaries that month: Arizona and Michigan, both held on February 28. While Arizona was expected to be an easy victory for Romney, he was surprised to find himself in a Michigan dogfight—a state considered essential to Romney regaining control of the race. Despite his status as a native son and political scion, Romney faced a significant challenge from Santorum. To fend him off, Romney and his super PAC launched an all-out assault on Santorum's conservative credentials, linking him to the billions of dollars in earmarks he had supported while in the Senate. By the middle of the month, Santorum's super PAC started running ads in Michigan attacking Romney in return. In an effort to deflect the negative attacks, Romney created his own spot called "Growing Up," featuring him driving a car and reminiscing about growing up in Detroit. Unfortunately, this feel-good nostalgia was dampened by steady reminders about Romney's 2008 *New York Times* op-ed piece headlined "Let Detroit Go Bankrupt." Romney furthered perceptions that his vast wealth made him out of touch with middle America with a series of statements that indicated he "had a tin ear, that he continues to say things like, you know, 'I don't really follow NASCAR, but I know the guys who run it,' and 'My wife has two Cadillacs' and 'Nice poncho. You really spent a lot of money on that.'"[84]

Romney was not alone in courting negative attention. Santorum invited controversy when his campaign launched robocalls across Michigan that invited Democrats to take part in the state's open primary. This did not go over well with his competitors: "The unusual tactic . . . drew an angry rebuke from Mr. Romney. He called it a 'dirty trick' in a television interview and returned to the topic during a press conference with reporters," calling it a "'real effort to kidnap our primary process.'"[85] Romney eked out a Michigan victory, although it was closer than he would have liked. For his part, Santorum considered it a victory that he had made Michigan—Romney's home state—competitive. Coupled with a resounding victory in Arizona, Romney hoped this would be enough to launch a successful campaign into early March's Super Tuesday.

By this point, candidates and their advisers were sending clear messages to donors: They needed to hunker down for a long, drawn-out, hard-hitting campaign. Money would be needed to help define the opposition and defend themselves against attacks. Delegate math would ultimately determine the nominee; some were beginning to speculate about a brokered convention.[86] As February drew to a close, these first two months of voting could be summed up as such for Mitt Romney: "After 5 caucuses, 6 primaries, 20 debates and $30 million in television commercials, [he faces] the same stubborn question: Can a onetime Northeastern governor with a history of ideological migration win the Republican presidential nomination in the era of the Tea Party, with all its demands of political purity and passion?"[87]

NOTES

1. Chris Wallace, Carl Cameron, and Bret Baier, "Candidates Prepare for the Iowa Caucuses; Interview with Republican Presidential Candidate Texas Representative Ron Paul; Interview with Republican Presidential Candidate Minnesota Representative Michele Bachmann; Interview with Republican Presidential Candidate Texas Governor Rick Perry; Interview with Iowa Republican Governor Terry Branstad," *Fox News Network: Fox News Sunday*, January 1, 2012, LexisNexis Academic.

2. Jeff Zeleny, Jim Rutenberg, Katharine Q. Seelye, Trip Gabriel, and Susan Saulny, "Last-Minute Scramble as Caucus Night Nears," *New York Times*, January 1, 2012, National Desk, Factiva.

3. Huntsman had focused his strategy on a strong New Hampshire performance and thus was not actively campaigning in Iowa during this period.

4. Andrea Mitchell, "For January 2, 2012," *MSNBC: MSNBC Special*, January 2, 2012, LexisNexis Academic.

5. Megyn Kelly, Bret Baier, Bill Hemmer, Mike Huckabee, John Roberts, and Brit Hume, "Caucus Night—Fox 2030 Half Hour," *Fox News Network: Live Event*, January 3, 2012, LexisNexis Academic.

6. Rachel Maddow, Al Sharpton, Lawrence O'Donnell, Ed Shultz, Chris Matthews, and Kelly O'Donnell, "MSNBC Coverage of the Iowa Republican Caucuses 0000 Hour; MSNBC," *MSNBC: MSNBC Special*, January 4, 2012, LexisNexis Academic.

7. Jim Rutenberg and Sam Tanenhaus, "For Divided G.O.P., Signs of a Long Road to November," *New York Times*, January 4, 2012, National Desk, Factiva.

8. Sean Hannity, "Interview with Sarah Palin," *Fox News Network: Hannity*, January 4, 2012, LexisNexis.

9. Wolf Blitzer, Jack Cafferty, Will Cain, Lisa Sylvester, Mary Snow, Gloria Borger, Jeanne Moos, Jim Acosta, Brian Todd, and Dana Bash, "Obama Appoints Consumer Watchdog, Defying Senate Republicans; Analysis of Iowa Caucuses; South Carolina: We Pick Winners; No Perfect GOP Candidate," *CNN: The Situation Room*, January 4, 2012, LexisNexis Academic.

10. Dan Balz, "Romney: Still Strong, Still Unable to Shake Doubts," *Washington Post*, January 9, 2012, A-Section, Factiva.

11. Soledad O'Brien, Ron Brownstein, and Christine Romans, "Huntsman Endorsed by 'Boston Globe'; Interview with Eric Fehrnstrom, Mitt Romney's Top Guy; New Hampshire Voters Speak; For Sushi and Country; What's in Store for Your Money?; Candidates Pin Hopes on South Carolina; Video Message Made by Casey Anthony; Cornell High Basketball Video Shows Officials Not Calling Fouls," *CNN: Starting Point with Soledad O'Brien*, January 4, 2012, LexisNexis Academic.

12. Candy Crowley, "Interview with Jon Huntsman; Interview with Bob Walker, John Sununu; Interview with Nancy Pelosi," *CNN: State of the Union with Candy Crowley*, January 8, 2012, LexisNexis Academic.

13. Wolf Blitzer, Dan Rivers, Ted Rowlands, Lisa Sylvester, Jack Cafferty, Gloria Borger, Joe Johns, Brian Todd, and Jeanne Moos, "Two Americans Still Missing From Cruise Ship Crash; Gingrich Urges Santorum, Perry To Drop Out; Rick Perry Interview; Salvage or Scrap Costa Concordia?; Perry Stands By Controversial Turkey Comment," *CNN: The Situation Room*, January 17, 2012, LexisNexis Academic.

14. Bret Baier, Megyn Kelly, and Brit Hume, "Caucus Night—Fox 2230 Half Hour," *Fox News Network: Live Event*, January 3, 2012, LexisNexis Academic.

15. Bill O'Reilly, "Talking Points Memo and Top Story," *Fox News Network: The O'Reilly Factor*, January 11, 2012, LexisNexis Academic.

16. Rachel Maddow, Chris Matthews, Tom Brokaw, Chuck Todd, and Howard Fineman, "New Hampshire Primary Coverage 2200 Hour," *MSNBC: MSNBC Special*, January 10, 2012, LexisNexis Academic.

17. O'Reilly, "Talking Points Memo."

18. Trip Gabriel and Nicholas Confessore, "PAC Ads to Hit Romney's Role at Equity Firm," *New York Times*, January 9, 2012, National Desk, Factiva.

19. Neil King Jr., Brody Mullins, and Danny Yadron, "Romney Lashes Back on Bain—As Campaign Moves to South Carolina, GOP Split Over Attacks on Private Equity," *Wall Street Journal*, January 12, 2012, A5, Factiva.

20. Jeff Zeleny, "Certainty Fades as Romney Falters," *New York Times*, January 22, 2012, National Desk, Factiva.

21. Philip Rucker, "Romney Takes Tough Tone in Face of Defeat," *Washington Post*, January 22, 2012, A-Section, Factiva.

22. Ed Lavandera, Chris Lawrence, Gloria Borger, Jim Acosta, John King, Ed Lavandera, Dana Bash and Kate Bolduan, "Exclusive Reports from Syria, Yemen; President Takes Personal Role in Debt Ceiling Negotiation; Rep. Bachmann Enters Presidential Race," *CNN: John King*, January 5, 2012, LexisNexis Academic.

23. Ibid.

24. Ed Schultz and Eugene Robinson, "The Ed Show for January 5, 2012," *MSNBC: The Ed Show with Ed Schultz*, January 5, 2012, LexisNexis Academic.

25. Sandhya Somashekhar, "Some See Racial Tinge to Gingrich Remarks," *Washington Post*, January 18, 2012, A-Section, Factiva.

26. Schultz and Robinson, "January 5, 2012."

27. Ed Larendera, Chris Lawrence, Gloria Berger, Jim Acosta, Jon King, Dana Bash, and Kate Bolduan, "Interview with Presidential Candidate Jon Huntsman; U.S. Citizens Deported By Mistake." CNN: John King, USA, January 5, 2012, LexisNexis Academic.

28. Ed Schultz and E. J. Dionne, "The Ed Show for January 9, 2012," *MSNBC: The Ed Show with Ed Schultz*, January 9, 2012, LexisNexis Academic.

29. Jeff Zeleny and Jim Rutenberg, "Romney Unleashes Attack with Gingrich Sole Target: Sharp Exchanges—Ex-Speaker Sees Desperate Ploy," *New York Times*, January 24, 2012, National Desk, Factiva.

30. Fredricka Whitfield, Joe Johns, Wolf Blitzer, and John King, "Cain Endorses Gingrich; Debates Place in Campaigns; Latest from the Campaigns in Florida," *CNN: CNN Newsroom*, January 29, 2012, LexisNexis Academic.

31. Ibid.

32. Jeremy W. Peters, "Going Negative: In Florida, a Sea of Attack Ads," *New York Times*, February 1, 2012, National Desk, Factiva.

33. Chris Wallace, "Interview with Newt Gingrich," *Fox News Network: Fox News Sunday*, January 29, 2012, LexisNexis Academic.

34. Bill O'Reilly, "Interview with Rick Santorum," *Fox News Network: The O'Reilly Factor*, January 30, 2012, LexisNexis Academic.

35. Ibid.

36. Michael D. Shear, "Romney Embraces Attack Style against Gingrich," *New York Times*, January 26, 2012, National Desk, Factiva.

37. Dan Balz, "Romney Rebounds with Florida Victory," *Washington Post*, February 1, 2012, A-Section, Factiva.

38. Amy Gardner, "Gingrich Counting on Delegate Math," *Washington Post*, February 6, 2012, A-Section, Factiva.

39. Jim Rutenberg, Jeff Zeleny, Richard A. Oppel Jr., and Malcolm Gay, "Another Twist for G.O.P. as Santorum Fares Well," *New York Times*, February 8, 2012, National Desk, Factiva.

40. Jeff Zeleny, Kirk Johnson, Ashley Parker, and Jim Rutenberg, "Romney Faces Rebels on the Right and Softness in the Middle," *New York Times*, February 9, 2012, National Desk, Factiva.

41. Ashley Parker, "Romney Quotes His Favorite Patriotic Songs and Offers Voters an Interpretation," *New York Times*, January 1, 2012, National Desk, Factiva.

42. Philip Rucker, Amy Gardner, and Rosalind S. Helderman, "Romney Rides His Fla. Win to Nevada," *Washington Post*, February 2, 2012, A-Section, Factiva.

43. Wolf Blitzer, Ivan Watson, Brian Todd, Jack Cafferty, Barbara Starr, Jessica Yellin, Dana Bash, Jim Acosta, John Zarrella, and Jeanne Moos, "Al-Assad 'Is Killing Children'; Slaughter 'Too Shocking to Ignore'; Iran's Role in Syria Crackdown; Stunning Images of Syria Under Siege; Big Pentagon Move Puts Women Closer to Combat; Mortgage Deal Could Bring Billions in Relief; Deep Space Health Problem; FBI File Reveals Gripping Details of Steve Jobs' Life," *CNN: The Situation Room, February 9, 2012, LexisNexis Academic.*

44. Lawrence O'Donnell, Chris Matthews, Chuck Todd, Andrea Mitchell, and John Heilemann, "The Last Word for January 9, 2012," *MSNBC: The Last Word with Lawrence O'Donnell*, January 9, 2012, LexisNexis Academic.

45. Phillip Rucker and Dan Balz, "Romney Faces Mounting Pressure to Release Tax Returns Sooner," *Washington Post*, January 19, 2012, A-Section, Factiva.

46. Rachel Maddow, "The Rachel Maddow Show for February 23, 2012," *MSNBC: The Rachel Maddow Show*, February 23, 2012, LexisNexis Academic.

47. Anderson Cooper, Wolf Blitzer, John King, Erin Burnett, Candy Crowley, Gloria Borger, and David Gergen, "Ron Paul to Finish Third in Iowa; Gingrich to Place 4th in Iowa," *CNN: CNN Live Event/Special*, January 3, 2012, LexisNexis Academic.

48. Trip Gabriel, "Advertising: Gingrich Takes a Harsher Tone," *New York Times*, January 6, 2012, National Desk, Factiva.

49. Ed Lavandera, Chris Lawrence, Gloria Borger, Jim Acosta, John King, Dana Bash, and Kate Bolduan, "Interview with Presidential Candidate Jon Huntsman; U.S. Citizens Deported by Mistake," *CNN: John King, USA*, January 5, 2012, LexisNexis Academic.

50. Rosalind S. Helderman and Felicia Sonmez, "Romney Edges Paul in Maine Caucuses," *Washington Post*, February 12, 2012, A-Section, Factiva.

51. Suzanne Malveaux, Dana Bash, John King, Alison Kosik, Dan Lothian, David Mattingly, Christine Romans, and Wolf Blitzer, "Michele Bachmann Suspends Presidential Campaign; Rick Perry Remains in Presidential Race; A Look at the Close Results in the Iowa Caucus; Where GOP Candidates Stand on Social Security; GOP Candidates Gear up for New Hampshire Primary; 2012 Could Be Good Year for Those Seeking Work; Republican Presidential Candidates Off to New Hampshire; Looking Ahead to South Carolina; Interview with Christine O'Donnell; O'Donnell Endorses Romney; McCain Set to Endorse Romney," *CNN: CNN Newsroom*, January 4, 2012, LexisNexis Academic.

52. Chris Hayes, Melissa Harris-Perry, Garrett Haake, and Anthony Terrell, "Maine Caucuses Coverage—1730 Half Hour," *MSNBC: MSNBC Special*, February 11, 2012, LexisNexis Academic.

53. Jodi Kantor, "At Harvard, a Master's in Problem Solving," *New York Times*, December 25, 2011, National Desk, Factiva.

54. Greta Van Susteren, "GOP Race for Presidential Nomination Still Up in the Air; Super-PACs Raise and Spend Millions; Interview with Rep. Michele Bachmann; Gasoline Prices and the 2012 Election," *Fox News Network: Fox on the Record with Greta Van Susteren*, February 21, 2012, LexisNexis.

55. Manny Fernandez, "Santorum Adjusting to Star Treatment on Trail," *New York Times*, February 10, 2012, National Desk, Factiva.

56. Danny Yadron, Patrick O'Connor, and Janet Adamy, "Election 2012: Campaign Watch," *Wall Street Journal*, February 2, 2012, A5, Factiva.

57. Bill O'Reilly, "Impact," *Fox News Network: The O'Reilly Factor*, February 14, 2012, LexisNexis Academic.

58. Sandhya Somashekhar, "Santorum Appears on Obama's Radar," *Washington Post*, February 18, 2012, A-Section, Factiva.

59. Rachel Maddow and Dave Weigel, "The Rachel Maddow Show for February 10, 2012," *MSNBC: The Rachel Maddow Show*, February 10, 2012, LexisNexis Academic.

60. Dan Balz, "A Race to Define Rick Santorum," *Washington Post*, February 19, 2012, A-Section, Factiva.

61. Mark Leibovich, "The Santorum of 2012 Comes From a Long History of Political Brawling," *New York Times*, January 7, 2012, National Desk, Factiva.

62. Sandhya Somashekhar, "Fine-tuning Santorum," *Washington Post*, February 12, 2012, A-Section, Factiva.

63. Andrea Mitchell, "Interview with Alice Stewart," *MSNBC: MSNBC Special*, February 15, 2012, LexisNexis Academic.

64. Danny Yadron and Patrick O'Connor, "Election 2012: Santorum to Face Romney Ad Blitz," *Wall Street Journal*, February 16, 2012, A5, Factiva.

65. Mike McIntire and Michael Luo, "When Santorum Left the Senate, Familiar Hands Reached Out," *New York Times*, January 6, 2012, National Desk, Factiva.

66. Richard A. Oppel Jr., Jeremy W. Peters, and Ashley Parker, "In Detroit, Santorum Defends Opposition to Auto Industry Bailout," *New York Times*, February 17, 2012, National Desk, Factiva.

67. Nia-Malika Henderson, "A Santorum Barrage in the Culture Wars," *Washington Post*, February 27, 2012, A-Section, Factiva.

68. Erin Burnett, Ari Fleischer, John Avlon, Paul Callan, Gloria Borger, Erick Erickson, James Carville, and Wolf Blitzer, "CNN GOP Debate; Interview with Cindy McCain; UVA Verdict," *CNN: Erin Burnett OutFront*, February 22, 2012, LexisNexis Academic.

69. Balz, "A Race to Define."

70. Brian Knowlton and Katharine Q. Seelye, "Santorum Is Questioned on Criticism of Feminists," *New York Times*, February 13, 2012, National Desk, Factiva.

71. Bret Baier, Martha MacCallum, Carl Cameron, Ed Henry, Mike Tobin, John Roberts, and James Rosen, "Political Headlines," *Fox News Network: Fox Special Report with Bret Baier*, February 28, 2012, LexisNexis Academic.

72. A. G. Sulzberger and Michael Barbaro, "Over Phones and Greasy Pizza, a Battle for Iowa," *New York Times*, January 1, 2012, National Desk, Factiva.

73. Bret Baier, Casey Stegall, John Roberts, and James Rosen, "Nevada Caucuses Coverage—2300 Hour; Newt Gingrich Press Conference," *Fox News Network: Fox Special Report with Bret Baier*, February 4, 2012, LexisNexis Academic.

74. Trip Gabriel, "Professorial Gingrich Shows What He Knows on the Road," *New York Times*, February 10, 2012, National Desk, Factiva.

75. Michael D. Shear, "A Conservative Call for Gingrich's Exit," *New York Times*, February 14, 2012, National Desk, Factiva.

76. Jon Scott, Jim Pinkerton, Judy Miller, Kirsten Powers, and Andrea Tantaros, "Fox News Watch for February 18, 2012," *Fox News Network: Fox News Watch*, February 18, 2012, LexisNexis Academic.

77. Chris Matthews, Ted Koppel, Milissa Rehberger, Howard Fineman, and Michael Steele, "For January 16, 2012," *MSNBC: Hardball*, January 16, 2012, LexisNexis Academic.

78. Richard A. Oppel Jr., "Among These Republicans, Paul Supporters Go from Outsiders to Vanguard," *New York Times*, February 2, 2012, National Desk, Factiva.

79. Joel Millman and Naftali Bendavid, "Campaign Journal—On the Stump: Paul Still in GOP; Tea-Party PAC Steps into House Race," *Wall Street Journal*, February 11, 2012, A5, Factiva.

80. Katharine Q. Seelye and Michael Barbaro, "Santorum Vows to Wage A Long, Fierce Battle," *New York Times*, February 26, 2012, National Desk, Factiva.

81. Bret Baier and Shannon Bream, "Fox News All-Stars," *Fox News Network: Fox Special Report with Brett Baier*, February 28, 2012, LexisNexis Academic.

82. Ibid.

83. Soledad O'Brien, Michael Holmes, Christine Romans, and Kyra Phillips, "Western Journalists Killed in Syria; Interview with Former Congressman J. D. Hayworth; Obama Corporate Tax Plan Revealed; Interview with Jon Huntsman's Daughters; New Clinton Documentary; Overturning Race Ruling," *CNN: Starting Point with Soledad O'Brien*, February 22, 2012, LexisNexis Academic.

84. Bill O'Reilly and Ann Coulter, "Is GOP Imploding?" *Fox News Network: The O'Reilly Factor*, February 29, 2012, LexisNexis Academic.

85. Michael Barbaro, Ashley Parker, Katharine Q. Seelye, Trip Gabriel, and Steven Yaccino, "Romney Admits Mistakes as Michigan Votes in Crucial Primary," *New York Times*, February 29, 2012, National Desk, Factiva.

86. If no candidate managed to earn the minimum number of delegates, the nominee could be decided during the convention. This is extremely rare in modern American electoral politics.

87. Jim Rutenberg, "Amid Victory, Echo of Doubt," *New York Times*, February 29, 2012, National Desk, Factiva.

Chapter Seven

Last Man Standing

March–April 2012

While four candidates were still officially in the race, by March it was clearly a two-man contest: Romney, the longtime frontrunner who had difficulty gaining real traction among voters, versus Santorum, the impassioned conservative who excited values voters but struck fear in the hearts of establishment Republicans who considered him unelectable. The two boiled down to what was becoming a powerful explanatory frame in the 2012 Republican primaries—pragmatism versus ideology. This frame worked for both understanding motivations among the electorate (pragmatists voted for Romney because he was the most electable, while those preferring Santorum believed he had a true commitment to their shared ideological values) as well as the two as political figures themselves. At this point, Romney's hope for a quick, decisive victory was a distant memory. Pundits and political observers now recognized that candidates were in for a state-by-state slog. MSNBC's Rachel Maddow credited Howard Fineman with having "coined the new term for how to think about this race. It is the big queasy. It's a big important race that's taking forever and that mostly just reflects unease."[1]

Coming out of Michigan's important primary, there was a real sense that this nominating contest could extend through the summer. Romney had eked out a victory, but the post-election narrative noted that he and his super PAC had vastly outspent Santorum—even though Michigan, as Romney's home state, should have been an easy win. At the same time, media coverage emphasized that he had avoided disaster. A loss in Michigan could have been a death knell for Romney and his candidacy, reinforcing concerns that he was unable to win in Rust Belt states because he could not win the approval of conservatives. At the same time, media framed the outcome as a missed opportunity for Santorum: "Michigan was Mr. Santorum's best shot at delivering a fatal blow to Mr. Romney. . . . Yet Mr. Santorum couldn't beat Mr. Romney mano-a-mano."[2]

A DELEGATE STRATEGY

With neither Romney nor Santorum delivering a decisive blow in Michigan, the campaigns looked to Super Tuesday as the next, best opportunity to make their cases to voters. There was widespread recognition that at this point the race had changed: "The first phase of the 2012 Republican presidential campaign, ending with the 10 states that vote . . . on Super Tuesday, has been about money and message. The next several months will be about maps and math."[3] With this revised framing came increasing recognition that Romney's vastly superior organization—a powerful, sizable force that he had been building and maintaining since 2007—would give him an advantage. Thanks to this, he could continue to win a war of attrition, outlasting his opponents through the sheer scope and scale of his campaign organization.

While Romney had not managed to capture the hearts of the Republican electorate and thus might not win the popular vote, he was a good bet to win the 1,144 delegates needed to earn the nomination. Of the three other candidates still in the race, only Paul had a similar level of organization at his disposal. Santorum and Gingrich, both considered no-hopers for much of the build-up to January voting, had failed to qualify for the ballot entirely in some states and only partially in others. This meant Romney could pick up delegates in key states, even if he did not win outright.

This delegate-focused approach to the nominating contest meant that the remaining candidates had to spend their time and money—both in short commodity at this point in the race—strategically campaigning in multiple states. Advertising continued to be a major factor, and campaigns were running spots in Ohio as early as February. Producing ads and buying time were expensive ventures, however, and this meant super PACs continued to play an essential role. In Ohio alone, Romney and his super PAC committed $3.4 million in advertising; Santorum and his supporters accounted for another half-million. While they were expensive, these spots were candidates' best way to define their opposition to the electorate and maximize their own chances to win. During the last ten days before Super Tuesday, campaigns spent almost $10 million across the board, and "about half of it came from Mitt Romney's campaign in the super PAC that supports him. . . . Yes, they are confident."[4]

During this period, media began to discuss more explicitly the potential implications of the increasingly narrow ideology of the Republican Party. This political homogeneity meant the candidates all fundamentally agreed, so they were forced to create contrasts where few actually existed. Some feared this could spell disaster in the general election, since "the uniformity of views this year—forcing candidates to distinguish themselves by showing rigid fealty to conservative ideology—strikes some veteran Republicans as misguided and electorally dangerous."[5] In the same *New York Times* article, Harwood writes, "This is the presidential primary campaign that political polarization has wrought. . . . As a result, the first Republican presidential primary in the Tea Party era lacks the straightforward ideological cleavages of earlier contests."[6]

This began to generate concern among seasoned Republican veterans that Romney, the likely eventual nominee, would be pushed so far to the right that it would hurt his chances in November. To win the approval of the conservative base, Romney had moved away from his earlier laser-like focus on the economy and instead was swept up in a firestorm of flashpoint social issues. The contest he had already described as a battle for the soul of the GOP was now a full-blown civil war. Would the Republican Party maintain its traditional positions, or would the Tea Party and its impassioned voters come to dominate the party's platform?

Supporters on either side claimed that a victory for the other group meant a loss in the general election. While Romney had thus far been winning on perceived electability against Obama, Santorum and Gingrich were offering a new argument: When Republicans nominate a moderate, they lose, since those moderate candidates cannot excite conservatives enough to get to the polls on Election Day. They also bucked against the assumption that Romney was a sure bet to win the nomination. As Santorum fumed, "What won't they resort to, to try to bully their way through this race, you know? If the govern-or thinks he's—you know, he's now ordained by God to win, then let's—let's just have it out."[7] He then reinforced the narrative that Romney's campaign was a machine prepared for battle, commenting, "We're running a race, energizing people, the man versus the machine. And you know, they got the machine and they got the—they got the—you know, the insiders and the—and the big money, and we've got the people."[8]

BUILD-UP TO SUPER TUESDAY

Within this context, the candidates and their campaigns began the push toward Super Tuesday, a one-day voting extravaganza on March 6 in which ten geographically diverse states simultaneously held their primaries. Of these, Ohio was considered the real prize. It not only was a must-win state for the general election; Ohio also was Romney's chance to prove his ability to win in the Rust Belt outside of his home state, and a prime opportunity for Santorum to permanently undermine his opponent's electability argument.

Furthermore, Santorum increasingly was attempting to make the case that he could beat Obama in November precisely because of his appeal to blue-collar voters in swing states, citing his Pennsylvania roots as evidence of his credibility with this population.

In the days leading up to Super Tuesday, Ohio polls indicated that the race would be quite close. Continuing his focus on solidifying support among the Republican establishment, Romney boasted considerable support from prominent Ohio politicians, including Senator Rob Portman and former senator George V. Voinovich. Romney felt confident about his chances in the Midwestern state. According to CNN's Jim Acosta, "They are feeling the big mo' in Ohio. You heard Governor Romney . . . say if he could win Ohio, he feels he could win the GOP nomination. This is not something you send a candidate out to say on the day before Super Tuesday unless you're feeling pretty good."[9]

Romney experienced a rare establishment rejection, however, when former senator and current Ohio Attorney General Mike DeWine rescinded his endorsement and shifted his loyalty to Santorum. DeWine was an outspoken and enthusiastic surrogate for the candidate, advocating for him across the state and in the media. DeWine framed Ohio as a battle between momentum and money: "What you really have in Ohio in the last several weeks is tremendous energy behind Rick Santorum and a lot of money behind Governor Romney. It's the most massive amount of money that's ever been spent in Ohio in a short time by one candidate."[10] Even with that boost, Santorum faced an uphill battle on Super Tuesday after being "outspent and out organized."[11] While he continued to cement support from evangelical and Tea Party voters, Santorum had to prove he could reach a more mainstream Republican audience. To help broaden his appeal, Santorum began to shift focus away from his typical social issues and instead emphasized jobs and the economy. This messaging began to take hold, and in early March he "appear[ed] to be gaining strength among working-class voters with his message about jobs, energy, and manufacturing."[12]

While most coverage focused on Super Tuesday, the first five days in March also included caucuses in Wyoming and Washington. Romney victories in both states added credibility to his arguments that his message had broad appeal coming into the pivotal March election day. March 3 also marked a momentous milestone: After twenty-seven meetings over a ten-month period, the debates were finally over. A final event, Huckabee's third Fox News forum, was held in Wilmington, Ohio, with Romney, Santorum, and Gingrich in attendance. When CNN attempted to schedule another debate, only Gingrich agreed to participate. The meeting was canceled and no more were on the books.

As Super Tuesday approached, drumbeats calling to end the primary and settle on a nominee began to quicken: "A methodical effort is under way among governors, donors, and top Republicans to make the case that a long nominating fight could weaken the party's chances to win the White House, maintain control of the House and gain a majority in the Senate."[13] To benefit from this movement, however, a candidate needed to demonstrate once and for all that the all-important momentum was on his side.

NO CLEAR WINNER ON SUPER TUESDAY

Republican voters in ten states cast their ballots on March 6: Alaska, Georgia, Idaho, Massachusetts, North Dakota, Ohio, Oklahoma, Tennessee, Virginia, and Vermont. Not surprisingly, Gingrich won his home state of Georgia—a victory he hoped would spark yet another resurgence for his campaign. Santorum was the victor in North Dakota, Oklahoma, and Tennessee, buttressing his argument that he held more appeal in southern and conservative states than Romney. Along with geographically large states like Alaska and Idaho, Romney won contests in New England (Massachusetts and Vermont) as expected. His decisive win in Virginia was tempered by the failure of Gingrich and Santorum to qualify for the ballot.

Romney also eked out a victory in Ohio by a minuscule margin, earning 38 percent of the vote to Santorum's 37, along with delegates in areas where Santorum had not qualified. While this technically was a win, the closeness of the contest meant Romney could not claim momentum coming out of Super Tuesday. No clear victor emerged. The race would continue: "And again voters upended the expectations set in campaign war rooms and New York newsrooms, splitting their preferences in ways that exposed continued divisions within the restive party between pragmatism and passion, political expediency and ideological purity."[14]

Once again, Romney had not managed to attract conservative voters away from his opponents, despite vastly outspending them and their super PACs. This was chalked up to a campaign that was lethargic and unexciting, exemplified by its emphasis on delegate counts and campaign math. The continuing frame that Romney had difficulty connecting with or exciting voters also exacerbated this "uninspired" narrative. According to Rick Tyler, senior adviser for Gingrich super PAC Winning Our Future, "Romney comes off as inauthentic because he is inauthentic. . . . There's no wonder he doesn't relate to the grassroots of the party and can't seal the deal. He currently spends four to twelve times as much as every other candidate and still can't win the nomination."[15]

ROMNEY: NO EXCITEMENT, NO INSPIRATION

Coverage of Romney during this period continued to reinforce the same ostensibly positive frames evidenced throughout his coverage, emphasizing his superior organization, fundraising prowess, and establishment support. Romney was running a smart, defensive campaign designed to accumulate enough delegates to block anyone else from winning the nomination, a strategy successfully employed by Obama in 2008. This was proving to be not quite enough, however, and conservative commenters began to criticize him for failing to wrap up the nomination. On Fox News, Charles Krauthammer offered this analysis: "Now, he'll say, you know, I didn't win by much, but I won by enough. . . . But it tells you that every time he's got a chance to close the deal, and he has the one opportunity, it doesn't happen."[16]

Within the context of Romney failing to "close the deal," these frames pointed toward an overarching problem with Romney's campaign: his by-the-book strategy may be smart, but it was not resonating with or exciting voters. After all, this approach was predicated on winning delegates, not the popular vote; once again, Romney and his team seemed to be ignoring the intangibles in favor of a mathematical, methodical, soulless path to victory. He was running a defensive campaign, focusing on the flaws of his competitors rather than inspiring Republicans to vote for him. True to Romney's form, his campaign's strategy focused on mind over heart, logic over emotion, and not losing over winning convincingly. Steve Hayes from *The Weekly Standard* offered this insight on Fox News: "They have to be careful—the argument about inevitability, look at the math, he is going to get elected—I think may turn off voters he is seeking to convert, because they don't want to hear that. They have been hearing he is inevitable forever." With that in mind, Hayes suggested, "They want to hear an issues message. . . . Discussions about process don't work. Discussions about vision and issues where he can get passionate about something, that is the kind of thing that will appeal to conservatives."[17]

Coverage so frequently framed Romney as not inspiring excitement among voters that it was notable when an article or program did highlight enthusiastic supporters. Even in this context, however, they were framed as worthy of coverage precisely because they were members of a rare breed: "To be clear, these 'Romniacs' are not Wall Street bigwigs or paid campaign operatives. Many of them, but not all, are Mormons like Romney. What unites them is a powerful—and unusual—excitement for a candidate who struggles to excite anybody else."[18]

Reiterating this frame was Romney's decision to continue going negative, characterized as a decision made to offset his inability to generate excitement on his own merit. He continued to destroy his competition through cutthroat advertising, spending millions of dollars to run negative spots. The cost of advertising added to his considerable expenditures; although the campaign raised $11.5 million in February, its January reports "showed a campaign that was far outspending what it raised."[19] Romney had relied on big donors throughout his campaign, asking for and often receiving the maximum donation individuals could offer. Because that pool was mostly maxed out, Romney now needed to appeal to small donors—those who could offer incremental donations that would add up over time. The challenge he faced, however, was how to convince people living paycheck to paycheck to donate money to a multimillionaire.

While all of the remaining candidates were wealthy in their own rights, Romney was the only candidate for whom this was a defining feature. The frame that he was an out-of-touch millionaire continued to be reiterated, both in media coverage and when prompted by his competitors and Obama's surrogates. As comedian Dean Obeidallah commented on CNN, "Mitt Romney has opened a door on questions about is he out of touch with his wealth. The $10,000 bet, saying things [like] I like to fire people, saying my wife drives two Cadillacs. Mitt's got to do something to connect with average voters during these tough economic times."[20] To help deflate the potency of this frame, Romney continued trying to turn his wealth into an asset by positioning himself as a conservative businessman who enjoyed great success because he understood the private sector, unlike his professional politician opponents. While that argument had merit, his continual off-the-cuff statements inadvertently calling attention to his extraordinary wealth offered primacy to the negative frame as well as a reason to employ it. By this point, his "fortune has become a central topic in the 2012 campaign,"[21] reinforced by his refusal to disclose his tax information or reluctance to discuss his banking and investments.

Seemingly incapable of learning from past mistakes, Romney once more elicited the frame that he was an out-of-touch multimillionaire when he told Ohio college students that they should ask their parents for money to pay for college or fund their career ambitions. As MSNBC's Lawrence O'Donnell lamented to economist and *New York Times* columnist Paul Krugman, "He seems to think, Paul, that when we say students can't afford a college education, he thinks we literally mean just that student. We mean the student, their parents, their cousins, everybody who they could possibly get any money from are tapped out. They can't afford it."[22] Krugman concurred, noting, "Yes, there is a special Romney touch, which is this apparent complete inability to put himself in the shoes of someone else. . . . I don't think we have ever seen anything quite that obtuse, if you like, in a candidate before."[23]

Romney had spent much of the primary season trying to prove his conservative credibility, moving to the right in an effort to ward off competition. On CNN, contributor Paul Begala claimed, "Well, when you're to the right of Rick Santorum on contraception [and] to the right of Rick Perry on immigration, you're too far to the right to win swing voters in November."[24] During March, however, Romney began making an effort to distance himself from Santorum's brand of absolute social conservatism, saying "I'm not willing to light my hair on fire to try and get support. I am who I am."[25] While this statement might have appeal to moderate voters down the road, it did little to engage conservative voters immediately, instead reinforcing concerns that he lacked core conservative values.

While Romney had long been framed as being robotic, this narrative became more explicit in March; by now, Romney was a "somewhat awkward candidate who, despite massive financial and organizational advantages, hasn't been able to lock down the Republican nomination."[26] To counter this, Romney's supporters began to call for his campaign to humanize him by showing ways he was authentic and relatable. On CNN, Huntsman's daughter Abby Livingston noted, "I'm surprised that the Romney boys haven't been out there more, because I think they could help humanize their dad. You know, I think he's had a tough time connecting."[27] While his robotic persona and campaign offered precision and a methodical approach that likely would result in the nomination, this reiterated the larger frame that Romney would not—or could not—inspire Republican voters. He had establishment support and more money than his competitors, but Romney just did not generate excitement: "And you know, Mitt Romney can buy a lot of things, [but] he can't buy Rick Santorum's conservative message, and that's why he's having so much trouble. Certainly, there's an enthusiasm gap about . . . Mitt Romney or he'd be doing better."[28]

SANTORUM'S WILD RIDE

March was a rollercoaster month for Santorum. He had fought pitched battles both in states where his message would be easily received and in those where his brand of hardcore conservatism was a tougher sell. Across the board, however, he remained competitive, forcing Romney to spend money and time fending off his advances and attacks. His campaign often framed this as a battle of David versus Goliath, the little guy using his wiles to ward off the campaign behemoth that was Mitt Romney. After all, "Rick Santorum and the people don't have the machinery. They don't have the money. But what they have is a finger on the pulse of the Republican Party of today, which . . . is a faith-based party."[29] Santorum argued that he was the party's best chance to offer a candidate who was decidedly different from the sitting president, accusing Romney of being a "Republican Obama" and saying, "This election, we need a choice . . . We don't need a choice between Tweedledum and Tweedledee. We need a clear choice."[30]

Santorum's ability to reach conservative evangelical voters had sustained his candidacy throughout the race. His ability to inspire everyday citizens was evidenced by his fundraising: While Romney depended on big-money guys capping out their investments, Santorum's coffers were filled by smaller individual donations. By mid-March, two-thirds of Santorum's donors had contributed less than $100 each, meaning they were ripe for additional fundraising efforts.

As he increasingly was perceived as the main obstacle to Romney's nomination, Santorum underwent the frontrunner treatment and faced an increasing barrage of attacks on his character as Romney and his super PAC attempted to define him. Questions continued to be raised about Santorum's ethics, particularly concerning his close relationship with steel companies as senator that later proved financially beneficial. These ethical concerns were framed within a broader "Washington insider" narrative that did not allow Santorum to continue positioning himself as the candidate with the greatest distance from the Beltway. During this period, Santorum also continued to be characterized as a bully who tried to intimidate others into getting his way. The candidate accused the Michigan Republican Party of "thuggery"[31] for not allocating delegates in a way that favored him, and the media framed his efforts to elicit a different outcome as being demanding and petulant. This was a candidate not afraid to play hardball, taking aggressive stances to defend his positions and attack his opponents.

Simultaneously (and often relatedly), Santorum framed himself as a victim to the party's and Romney's machinations. In this frame, media and party elites already had sanctified Romney as their candidate of choice; as such, Santorum was being unfairly treated in an effort to stifle his candidacy. This framing was thought to be an effective tool for eliciting support among voters disenchanted with mainstream media and the political status quo. On MSNBC's *Hardball*, Susan Mulligan of *U.S. News and World Report* commented that Santorum was "painting himself a little bit as a victim and that's probably going to help his ratings as well."[32]

To help parse and understand Santorum's appeal as a candidate, his coverage frequently addressed and/or examined the role his faith as a strict Roman Catholic played in his life. Santorum was characterized as deeply religious and highly traditional. His wife homeschooled the couple's many children. He vehemently opposed marriage equality. Santorum was staunchly anti-abortion and spoke out against contraception, often citing his own personal experiences with premature and sick children for support. While Catholics frequently did not vote for him in the primaries, he found considerable support among evangelical Protestants. While this "could be seen by cynics as a coalition of zealots, held together by intolerance . . . his candidacy offers proof of a growing tolerance on the part of evangelical Christians, a willingness to shed ancestral religious prejudices."[33]

Santorum's appeal to these voters offered him a chance to wrest control of the election from Romney—if only he could consolidate their support. True to the predictions of Iowa's evangelical leaders, Gingrich staying in the race meant the conservative support was split.

GINGRICH AND PAUL: STILL RUNNING, TOO

Despite not winning any state besides Georgia since his surprise victory in South Carolina, Gingrich refused to drop out of the race. He insisted that his next resurgence could be right around the corner, and he continued to fight for relevance in southern states. Coverage was clear, however, that some Republicans felt he needed to consider dropping out for the good of the conservative electorate: "If Gingrich were to lose both [Mississippi and Alabama] . . . a lot of people in the conservative community would be saying, but, Newt, you ought to put your loyalty to conservatism above your ego. You ought—you ought to give us a shot, a clean shot at Romney with only one candidate."[34]

As it stood, Gingrich was framed as a spoiler. His continued presence in the race served as a distraction from the two-man contest and took votes that otherwise might have put Santorum over the top. As CNN's chief political analyst Gloria Borger put it, this worked in Romney's favor: "Governor Romney needs Rick Santorum and Newt Gingrich right now. . . . If it weren't for them splitting the conservatives—the very conservative, the evangelicals, the Tea Party voters, Mitt Romney would not be within sort of a position to win."[35] Others refuted this, noting that exit polls indicated that Santorum did not have a lock on the "second choice" slot for Gingrich voters.

Gingrich's refusal to step down from the race to open a path for Santorum generally was framed by conservative pundits and the media in two ways: as evidence of an ego-driven candidacy or, not completely unrelated, fueled by anger at Romney for his attacks in Iowa. Unsurprisingly, Gingrich himself argued that his presence in the race was a boon to the conservative cause, since his continued accumulation of delegates would prevent Romney from clinching the nomination. According to the media's interpretation of this narrative, Gingrich would rise up in a brokered convention and be named the Republican nominee. No matter his true reasons, however, most agreed that this ultimately served Gingrich's permanent goal: keeping the spotlight on him and his ideas.

If Gingrich was considered a spoiler who needed to get out of the race to help a conservative win, Paul was just not considered at all. There was very little coverage of Paul specifically during this period. Instead, he was discussed in relation to his vote totals, often within the context of trying to puzzle out the reasons for his lack of appeal. After a fairly strong start in

Iowa, Paul had petered out almost completely. His continued presence in the race was not questioned, since earlier coverage had clearly indicated Paul's intention to stay in through the convention in order to wield some influence over the platform, but his continued inclusion on ballots was not thought to help or harm anyone else. While Gingrich might have been a spoiler, this was primarily a two-man battle.

MID-MARCH MADNESS

Once more, candidates quickly moved from state to state in an effort to build both momentum and delegate totals. Just four days after Super Tuesday, voters met once more in Kansas, the Virgin Islands, Guam, and Northern Mariana Islands. Santorum continued his heartland streak, winning Kansas by a stunning 57 percent to Romney's 21, but his opponent argued that he had come away a victor since he won more delegates in that day's contests. While this was technically true, it was not a message designed to inspire voters or donors.

The next major day of voting, March 13, featured four contests: Alabama, Mississippi, Hawaii, and American Samoa. Much emphasis was put on the two southern states, although none of the candidates was considered ideal: "A common wish is for some combination of the three current frontrunners, a candidate described by one caller to an Alabama talk radio show as having Mr. Romney's looks, Mr. Gingrich's brains, and Mr. Santorum's moral fiber."[36] For Romney, these two primaries would "test [his] ability to reach evangelical Christians and conservative Republicans, who have been slow to embrace him in a number of prior contests."[37] Upending the horse race one more time, Santorum won both states, with Gingrich and Romney rounding out the top three. Going into the primaries Romney had predicted that he would do well, a real miscalculation from his campaign in terms of managing expectations. In an effort to defuse commentary on the failure of his southern strategy and reinforce the frame that Romney was not a sure bet, Gingrich noted, "If you're the frontrunner and keep coming in third, you're not much of a frontrunner."[38]

Despite his failure to thrive in southern and heartland states, the argument that Romney was likely to be the Republican nominee was gaining credibility by the middle of the month. National polls showed GOP voters favoring him over Santorum 33 percent to 24 percent. To continue this slow-build momentum, Romney attempted to go back to his roots and refocus his attention on the economy. His continuing efforts to position himself as the definitive frontrunner and paint Santorum as unelectable against Obama were helped when Santorum committed a major error while campaigning in Puerto Rico. He incited a substantial backlash when he implied that Puerto Ricans should be required to learn English if they were to become a state. Reflecting his self-promoted "victim" frame, Santorum insisted that "his earlier comments had been 'maliciously' twisted."[39] In the wake of this, a delegate quit rather than support Santorum at the convention. Romney went on to dominate the territory, winning a spectacular 84 percent of the vote on March 18.

Two days later, voters in Illinois had their say in the nomination. The state was known for choosing moderate Republicans, although the impact of the Tea Party meant more conservative candidates had the opportunity to take the race. As was the case in fellow Great Lakes state Ohio, Santorum failed to qualify for the ballot in several districts; he only was eligible for 44 out of the 54 available delegates. Romney and his surrogates pointed to this as further evidence that Santorum was not equipped to run a campaign against Obama. Romney outspent Santorum at least six to one in the Midwestern state in an effort "to bury him in negative advertising." He tried to position Santorum as an economic lightweight and questioned his policy abilities. The vitriol went both ways, however, with Santorum attacking Romney for lacking core convictions. When polls closed, Romney had won Illinois by a decisive twelve-point margin, accruing almost half of the votes cast. His victory was credited to his superior campaign organization and the argument that he was best positioned to beat Obama.

As had become an unfortunate tradition within his campaign, however, this victory was quickly overshadowed by yet another high-profile verbal gaffe. When asked about how Romney's conservative positions would play in a general election, communications director Eric Fehrnstrom likened the transition to a children's drawing toy that erases when you shake it: "I think he hits a reset button for the fall campaign. Everything changes. It's almost like an Etch-A-Sketch. You can kind of shake it up and we start all over again."[40] While this analogy likely would have caused problems for any candidate, it was particularly problematic for Romney since it so clearly reinforced the "flip-flopper" and "conservative of convenience" frames. If his campaign team openly acknowledged the transience of Romney's already-questionable conservative bona fides, how could voters trust that he would continue to reflect their values both in a general election and as president? As Jeff Zeleny and Jim Rutenberg wrote in the *New York Times*, this mistake "followed a Romney campaign pattern of committing unforced errors after major victories. And they flared throughout the day from both Republicans and Democrats alike, moving beyond politics into a hard-to-forget moment of popular culture that could be difficult for Mr. Romney to shake."[41]

Despite concerns reinforced by the Etch-A-Sketch comment, calls for Santorum to cede the race to Romney so Republicans could shift focus to Obama and November increased toward the end of the month. Santorum's March 24 victory in Louisiana failed to quash this narrative, particularly since it was framed as doing little to indicate his appeal extending outside his base of social conservatives. In early April, the message from the Republican establishment was "unmistakable: The nomination battle has gone on long enough. It's now time to let Mitt Romney, the presumptive nominee, and the rest of the party concentrate on the general election campaign against President Obama."[42] Prominent Republicans continued to fall in line behind Romney, including former Florida governor Jeb Bush, current Florida Senator Marco Rubio, and Wisconsin Congressman Paul Ryan. Santorum, however, vowed to stay in the race, saying "I'm not talking about this anymore."[43]

While calls for Santorum to drop out were primarily grounded in concerns that the extended primary—a battle that was overwhelmingly negative—was permanently damaging the eventual nominee and sucking up much-needed resources, Republicans also were beginning to grow concerned that the economy was showing signs of improvement. Romney's case was built on being a financial fix-it man, the sole candidate prepared to step in and save the American economy. It was unclear how that position would play in the case of a clear recovery.

The negativity of the primary also was framed as dampening enthusiasm among the Republican electorate. Throughout the last year, politicians and pundits were in agreement that the GOP voters were charged up enough about wanting Obama out of office that they would turn out for any nominee. As the nominating process began to wind down, however, this conventional wisdom came under question: After months of being told Romney was a shape-shifting, flip-flopping, robotic, emotionless multimillionaire vulture capitalists who was out of touch with the middle class, what motivation would voters have to support the "eat-your-veggies" candidate?

APRIL: THE RACE WINDS DOWN

Buoyed by these displays of support, Romney dominated in three early-April contests, winning handily in the District of Columbia, Maryland, and Wisconsin. The latter primary was particularly important. A seventeen-point victory for Romney in the Midwestern state was characterized as the beginning of the end for Santorum since it "effectively forecloses any chance that the former Massachusetts governor might not be the GOP nominee in the fall."[44] After losing in Michigan, Ohio, Illinois, and Wisconsin by increasingly large margins, Santorum could no longer make the argument that he was best positioned to engage Rust Belt voters in the general election. While four candidates were still officially in the mix, the race was framed as over. Instead of asking if Santorum would quit, the question now posed was when his decision would be announced.

In the wake of his Wisconsin loss and aware of dropping poll numbers in his home state of Pennsylvania, Santorum met with conservative leaders to hash out his next steps. There was no obvious path available to him, no game-changing states on the horizon that might break in his favor. On April 10, Santorum officially declared that he was out of the race. While he would not be president in 2012, this decision was considered the smart move for his future political career. Santorum's success in the primaries rejuvenated a reputation that had been seriously damaged after losing his Senate reelection bid. A loss in Pennsylvania could have undone much of that progress. As it stood, Santorum could adopt the mantle of taking one for the team, stepping aside for the good of the party after a performance that "revived the career of this 16-year congressional veteran who had been written off when he last exited from the national political stage in 2006, after a humiliating defeat. The question now is what his improbable success in the most recent contest suggests for Mr. Santorum's political future."[45]

While coverage of Santorum's decision to leave the race was generally framed as a savvy political decision, reporters and pundits also noted that his campaign had been deeply flawed. Organizational challenges limited his ability to compete against Romney in terms of delegate totals. More problematically, "at his moment of greatest opportunity, Santorum swung and missed. He veered far off message by refusing to back down from comments . . . [that] drew an avalanche of negative headlines, forcing Santorum to take the defensive in the days leading up to the Michigan vote."[46] Verbal gaffes including saying Kennedy's speech on the separation of church and state nauseated him and calling Obama a snob reinforced perceptions that Santorum was hot-headed and, perhaps more importantly, just not presidential. He never fully recovered.

ROMNEY: THE LAST MAN STANDING

After a long, bruising primary contest, Romney had to begin repairing the damage. He immediately turned his sights once more toward Obama and simultaneously trying to shore up support among groups like the National Rifle Association and gun enthusiasts. While this was not a natural fit for him, during Romney's speech to the NRA he "received a standing ovation with muted applause . . . but the crowd seemed to warm to him as he spoke."[47] This quote exemplifies coverage of Romney's candidacy during this time; while he would engender (sometimes reluctant) support from the Republican base, he still had much to prove and a long way to go to generate enthusiasm: "Across the country, some Republicans are coming to terms with the likelihood that the man they never really liked will probably be their party's presidential nominee."[48]

While Romney was making inroads with the Republican electorate, concerns were raised about whether he and his party would be able to appeal to groups outside of the GOP mainstream. Pundits expressed concerns that he could not reach or engage with women or minorities. Moving to the right on immigration during the primaries left him operating at a deficit with Hispanic voters, although by late April the "Romney campaign appears to have begun shifting to the center on immigration, after staking out a position to the right of opponents like former Speaker Newt Gingrich and Gov. Rick Perry of Texas."[49] Others noted that he had alienated women, including CNN's David Gergen: "You can't measure how much damage has been done to Romney. . . . That on this issue of women and contraception, Planned Parenthood, Mitt Romney has been sucked to the right on social issues by Santorum. . . . There are a lot of women who . . . are now fired up. They're angry."[50]

Although both Gingrich and Paul were still officially running, on April 25 Romney was named the presumptive nominee for the Republican Party. His campaign refocused on Obama and tried to start moving Romney back to the center, where he would have better luck appealing to moderates and Independent voters. The longstanding frames established during the primary process could not be escaped so easily, however, particularly since Obama and his campaign team embraced characterizations of Romney as an out-of-touch millionaire who could not understand or inspire middle-class voters. With the economy showing slow but steady signs of improvement, Obama's chances for reelection looked better than ever. After all, Obama's message boiled down to this statement from Vice-President Joe Biden: "If you're looking for a bumper sticker to sum up how President Obama has handled what we inherited, it's pretty simple: Osama bin Laden is dead and General Motors is alive."[51] Romney's bumper sticker was as yet unclear.

NOTES

1. Rachel Maddow, Chris Matthews, Ed Schultz, Lawrence O'Donnell, Al Sharpton, Steve Schmidt, Howard Fineman, and Michael Steele, "Special Coverage 2300 Hour," *MSNBC: Special*, March 6, 2012, LexisNexis Academic.

2. Karl Rove, "Romney Takes the GOP Lead," *Wall Street Journal*, March 1, 2012, A13, Factiva.

3. Michael D. Shear, "Romney Traces Obama's Path on Delegates," *New York Times*, March 4, 2012, National Desk, Factiva.

4. Bret Baier, Megyn Kelly, Brit Hume, Stephen Hayes, Carl Cameron, Bill Hemmer, Jenna Lee, Martha MacCallum, Chris Wallace, and Karl Rove, "Coverage of Super Tuesday— 2000 Half Hour," *Fox News Network: Live Event*, March 6, 2012, LexisNexis Academic.

5. John Harwood, "Candidates Scramble to Create Differences," *New York Times*, March 1, 2012, National Desk, Factiva.

6. Ibid.

7. Chris Matthews, Chuck Todd, Amanda Drury, and Eugene Robinson, "For March 7, 2012," *MSNBC: Hardball*, March 7, 2012, LexisNexis Academic.

8. Ibid.

9. Fareed Zakaria, Gloria Borger, Jim Acosta, Jessica Yellin, John King, Dana Bash, Lisa Sylvester, Erick Erickson, and Kate Bolduan, "Interview with Senator John McCain; President Obama Meets with Israeli Prime Minister; Candidates Prepare for Super Tuesday," *CNN: John King*, March 5, 2012, LexisNexis Academic.

10. Soledad O'Brien, Christine Romans, Tom Foreman, Carol Costello, and Sanjay Gupta, "Interview with Congressman Aaron Schock of Illinois; Pay for Pain; GOP Presidential Candidates Prepare for Super Tuesday; Interview with Ohio Attorney General Michael DeWine; Strong Stance on Iran; Never Too Old," *CNN: Starting Point with Soledad O'Brien*, March 6, 2012, LexisNexis Academic.

11. Bret Baier, Dan Springer, Carl Cameron, Jonathan Serrie, Shannon Bream, and Bob Beckel, "Washington Primary Coverage; Super Tuesday Preview," *Fox News Network: Fox Special Report with Bret Baier*, March 3, 2012, LexisNexis Academic.

12. Richard A. Oppel Jr., Trip Gabriel, and Jeremy W. Peters, "To Forge a Comeback, Santorum Focuses on Ohio," *New York Times*, March 1, 2012, National Desk, Factiva.

13. Jeff Zeleny, Jim Rutenberg, Ashley Parker, Robbie Brown, and Richard A. Oppel Jr., "Before Pivotal Tuesday Votes, Big Names Rally to Romney," *New York Times*, March 5, 2012, National Desk, Factiva.

14. Jim Rutenberg, Ashley Parker, Allison Kopicki, and David R. Jones, "Romney Appears the Ohio Winner; Santorum Strong," *New York Times*, March 7, 2012, National Desk, Factiva.

15. Lawrence O'Donnell and Howard Fineman, "The Last Word for March 14, 2012," *MSNBC: The Last Word with Lawrence O'Donnell*, March 14, 2012, LexisNexis Academic.

16. Megyn Kelly, Bret Baier, Steve Brown, Chris Wallace, and Bill Hemmer, "Special Coverage 2300 Half Hour," *Fox News Network: Live Event*, March 6, 2012, LexisNexis Academic.

17. Bret Baier, Bill Hemmer, and Doug McKelway, "Fox News All-Stars," *Fox News Network: Fox Special Report with Bret Baier*, March 8, 2012, LexisNexis Academic.

18. David A. Fahrenthold, "'Romniacs' Have Rare Passion," *Washington Post*, March 28, 2012, A-Section, Factiva.

19. Sara Murray, Elizabeth Williamson, Carol E. Lee, and Janet Hook, "Election 2012: Campaign Watch," *Wall Street Journal*, March 8, 2012, A5, Factiva.

20. Carol Costello, Paul Steinhauser, David Mattingly, Dan Lothian, Christine Romans, Barbara Starr, Robert Zimmerman, Elise Labott, Ali Velshi, and Mark Preston, "'Super Tuesday' Voting Under Way; GOP Candidates Fight for Ohio; Candidates Address Pro-Israel Lobby; Obama's Plan to Help Homeowners; Gingrich Leans on Home State; Georgia Has Today's Biggest GOP Prize; Interview with Georgia Governor Nathan Deal; McCain: Time for U.S. to Bomb Syria," *CNN: CNN Newsroom*, March 6, 2012, LexisNexis Academic.

21. Tom Hamburger, "Romney Uses Rule to Cloak Wealth," *Washington Post*, April 6, 2012, A-Section, Factiva.

22. Lawrence O'Donnell, "The Last Word for April 2, 2012," *MSNBC: The Last Word with Lawrence O'Donnell*, April 2, 2012, LexisNexis Academic.

23. Ibid.

24. Wolf Blitzer, John King, Anderson Cooper, Ari Fleischer, Paul Begala, Alex Castellanos, Donna Brazile, Gloria Borger, Jessica Yellin, David Gergen, Joe Johns, and Jim Acosta, "Super Tuesday; Gingrich Wins Georgia," *CNN: CNN Live Event/Special*, March 6, 2012, LexisNexis Academic.

25. Donna Brazile, Ari Fleischer, Alex Castellanos, Joe Johns, Jim Acosta, Candy Crowley, Tom Foreman, Wolf Blitzer, Paul Begala, John King, Anderson Cooper, Gloria Borger, David Gergen, Erin Burnett, Jim Spellman, and Jessica Yellin, "Super Tuesday Showdown; Interview with Texas Congressman Ron Paul," *CNN: John King*, March 6, 2012, LexisNexis Academic.

26. Chris Cillizza, "Five Signs of an Impending Race," *Washington Post*, March 28, 2012, A-Section, Factiva.

27. Soledad O'Brien, Christine Romans, and Carol Costello, "Interview with Senator John McCain; Gas Prices Up for 27 Days Straight; North Korean Leader's DMZ Visit; Interview with Newt Gingrich; Earthquake in San Francisco Area; Super Tuesday Countdown," *CNN: Starting Point with Soledad O'Brien*, March 5, 2012, LexisNexis Academic.

28. Maddow et al., "Special Coverage 2300 Hour."

29. Ibid.

30. Philip Rucker and Rosalind S. Helderman, "Super Tuesday's Prize is Spelled Ohio," *Washington Post*, March 3, 2012, A-Section, Factiva.

31. Katharine Q. Seelye, "Santorum Says Michigan Misawarded Delegates," *New York Times*, March 2, 2012, National Desk, Factiva.

32. Matthews et al., "For March 7, 2012."

33. Samuel G. Freedman, "In Surprising Shift, Many Evangelical Voters Are Turning to Santorum, a Catholic," *New York Times*, March 24, 2012, National Desk, Factiva.

34. Wolf Blitzer, John King, Anderson Cooper, Ari Fleischer, Paul Begala, Mary Matalin, Hilary Rosen, Gloria Borger, David Gergen, Jim Acosta, Joe Johns, Dana Bash, Shannon Travis, Candy Crowley, and Jessica Yellin, "The Mississippi and Alabama Primaries," *CNN: CNN Live Event/Special*, March 13, 2012, LexisNexis Academic.

35. Wolf Blitzer, John King, Anderson Cooper, Ari Fleischer, Paul Begala, Mary Matalin, Hilary Rosen, Gloria Borger, David Gergen, Dana Bash, and Shannon Travis, "Mississippi, Alabama Hold Primaries; Tight Race in Mississippi," *CNN: CNN Live Event/Special*, March 13, 2012, LexisNexis Academic.

36. Campbell Robertson and Trip Gabriel, "Tight Primaries Suggest Less-Predictable South," *New York Times*, March 12, 2012, National Desk, Factiva.

37. Janet Hook and Cameron McWhirter, "Election 2012: Race Heads South, Evangelical Terrain," *Wall Street Journal*, March 7, 2012, A6, Factiva.

38. Ed Schultz, Rachel Maddow, Chris Matthews, Al Sharpton, Chuck Todd, Karen Finney, Eugene Robinson, and Richard Wolffe, "Primary Coverage—2300 Hour," *MSNBC: The Ed Show with Ed Schultz*, March 13, 2012, LexisNexis Academic.

39. Neil King Jr. and Sara Murray, "Election 2012: Campaign Watch," *Wall Street Journal*, March 16, 2012, A4, Factiva.

40. Bret Baier, Ed Henry, Jim Angle, Greg Palkot, Carl Cameron, Mike Emanuel, Shannon Bream, and James Rosen, "Political Headlines," *Fox News Network: Fox Special Report with Bret Baier*, March 21, 2012, LexisNexis Academic.

41. Jeff Zeleny, Jim Rutenberg, and Ashley Parker, "Romney's Day to Relish Is Marred by Aide's Gaffe," *New York Times*, March 22, 2012, National Desk, Factiva.

42. Dan Balz, "Santorum Defies Mounting Pressure to Bow Out," *Washington Post*, April 3, 2012, A-Section, Factiva.

43. Ibid.

44. Chris Cillizza and Philip Rucker, "Romney's Wisconsin Win Means the Beginning of the End," *Washington Post*, April 4, 2012, A-Section, Factiva.

45. Patrick O'Connor and Peter Nicholas, "Election 2012: Race Over, Santorum Considers Next Steps," *Wall Street Journal*, April 11, 2012, A4, Factiva.

46. Chris Cillizza, "The Once and Future Candidate?" *Washington Post*, April 11, 2012, A-Section, Factiva.

47. Rosalind S. Helderman, "Romney Seeks to Reassure NRA, Gun Enthusiasts," *Washington Post*, April 14, 2012, A-Section, Factiva.

48. Rosalind S. Helderman and Sandhya Somashekhar, "Romney Slowly Gaining Conservatives' Support, If Not Their Full Hearts," *Washington Post*, April 20, 2012, A-Section, Factiva.

49. Jonathan Weisman, "Rubio, in Appeal to GOP Conscience, Urges Compromise on Dream Act," *New York Times*, April 20, 2012, National Desk, Factiva.

50. Blitzer et al., "Mississippi, Alabama Hold Primaries."

51. *Washington Post*, "If You Are Looking for a Bumper Sticker to Sum up How President Obama Has Handled What We Inherited, It's Pretty Simple: Osama bin Laden Is Dead and General Motors Is Alive," *Washington Post*, April 30, 2012, A-Section, Factiva.

Chapter Eight

Conclusion

After almost an entire year of nonstop debates, rallies, stump speeches, primaries, and caucuses, the 2012 presidential contest was finally set: Incumbent Barack Obama would face off against Republican challenger Mitt Romney. While the conventions were still months away, no rest was to be had. In today's political environment, the breathing room between primaries and the general election campaign has all but vaporized. Romney's bruising (and expensive) primary battle was barely in his rearview mirror before he and his team had to immediately look toward November. Recovery was on the fly, with Romney returning to the road to raise the money he so desperately needed to compete against Obama. By now, the frames mainstream media used to shape narratives about and around Romney were clear and consistent. He and his campaign team faced a daunting challenge: How do you convince voters to support someone they believe to be a shape-shifting, flip-flopping millionaire robot?

FRAMING CANDIDATES AND ISSUES

As the only candidate to begin and end the contest in the top tier of candidates, Romney's frames were remarkably stable throughout the contest. What was notable, however, was that the valence changed after Romney began to lose his aura of invincibility post–South Carolina. The same frames that were treated positively during the months leading up to voting—a methodical and meticulous campaign characterized by impressive discipline, incomparable business acumen needed to save the economy—turned negative. Because his campaign was so well run with exceptional attention to detail, all mistakes were framed as magnified and no quarter was given.

This held true for Romney's lapses in discipline as well. When he started having to fight his way back into the mix, Romney finally showed the passion voters wanted, but this seemed to correspond with an inability to keep himself from making incidental comments that would immediately go viral. His wife's two Cadillacs, being friends with NASCAR owners, making $10,000 bets—the list went on. While Romney had made the occasional gaffe earlier in the campaign, the alarming frequency of these statements indicated that the candidate was rattled. Because they violated the expectations established by the "methodical and disciplined" frame, Romney's foibles were presented as notable for being outside the norm—even when they probably should have been expected.

Those same comments alluding to his vast wealth and powerful connections also reinforced the negative side of the "successful businessman" narrative. Rather than being treated as evidence of his ability to save the American economy, Romney's business background was discussed within the context of what Bain Capital did and how much money he made there. No longer was he perceived to be a capable steward of the economy; instead, he was an out-of-touch millionaire who was unable to relate to or understand middle-class American voters.

Coming out of the nominating contest, Romney's negative frames were clear. Unfortunately for his candidacy, he and his team did not—or could not—counteract them. For a candidate who was consistently framed as a robot with difficulty engaging voters emotionally, the worst possible argument you can make is that you will win because of *math*. While their delegate count strategy was smart, it certainly did nothing to address concerns about who Romney was as a candidate or as a man. Focusing on the delegate strategy could be interpreted as not caring what voters thought of him. Instead, Romney would win due to sheer preparation, planning, and resource allocation. In some ways, this represented the difference between *inevitable* versus *invincible*: It was not a show of strength as much as an attempt to just wear everyone else down.

A particular challenge that Romney faced throughout his campaign was the perception that he lacked a true north. He was framed as a shape-shifter and flip-flopper who thus was not trustworthy. Voters did not know where he really stood on issues, and they often did not believe he was telling the truth. Comments from his adviser comparing the transition to the general election to an Etch-A-Sketch reinforced this perception. While both Romney and his campaign often gave cause for this frame to be used, media coverage likely exacerbated this perception. From the earliest coverage included in this study, however, almost every decision Romney made was framed as being politically motivated; if he opted to continue supporting the contention that humans were contributing to climate change, it was framed in the media as being easier to defend than yet another shift in positions (as discussed in chapter 2). Romney could not win.

While Romney's frames remained consistent, other candidates experienced more of a dramatic shift. Early coverage (although sometimes scarce) tended to treat the lower-tier candidates generously. Their biographies were addressed and their names included in lists of potential nominees, but controversies in their backgrounds tended to be overlooked. This changed as soon as a candidate experienced a bounce, however. Once he or she became a potential nominee, thanks to debate performance or a polling surge, the media began to perform a more thorough vetting. This transpired whether or not they were perceived to have any realistic chance at winning the nomination. Thus, candidates like Michele Bachmann and Herman Cain, who were generally treated lightly in the early days of their campaigns, found themselves wilting under the blistering glare of the frontrunner spotlight. Bachmann's misstatements and untruths were highlighted, and media spent time digging into the backgrounds of both her and her husband. Cain, originally framed as a candidate whose good humor and crowd-pleasing oratory skills added entertainment value to the field, suddenly faced revelations about indiscretions past and present. Their honeymoon periods were over, as were their candidacies.

Not surprisingly, issue coverage during this period was fairly limited. Issues primarily were discussed within the context of controversy: either candidates attacking each other for unpopular positions or discussions of a single candidate shifting positions over time. What was interesting about issue coverage was how media framed issues in terms of how a position affected (or might affect) the horserace rather than what was right, moral, or an honestly held point of view. When a candidate voiced an unpopular position, coverage focused on how that would impact his or her standing in the polls rather than using it as a springboard to examine the issues from a variety of perspectives. For example, when Gingrich expressed his belief that illegal immigrants who had been in the States for decades might merit some path to permanent residency, coverage emphasized the backlash Perry had already experienced for his immigration position as well as speculation that this would bring Gingrich's surge to a screeching halt. Rather than exploring the perspective Gingrich raised—that law-abiding men and women who had built lives in the States over extended period of times might deserve to stay—media coverage focused overwhelmingly on what that position would do to Gingrich the candidate.

Interestingly, citizens rather than the candidates or political leaders often drove the issues covered. Illegal immigration was not thought to be a top concern, but when voters kept bringing it up during town halls and question-and-answer periods with the candidates, it began to drive a narrative. At the beginning of the period included in this study, media expected the attention to be focused almost exclusively on the economy. The preponderance of social issues—the same social issues that forced candidates to go on the record with conservative positions—were brought into the discussion by voters asking about things that mattered to them. No matter the state of the economy, many voters still wanted a candidate who would enthusiastically and wholeheartedly represent their own values and beliefs.

IMPACT OF THE TEA PARTY

After an exhaustive examination of a year's worth of media coverage and identifying a series of frames that helped shape our knowledge and understanding of Republican candidates, what did we learn? What did this coverage tell us about the Republican Party specifically and the state of politics in the United States more generally? What can we learn from the 2012 GOP nominating contest that can help us make sense of our current political context? Underlying each of those questions is one element: the impact of the Tea Party on the Republican nominating contest.

The influence of the Tea Party informed coverage throughout the year included in this research. Framed as oppositional to mainstream or traditional Republicans, this dynamic was very much perceived to be one of fundamental conflict. As Romney said, this was no less than a battle for the soul of the Republican Party. Despite the centrality of the Tea Party to the discussion, media tended to conflate that group and evangelicals, using "conservative" as a catchall to accommodate both groups, often notably leaving out pure fiscal conservatism entirely. They generally were treated as one unit rather than recognizing potentially distinct or divergent interests and motivations, and the assumption was the benefits of appealing to one group would extend to support from the other as well. While there was substantial overlap between the Tea Party and evangelical voters, they clearly were not monolithic. Ron Paul, for example, found favor with the fiscal conservatives and Tea Partiers with libertarian leanings, but evangelicals did not embrace his message. Bachmann, the "darling" or "sweetheart" of the Tea Party, managed to appeal to both groups—for a while at least.

These "conservative" voters, whether operating from the Tea Party or evangelical viewpoints (or in many cases, both), were framed as being surprisingly resistant to following the Republican line. As discussed in chapter 6, GOP voters historically fell in line, if not in love; this sentiment echoed earlier coverage from the summer months that considered the unsettled field to be both unusual and notable. Despite fairly direct instruction from Republican Party leaders and elected officials, these voters refused to cooperate. They would not blindly line up and offer fealty to Romney because he was the party's choice. They wanted their own voices heard. These voters were actively resistant to the status quo, at least until it became clear that Romney's machine could not be stopped. Their fury toward Washington was not reserved for Obama or Democrats. This was an insurgent voice brimming with anger and disdain for standard operating procedure. They wanted change, and they were desperate to find a candidate who could represent their views with passion and aplomb. This was happening at the expense of the national party, a group that was losing control of its nominating process in the most public of ways.

From a media-framing perspective, the Holy Grail in the 2012 nominating contest would be the emergence of a candidate who could appeal to both the conservative (including Tea Party and evangelical) voters while also maintaining a modicum of attractiveness to moderate and establishment Republicans. Early coverage frequently framed the declared pool of candidates as less than appealing; once potential saviors like Mitch Daniels, Mike Huckabee, and Chris Christie opted out, voters were being asked to vote for the best choice out of a generally uninspiring group. This was why Perry was so eagerly anticipated; before he actually entered the race and started falling apart, he was thought to be one of the handful of candidates who could unite the factions behind the banner of the GOP. Once Perry fell from grace, none of the remaining candidates was thought to be able to bridge this divide.

As coverage clearly demonstrated, however, the odds of finding any politician who can offer crossover appeal to both sides is nearly impossible: the same positions, beliefs, and attitude that appeal to Tea Partiers and evangelical voters turn off many moderates and independents—two groups needed for any Republican to win the presidency. This was exacerbated by a primary contest that focused on winning over the most conservative of voters. To do so, candidates tried to out-conservative each other on social issues, throwing "red meat" to the masses to generate outrage that they hoped would translate to support. Their fiscal policies often were considered untenable or unrealistic and did not hold up under scrutiny, a surprising turn of events for the party more closely associated with business interests and free market capitalism. It is important to note that the Tea Party's rise also corresponded with (if not inspiring) a narrowing of the definition of what it means to be conservative. In 2008, a pro-choice politician—Rudy Giuliani—was considered a viable candidate. During the primaries that year, Romney was framed as the conservative alternative to McCain. Clearly, the ensuing four years were characterized by a seismic shift in the Republican electorate, exemplified by the Tea Party's astounding success in the 2010 elections.

Considered within the context of coverage of these primaries, it is possible (if not likely) that the Tea Party and its candidates are better suited for local and state elections than national contests. A fairly homogeneous audience is required for these uber-conservative messages to hit home. This helps explain the success of the Tea Party in the 2010 contests; since midterm elections tend to have lower turnouts than in presidential years, the impact of these passionate true believers can belie their actual representation within the electorate. Based on this understanding of the Tea Party and its influence, accusations that Romney did not win against Obama because he was not conservative enough or that a more authentically conservative candidate would have triumphed seem unlikely and misguided. If anything, Romney being forced to go on record with conservative positions—likely with stronger and more impassioned rhetoric than he might have used otherwise—turned off voters outside of the right wing of the party. Seeds planted about the GOP's "war on women" and minority-unfriendly positions during the primaries took root during the general election campaign, exacerbated by party nominees and prominent Republican voices making inflammatory comments. The Republican Party of the 2012 nominating contest was framed as one intended to represent straight, Christian, white voters. Much of this was not Romney's doing and was out of his control, yet these factors influenced the context in which he ran for president.

WHAT HAPPENED IN 2012?

This is not to say that Romney was a perfect candidate. The frames that emerged and gained currency during his fight to win the nomination highlighted his weaknesses. From my reading of the coverage, one particular element stands out as pivotal to understanding the challenges Romney faced: South Carolina. Angered by Romney's attacks in Iowa that stunted his surge, Gingrich went on the offensive. The other conservative candidates quickly joined him as they test-drove the Democrats' lines of attack for the general election: Romney was a vulture capitalist, the embodiment of a greedy rich guy who made his fortune by destroying those in his way. In this narrative, rich and successful equals evil and heartless. This was a powerful argument to offset Romney's claims that his business success made him an ideal steward for the economy. While other Republicans quickly repudiated these attacks, the damage was done. Romney had been framed as an out-of-touch millionaire who would ruthlessly put Americans into the poorhouse to serve the almighty bottom line, a perception that continued to haunt him through November.

While he went on to win the nomination, Romney never really recovered from this experience. To save his campaign in the wake of South Carolina, Romney turned up the heat—embodying the political version of that ruthless businessman. As is often the case, going on the attack increased his negatives. For Romney, however, this was particularly problematic. His campaign was built on being neutral, fighting a war of attrition. Romney's battle plan was framed as being the last candidate standing rather than an inspiring, positive choice.

Compounding Romney's challenge was the unexpected length of the primary season. Having to fight for the nomination for an extended period sucked up resources (including goodwill) that likely would have helped his performance in the general election. Instead of focusing on Obama, Romney was forced to face off against opponents whose chances at election were limited at best. Two factors helped facilitate this: the extensive debate schedule and super PACs.

With twenty-seven debates held between May 2011 and March 2012, any candidate who qualified suddenly had a national platform to reach audiences. For those whom the media suspected were in the race just to raise their profiles and possibly improve book sales, these were golden opportunities. Once no-hopers signed up, frontrunners had to participate as well or run the risk of being perceived as running scared. In the 2012 campaign, these debates were notable for their emphasis on entertainment. Candidates who could perform well in this context earned substantial bumps in the polls, catapulting them into the top tier. Those who did not excel were lost; debates undermined the candidacies of both Pawlenty and Perry. Catchphrases (including 9-9-9) and one-liners became water cooler topics, distracting from more substantive discussions among the candidates.

Comparisons to reality shows and wrestling matches were apt. The emphasis was on spectacle rather than substance, and they allowed those who were facile with attacks to insert themselves into the discussion. While this was not automatically a bad result—in fact, it can be argued that this diversity of opinions is central to the democratic process—in this instance they created a mediated environment with unexpected influence that subverted the process. Rather than focusing on reaching voters in key states, candidates ran a national campaign into citizens' living rooms. Iowa and New Hampshire voters, accustomed to the one-on-one interactions that let them evaluate the candidates and weed out the weakest, were left in the cold.

While the excessive number and frequency of debates shifted the dynamic of the race, the impact of the Citizens United decision cannot be underestimated. Unlimited donations to candidate-affiliated super PACs meant a wealthy true believer could keep a candidate in the mix long after his sell-by date. These candidates became distractions who often drove the narrative rather than just petering out as they had done in the past. For all that Gingrich argued his continued presence would prevent Romney from collecting a sufficient number of delegates to clinch the nomination before the convention, it seems more likely that his refusal to drop out cannibalized support from Santorum and forced all candidates to spend more money. His attack ads continued to cause damage to Romney's campaign, making his transition to the general election more difficult than it might have been otherwise.

Rather than a quick wrap-up, the contest became a state-by-state slog that cost valuable time, money, and goodwill.

PRAGMATISM VERSUS IDEOLOGY

The 2012 Republican primaries represent a struggle the party will continue to face moving forward: pragmatism versus ideology. Pragmatic politicians govern—they have experience working across party lines and recognize that compromise is required in a world that is not black and white. Ideologues, on the other hand, excel at campaigning rather than governing. They focus on raising ire and spewing invective, rallying the faithful by stoking the potent flames of rage and fear. If voters believe they are under attack, they need leaders who will defend them. Ideologues offer this promise. Unfortunately, this makes governing nearly impossible. Compromise is an essential part of the democratic process. If elected officials are so terrified of being framed as wishy-washy or inauthentic and therefore risk losing their party primaries (and thus their seats), governing grinds to a halt. This is not a sustainable model for running a country.

To win in this political environment, Romney the pragmatist tried to fight off his ideologue opponents by playing their game. Unfortunately, this approach forced him to go on the record on social issues in ways that turned off mainstream and moderate Republicans. His strategy was designed to give reasons to vote *against* someone else rather than *for* him. People did not have to like him as long as they liked the other guy less. While this worked for the primaries, it was not enough to win the general election. Romney's strategy was carefully calibrated to conditions as they existed at the beginning of the campaign. When conditions changed—the economy improved, Obama's approval ratings went up post–Hurricane Sandy—Romney could not adapt or adjust. He did not have a strong enough message to pull him through, and his defensive strategy lacked inspiration or goodwill. A message consisting of "better than the other guy" can only take you so far. For Mitt Romney and Republicans in 2012, it was not far enough.

Appendix

Methods

In order to effectively and rigorously examine mainstream media coverage of the Republican presidential candidate debates and primaries, I analyzed 6,615 articles and transcripts using techniques associated with textual analysis. This appendix offers a complete explanation of my data collection and analysis techniques.

DATA COLLECTION

Data collection for this project required use of two separate databases: Factiva for newspaper articles and LexisNexis Academic for transcripts. While ideally one database would have sufficed, we wanted to include specific media outlets in our study that represented differing views on the political spectrum. In order to access the *Wall Street Journal*, Factiva was required; unfortunately, it does not offer transcripts from cable news networks. Thus, we turned to LexisNexis for that material. The selection process for both newspaper articles and cable news transcripts are described in detail below.

Newspaper Articles

The initial sample of newspaper articles were derived from Factiva using the names of each candidate who had declared candidacy in Republican primaries: Michele Bachmann, Herman Cain, Newt Gingrich, Jon Huntsman, Gary Johnson, Ron Paul, Tim Pawlenty, Rick Perry, Mitt Romney, and Rick Santorum. Three newspapers were included for study: the *New York Times*, the *Wall Street Journal*, and the *Washington Post*.[1] In our initial data pull, all articles that included at least one name were found from May 1, 2011 (the month of the first debate) until April 30, 2012 (the month Romney was officially named the Republican presumptive nominee). Articles were pulled in month-long batches, and each batch (separated by month and newspaper) was reviewed separately. The initial data pull had a total of 7,328 articles: 2,684 from the *Times*; 1,438 from the *WSJ*; and 3,206 from the *Washington Post*.

Because this study specifically examined the emergent news frames, research assistants reviewed the initial data pull to identify those that merited inclusion in the final sample. Articles were excluded from the final sample if they were not in the News section (e.g., Style, Opinion, and Metro articles were eliminated) or if they mentioned the candidate peripherally within the context of another story. Two research assistants reviewed each article for inclusion; in case of disagreement, the two would discuss the article and come to a decision. The total number of articles included in this study can be found in Table A.1.

Table A.1. Newspaper Articles Included in Study

Newspaper	Initial Sample	Final Sample
New York Times	2,684	942
Wall Street Journal	1,438	570
Washington Post	3,206	980
Total	7,328	2,492

LexisNexis Academic was used to establish the initial pool of cable news transcripts. Following the same process in the data pull as outlined above for newspapers, we used the names of declared Republican candidates who participated in at least one televised debate as search terms. Data included transcripts from the three major cable news networks: CNN, Fox News, and MSNBC. Transcripts were pulled in month-long batches, beginning on May 1, 2011, and continuing through April 30, 2012. The initial sample included a total of 4,531 articles: 2,291 from CNN; 1,356 from Fox News; and 884 from MSNBC. During analysis, we realized that Fox News was missing a batch of transcripts from January 21–31. A second pull was conducted with the slightly broader search terms of "Republican and primary"; an additional 75 transcripts were uncovered. All data from this second pull were included in the final analysis.

While the Factiva database allowed us to follow identical processes for each batch regardless of the original newspaper source, in LexisNexis cable news transcripts are not stored in identical formats: Fox News will return only relevant segments, but CNN and MSNBC's transcripts include entire programs, even if multiple and varied subjects are included. To accommodate this, a three-step review process was implemented for CNN and

MSNBC. First, initial batches were pulled using the candidate names. A research assistant then edited down transcripts to only include potentially relevant segments, eliminating any material that clearly was not related to the Republican candidates, primary politics, and/or campaigning. In step three, two researchers then went through each transcript individually to determine which segment transcripts were relevant for inclusion. Transcripts were eliminated if candidates were peripheral to another topic or issue rather than central to the story. This included the removal of stories that ended with "teases" indicating that a piece about candidates was coming up next.

While we only included stories officially classified as News in the newspaper sample, this was much more complicated and difficult for cable news. Since the line separating "news" and "opinion" is quite nebulous for these networks, we decided to include all transcripts that dealt specifically with the candidates and their primary campaigns. As was the case with newspaper articles, two research assistants reviewed each transcript for inclusion. When their initial assessments diverged, they were charged with discussing their concerns and coming to consensus. In all instances, agreement was reached with minimal discussion. The total breakdown of transcripts is detailed in Table A.2.

Table A.2. Cable News Transcripts Included in Study

Cable News Transcripts	Initial Sample	Final Sample
CNN	2,291	2,041
Fox News Channel	1,356	1,257
	75 (second pull)	75
MSNBC	884	825
Total	4,606	4,198

Drawing the Sample

When determining how to best define the sample for this study, we experimented with a number of search terms (including Republican, primary, candidate, and various permutations of the three). A brief overview of results, however, indicated that each of these combinations left gaps in our analysis. By using candidate names, we could best represent the breadth of articles covering the primary while eliminating those that were not relevant for a framing study.

When we decided to use the candidate names, we discussed the wisdom of including those who were flirting with candidacy but never officially declared, including Sarah Palin and Donald Trump. Ultimately, we determined that the core purpose of this book—to understand how the mainstream media framed Republican candidates for the party's presidential nomination—meant that focusing specifically and exclusively on declared candidates made the most sense. While both Palin and Trump are discussed in our analysis within the context of articles included in our sample, adding their names as search terms on their own subverted the purpose of this book. Perhaps more importantly, including high-profile potential candidates like Palin and Trump would open a Pandora's box in terms of determining who merited an individual search term. Instead, limiting the pool to those who officially declared and thus took part in official debates and were represented in primary-season contests seemed the most accurate way to make sense of media framing within the 2012 Republican primary season.

TEXTUAL ANALYSIS

While scholars often note that frame analysis is both a theory and a method, it still requires the use of specific data analysis techniques. Often, researchers turn to content analyses, using various units of analysis (word, sentence, paragraph, article) to identify frames and measure their frequency. These techniques provide important insights into the frames found in media messages, and their value is unquestionable. For this project, however, I was interested in looking past the specific words, aiming for a deeper, more holistic understanding of how audiences could read and interpret these texts. To do so, I turned to textual analysis.

Unlike content analysis, textual analysis emphasizes exploring likely interpretations of texts—in this case, newspaper articles and cable news networks. The goal is not to produce a report that claims to have identified the only possible understanding of relevant texts; instead, we recognize that multiple interpretations are likely. In his seminal book on textual analysis, McKee writes, "When we perform textual analysis on a text, we make an educated guess at some of the most likely interpretations that might be made of that text."[2] As such, what this book offers is one particular interpretation that identifies common themes found across a large number of media products. This is not to say in any way that all audiences would interpret them the same way; variation is not only expected, but desirable. By using textual analysis, however, I am better equipped to focus on understanding the interpretations rather than word counts.

McKee's version of textual analysis uses a post-structuralist approach to examine and understand likely—and possible—interpretations of various texts. In this model, a researcher is not attempting to create a single dogmatic representation of the only way a text can be understood. Instead, the post-structuralist perspective encourages a researcher to "look for the differences between texts without claiming that one of them is the only correct one."[3] This approach requires us to acknowledge that there never is one single interpretation of a text; there always will be variance in interpretations, based on the reader's own personal beliefs, attitudes, and experiences. McKee writes:

> In post-structuralist textual analysis, we don't make claims about whether texts are "accurate," "truthful," or "show reality." We don't simply dismiss them as "inaccurate" or "biased." . . . Rather, the methodology I'm describing seeks to understand the ways in which these forms of representation take place, the assumptions behind them, and the kinds of sense-making about the world that they reveal.[4]

This focus speaks to the purpose of this book. As I wrote in the introduction, my purpose was not to examine the veracity of claims; while the 2012 election year was called the "year of the Fact Checker,"[5] this was beyond the scope of what I wanted to do. Instead, this analysis specifically addresses the claims themselves—the frames used by the media, sometimes provided by candidates, but as often not. Textual analysis provided a means to examine and analyze these texts in order to develop an understanding of how these frames were likely understood by media audiences.

So, then, how do I—or any other researcher using textual analysis to understand media content—know what a likely interpretation is? McKee offers us three steps. In step one, a researcher needs to choose his or her questions carefully. This book is the product of a carefully defined and constructed research study, based on specific questions I had about how the media framed Republican candidates during the path to nomination. In step two, a researcher needs to collect as many relevant texts as feasible, with a clear directive to be as comprehensive as possible: "This is your empirical evidence. . . . Obviously, the more you can gather, the stronger your argument will be."[6] With an initial sample totaling almost 12,000 articles and transcripts, we undoubtedly have collected a comprehensive pool from which to draw conclusions.

Step three requires a researcher put primacy on contextualizing data and texts: "When you come to make your educated guess about the likely interpretations of a text, bear in mind: context, context, context."[7] For a researcher, this means transparency and honesty about your background and ideals, as well as recognizing the impact of time and culture on your interpretations. While conducting this research, the entire research team was charged with explicitly identifying and bracketing our own personal beliefs and opinions, recognizing that this transparency was essential to conducting a rigorous, high-quality research study. Furthermore, this analysis both implicitly and explicitly acknowledges and recognizes the social, cultural, economic, and political contexts of the relevant period, bringing those considerations into the analysis and discussion as necessary.

As media students and scholars recognize, at times the most important part of media coverage includes looking at what is not covered at all. This is particularly true in the case of coverage of something like political primaries, when candidates are vying to generate favorable media coverage for their own personal gain while masking issues and questions that might result in less favorable voter perceptions. To help address this, McKee also offers researchers three tricks to "make invisible discourses more visible,"[8] including exnomination, commutation tests, and structuring absences.

In exnomination, a researcher recognizes that the cultural privilege associated with something dominant is so accepted, it does not even need to be named. Instead, it is just normal, becoming the point of reference against which everything else is judged. Commutation tests, on the other hand, are thought experiments. In this process, a researcher replaces one element of a text with something culturally similar, but different (for example, imagining that a Michele Bachman quote was actually from Hillary Clinton or, depending on the context, one of her male competitors). This allows us to explore and subvert expectations in order to achieve a more balanced analysis. Finally, structuring absences—consciously examining what is *not* by analyzing what *is*—helps call attention to what has been systematically excluded from coverage. Together, these three strategies "can contribute to a methodology of textual analysis by making visible what might otherwise be too obvious to see."[9]

ANALYTIC PROCESS

As would be expected for a textual analysis grounded in the post-structuralist perspective, articles and transcripts were analyzed using traditional qualitative, interpretivist techniques. Rather than taking a quantitative approach designed to break articles into units, I opted instead to take a holistic approach, considering each story as a whole.

Once the sample was constructed, I read each story with an eye toward emergent themes. In order to address the fluctuation of frames over time, data were analyzed in chronological order, beginning with May 2011 and continuing through April 30, 2012. During my initial read of the media texts I also consciously employed McKee's strategies of exnomination, commutation tests, and structuring absences to better understand the subtleties of what was not explicitly said. My initial examination and analysis of the emergent media frames were then presented to the research team and readers as a form of "member checks." Because the research assistants had extensively engaged with the raw data, they provided an important check to ensure that the interpretations represented in this book were, in fact, likely.

A FINAL NOTE ON METHODS

The post-structuralist, interpretive design for this study allows for maximum sensitivity and flexibility while making sense of the extensive data included in the sample. Some scholars might argue that a more quantitatively oriented approach, such as content analysis, would provide a more useful examination. While I recognize the value offered by those studies, I prefer to utilize a more nuanced approach. Rather than reducing stories to smaller units to be counted, summed, and statistically analyzed, this approach offers a much-needed opportunity to look deeper into the data to understand the subtle, often unmarked frames that are used in mainstream media coverage of the selection of a major party candidate: the first steps on the road to the White House.

NOTES

1. Newspapers were selected to represent the paper of record (*New York Times*), a conservative paper (*Wall Street Journal*), and one that focuses on national politics in part because of its geographic location (*Washington Post*).

2. Alan McKee, *Textual Analysis* (Thousand Oaks, CA: Sage Publications, 2003), 1.

3. Ibid., 13.

4. Ibid., 17.

5. John Green, Steven Hook, Bill Adair, and Stephanie Warsmith, "Politics & Perception: The Role of a Responsible Press" (panel presented at the annual Poynter Kent State Media Ethics Workshop, Kent, Ohio, September 20, 2012).

6. McKee, *Textual Analysis*, 91.

7. Ibid., 92.

8. Ibid., 111.

9. Ibid.

Bibliography

Anderson, Christopher L. "Which Party Elites Choose to Lead the Nomination Process?" *Political Research Quarterly* 66 (2013): 61–76. doi: 10.1177/1065912911430669.

Ashbee, Edward. "Bewitched—The Tea Party Movement: Ideas, Interests and Institutions." *Political Quarterly* 82 (2011): 157–64. doi: 10.1111/j.1467-923X.2011.02175.x.

Benoit, William L., P. M. Pier, LeAnn M. Brazeal, John P. McHale, Andrew Klyukovski, and David Airne. *The Primary Decision: A Functional Analysis of Debates in Presidential Primaries.* Westport: Praeger, 2002.

Bevan, Tom, and Carl M. Cannon. "21 Reasons for Obama's Victory and Romney's Defeat." *RealClearPolitics.com*, November 7, 2012. http://www.realclearpolitics.com/articles/2012/11/07/21_reasons_for_obamas_victory_and_romneys_defeat_116090-full.html.

Bloomberg Editors. "The Supreme Court's Cowardice." *Bloomberg.com: Opinion*, June 26, 2012. http://www.bloomberg.com/news/2012-06-26/the-supreme-court-s-cowardice.html.

Carlin, Diana P. "Presidential Debates as Focal Points for Campaign Arguments." *Political Communication* 9 (1992): 251–65. doi:10.1080/10584609.1992.9962949.

Citrin, Jack, and David Karol. "Introduction." In *Nominating the President: Evolution and Revolution in 2008 and Beyond*, edited by Jack Citrin and David Karol, 1–26. Lanham: Rowman & Littlefield, 2009.

Cohen, Marty, David Karol, Hans Noel, and John Zaller. *The Party Decides: Presidential Nominations Before and After Reform.* Chicago: University of Chicago Press, 2008.

Drew, Dan, and David Weaver. "Voter Learning in the 1988 Presidential Election: Did the Debates and the Media Matter?" *Journalism & Mass Communication Quarterly* 68 (1991): 27–37 doi: 10.1177/107769909106800104.

Entman, Robert M. "Framing: Toward Clarification of a Fractured Paradigm." *Journal of Communication* 43 (1993): 51–58. doi: 10.1111/j.1460-2466.1993.tb01304.x.

———. *Projections of Power: Framing News, Public Opinion, and U.S. Foreign Policy.* Chicago: University of Chicago Press, 2004.

———. "Framing Bias: Media in the Distribution of Power." *Journal of Communication* 57 (2007): 163–73. doi: 10.1111/j.1460-2466.2006.00336.x.

Green, John, Steven Hook, Bill Adair, and Stephanie Warsmith. "Politics & Perception: The Role of a Responsible Press." Panel presented at the annual Poynter Kent State Media Ethics Workshop, Kent, Ohio, September 20, 2012.

Guardian (U.K.) Editorial. "21 Reasons for Obama's Victory and Romney's Defeat." *The-Guardian.com*, November 7, 2012. www.guardian.co.uk/commentisfree/2012/nov/07/obama-second-term-change.

Harnden, Toby. "Hindsight Will View Romney as a Poor Candidate with No Core Values Who Looked Deeply Uncomfortable." *MailOnline.com*, November 7, 2012. http://

www.dailymail.co.uk/news/article-2229083/US-Election-2012-analysis-Hindsight-view-Mitt-Romney-poor-candidate-says-Toby-Harnden.html.

Kamarck, Elaine C. *Primary Politics: How Presidential Candidates Have Shaped the Modern Nominating System*. Washington, D.C.: Brookings, 2009.

Lanoue, David J., and Peter R. Schrott. "The Effects of Primary Season Debates on Public Opinion." *Political Behavior* 11 (1989): 289–306. doi: 10.1007/BF00992301.

Levinson, Jessica. "Will the SEC Save Us from Citizens United?" *SacamentoBee.com: Viewpoints*, March 5, 2013. http://www.sacbee.com/2013/05/04/5394092/will-the-sec-save-us-from-citizens.html.

Liptak, Adam. "Justices, 5-4, Reject Corporate Spending Limit." *NewYorkTimes.com: Politics*, January 21, 2010. http://www.nytimes.com/2010/01/22/us/politics/22scotus.html?pagewanted=all.

McKee, Alan. *Textual Analysis*. Thousand Oaks, CA: Sage, 2003.

O'Hehir, Andrew. "Fox News' Dark Night of the Soul." *Salon.com*, November 7, 2012. http://www.salon.com/2012/11/07/fox_news_dark_night_of_the_soul.

Parker, Ashley. "The Scene at Romney Headquarters." *NewYorkTimes.com: Live Coverage of the Election Day*, November 29, 2012. http://elections.nytimes.com/2012/results/live-coverage.

Putnam, Joshua T. "The Impact of Rules Changes on the 2012 Republican Presidential Primary Process." *Society* 49 (2012): 400–4, doi: 10.1007/s12115-012-9573-5.

Reese, Stephen D. "Framing Public Life: A Bridging Model for Media Research." In *Framing Public Life: Perspectives on Media and Our Understanding of the Social World*, edited by Stephen D. Reese, Oscar H. Gandy Jr., and August E. Grant, 7–32. New York: Routledge, 2001.

Scheufele, Dietram A., and David Tewksbury. "Framing, Agenda Setting, and Priming: The Evolution of Three Media Effects Models." *Journal of Communication* 57 (2007): 9–20. doi: 10.1111/j.0021-9916.2007.00326.x.

Tewksbury, David, and Dietram A. Scheufele. "News Framing Theory and Research." *In Media Effects: Advances in Theory and Research*, 3rd ed., edited by Jennings Bryant and Mary Beth Oliver, 17–33. New York: Routledge, 2009.

Washington Post. "Romney Prepared Victory Speech for Election, but Delivered Concession Speech Instead." *Washington Post*, November 7, 2012. http://articles.washingtonpost.com/2012-11-07/politics/35504045_1_mitt-romney-romney-plane-romney-first.

Weaver, David A., and Joshua M. Scacco. "Revisiting the Protest Paradigm: The Tea Party as Filtered through Prime-Time Cable News." *International Journal of Press/Politics* 18 (2013): 61–84. doi: 10.1177/1940161212462872.

The Week Editorial. "Mitt Romney's Disastrous Ground Game and 7 Other Behind-the-Scenes Revelations." *Yahoo! News.com*, November 9, 2012. news.yahoo.com/mitt-romneys-disastrous-ground-game-7-other-behind-113000893-election.html.

Yawn, Mike, Kevin Ellsworth, Bob Beatty, and Kim Fridkin Kahn. "How a Presidential Primary Debate Changed Attitudes of Audience Members." *Political Behavior* 20 (1998): 155–81. doi: 10.1023/A:1024832830083.

Index